PSYCHOLOGICAL AND RELIGIOUS DEVELOPMENT

Maturity and Maturation

Charles C. L. Kao

UNIVERSITY
PRESS OF
AMERICA

LANHAM • NEW YORK • LONDON

Copyright © 1981 by

University Press of America,™ Inc.

4720 Boston Way
Lanham, MD 20706

3 Henrietta Street
London WC2E 8LU England

Library of Congress Cataloging in Publication Data

Kao, Charles C. L., 1932–
    Psychological and religious development.

    Bibliography: p.
    Includes index.
    1. Psychology, Religious. 2. Developmental
psychology. 3. Maturation (Psychology) I. Title.
BL53.K28   200'.1'9   80–5852
ISBN 0–8191–1759–5   AACR2
ISBN 0–8191–1760–9 (pbk.)

Dedicated to my parents, Mr. & Mrs. Sin-tek Kao,
in honor of their 50th wedding anniversary.

ACKNOWLEDGMENTS

Appreciation is hereby expressed to all
authors and publishers whose works have
contributed to the making of this book.

CONTENTS

x

Preface

In response to my previous book, <u>Search for Maturity</u>, a reader from Philadelphia wrote, "I think maturity is in short supply!" In addition to the energy crisis, we have the problem of "maturity crisis." Both are interrelated. We are caught between "two fires," as Lewis J. Sherrill observes. He says, "On the one hand, modern civilization requires that the individual be a person of extraordinary strength if he is to thrive in the midst of that civilization. . . And yet, on the other hand, modern society is producing, in vast numbers, persons who are rendered deficient because they cannot achieve precisely that kind of strength and maturity which our civilization demands."[1] Today, the problem does not get better. Instead, it is getting worse.

Following the unprecedented advancement in science and technology, the stockpile of human knowledge has increased more in the last few decades than in all the previous centuries. The human race is now entrusted with an unthinkable power, but the thinking of the people is increasingly utilitarian and partisan not only in industry and the business world but also in schools, universities, government agencies, and cultural institutions. Morality has become the rationalization of self-interest, and fear has turned out to be the mother of morality. The human race has learned many things, but its children are living in the fragmented tower of Babel. The technological mind has become specialized, but it has lost the capacity for common discourse; the technological ego rarely relaxes its control over the rest of the psyche and has become tyrannical; its preoccupation with the manipulation of nature has led to self-manipulation and the manipulation of others.

Modern society requires that its members possess the kind of character and inner strength which signify maturity and maturation. The theme placed over the portals of the 1933 Chicago World's Fair was prophetic: "Science Explores; Technology Executes; Man Conforms." The respect for the individual's inner spirit and for basic human values has vanished greatly, and the life of the inner world has been forgotten,

if not destroyed, under the dictatorship of materialism.
Intoxicated with gadetry and material possession, a lot
of people have let their good brains waste away, their
adventurous vitality drain, and have lost their capacity
of transcendence. Many people rebel against this cult
of material goods by seeking the ecstacies of religious
mysticism through drugs without the need to discipline
oneself in prayer. They are looking for something
which money cannot buy.

What is this "something"? In classical terms,
it is called "soul." Modern men and women have lost
their "souls," their "homes," and their God. They
have trusted in their misdirected intelligence and
physical power. Modern science and technology have
enabled us to destroy not only the physical world but
also the human "soul" and human identity, although
the scientific and technological brain has brought us
"a pot of porridge," namely, physical power, comforts,
and prosperity.

Albert Einstein changed our view of this universe
with his theory of relativity, but he could not find
the unified theory which he dreamed of even until the
last moment of his life. Ever since the world has
been dominated by the principle of uncertainty in the
physical world as well as in the spiritual world. We
share his dream. Like him, we look for certainty and
unity in the physical world and in our minds.

We live in a world in which "change is king."
Political and emotional tension permeates every corner
of our habitat. Our basic beliefs and religions have
been questioned, and all the fixed points of reference
in human life have become increasingly disconnected.
The Victorian concept of "will power" has been inva-
lidated by Freud's discovery of the human unconscious,
and a new image of being human has been formulated.
Consequently, the human mind's driving agent has become a passive recipient of the inner unconscious
forces and the external environment. Our self-image
is low in spite of the victory the scientific and
technological mind has declared over all but this
last thread of nature. Should twentieth century men
and women conquer that too, they will die like a fetus
cutting its own umbilical cord. The modern mind is

intoxicated with dynamism, change and process. One
day we may perish in total disintegration because we
have lost our "souls," our "homes," and our God. The
breakdown of authority is no surprise to us, because
this has happened. There is nothing to challenge our
youth to make a sacrifice and no one to command leadership among the disillusioned folks, because the "Center"
is gone. Under such circumstances, maturity is hard
to come by, the process of maturation is seldom un-
hampered, goals are vague, and direction is uncertain. Change itself has become the only thing constant, and non-direction becomes our "direction."

H. G. Wells was the "Prophet of Our Day," as
his biographer observed. In his old age, he recalled
his adolescent years and became convinced that "the
Fuhrer's mentality was almost twin of what his own
had been at the age of thirteen around 1879," and
that "Hitler and Mussolini were only pimples on the
adolescent face of humanity, and would vanish as
humanity grew up."[2] Modern culture is characterized
by adolescent features, such as rebellion, self-
assertion, hostility toward authority, here-and-now
mentality, dynamism, vitality, uncertainty, the quest
for identity and meaning, the lack of balance in
growth, etc. Modern society is full of rebellion,
self-assertion, protests and strikes. So, parents
rebel against the social expectations, because their
children rebel against them, or vice versa. Their
children are abused, because they have been abused.

We are proud of our culture of youth. Often
maturity is identified with the old age. But old age
does not necessarily signify maturity, nor does youth
immaturity. We live in a culture in which maturity
is not easily found. But maturity is needed, if we
are to survive the total destruction by misuse of the
physical power in our hands. Maturity is needed also,
if we are to overcome the energy crisis and population
explosion by changing dependent living habits to self-
restraint and self-reliance, as autonomous persons in
the true sense of the word. Can we outgrow our current
adolescent state and mature to adulthood? It depends
on our maturation as individuals and as a nation, and
above all, as a human species. If we do, the "pimples"
on the adolescent face of humanity would disappear.

Then, there would be regeneration in society; the breaking point would become the turning point; human rights would be accompanied by human responsibility; and egoistic self-assertion would be replaced by true democracy.

Our modern culture is notoriously characterized by differentiation, which is manifested in scientific analytical thinking and specialization, the search for individual identity, feelings of existential alienation in modern living, the increasing complexity and proliferation of social organizations, and so on. So often, our work is dissociated from the rest of life, and all are going to pieces. Even the atom is no longer the "uncuttable," as Democritus and other Greek thinkers insisted some 2,500 years ago. The smallest is no longer the smallest. Some elements, such as uranium and radium, break to pieces gradually by giving off rays and throw off some of the particles of their atoms. Unfortunately the first use of this knowledge was the atomic bomb and the destruction of millions of human lives. If this trend continues, the stable elements in the universe and human society may become no longer stable, and the whirlwind of total destruction may blow in every direction and cover every dimension of human existence. Such an uncertainty is likely to be our common experience in modern living. The divorce rate increases, because the unity and cohesiveness of family life are no longer there. Like the broken atoms, members of families are scattered. Children are as heart-broken as their broken-hearted parents.

The mental state of modern men and women is akin to that of the Prodigal Son running away to a distant land. The act of running away is an expression of a desire to be differentiated from the family of which he has been a part. In the process of maturation, differentiation is necessary. But when the Prodigal Son comes to his senses at a more mature stage, he will return to his Father and be reintegrated into his family. Our secular culture has thrown away the sacred for centuries. Its children are enjoying material wealth and prosperity, but are spiritually suffering severe disintegration. A society which works well in pushing high levels of technological

productivity may nonetheless create great stresses
for those living in it. There is no psychological
problem more stressful than the disintegration of our
personality in a highly fragmented society which offers
multiple choices without a guiding core of principles.
In order to protect ourselves from extreme differentiation and disintegration, we need to emphasize the principle of integration. There are increasingly more
men and women who are determined to do something to
prevent further disintegration of our lives. They
become more aware of the importance of the principle
of integration, which is essentially a part of human
growth. We need stability as much as excitement. The
principle of integration is important to stability.

Modern secularization seems to have reached its
peak, and a group of thoughtful men and women are
beginning to wonder whether science and technology
are really the saviors of the world. Their sense of
disillusionment may be comparable to, but no quite
the same as the disillusionment they have had with
traditional religion and politics. It is said that
the most secularized cities are very often the places
where cults and other quasi-religious groups flourish.
The sacred just does not go away, because it is part
of human nature. Freud, Marx, and Sartre, each in
his own way, criticized religion. One may say that
they only attacked the caricatures of religion, and
indeed these caricatures are found among a multitude
of believers, who are still in the infant and childish
stages of their faith. In spite of scientific progress
faith remains part of human life. The human quest for
meaningful life will continue, no matter how advanced
we are in science and technology. In their earnest
quest for meaningful life many young people have been
trapped by cults and victimized. This phenomenon is
certainly not limited to the young. The quest for
meaning rekindles in our hearts like an unquenchable
fire, even when we grow old. In every stage of human
life, there is a religious dimension, which is often
neglected if not avoided or detested, by the psychologists and social scientists who proclaim they will
have nothing to do with religion. Human ingenuity
of mechanization and automation has solved some problems, and yet it has also created the problems of air
pollution, chemical wastes, and others.

xv

There are two major principles in human growth which have been well discussed by psychologists and social scientists: the principle of integration, and the principle of differentiation. But there is another principle, which has been neglected for so long but is equally needed in human growth: the principle of transcendence. In some ways, it is integrally related to and interweaved with the other two. This may be the reason it has not been treated as a separate principle. But it seems to me that there is a significant dynamism correlating the three principles. The purpose of this book is to expound that dynamism, as it is manifested in maturity and maturation at every stage of life.

This book has come out of nearly a decade of personal interviews, biographical analysis, and literature survey in related fields. It attempts to present a comprehensive picture of human growth with depth and perceptive insight, (which may stimulate some psychologists and social scientists toward formulating new hypotheses in their empirical study). By integrating theories from the literature survey and the critical reflection on the study with the concrete life experiences from personal interviews and biographies, I wish to present a thorough picture of maturity and maturation to the reader with the hope that he or she may be engaged in pushing our present culture to a more mature stage.

Each person's view of maturity is culturally bound, and each individual has his or her unique life history and idiosyncracies, but there must be some common elements in our views. What are they? The answer to this question may help us determine our future direction. I invite the reader to participate in this endeavor for a common dialogue.

In reading this book, those who are familiar with developmental psychology may like to skip part Two except the section on the religious dimension of each stage; those who are practically-minded may like to read part One after the introduction, and then parts Two, Three ; those who are religiously-minded may like to read the sections on religious experience in each chapter first. Professors may like to con-

sider using this book in their courses. Likewise,
ministers may like to consider using it in their
adult groups.

Finally, I would like to express my deep appreciation and gratitude to the many scholars and friends
in the greater Boston area and other places who have
shared their life experiences and ideas for interviews, and offered valuable suggestions. It is impossible to list them. I began this project as a
Visiting Scholar at Harvard University in 1969, and
then continued it as an independent researcher in
dialogue with several members of the faculty at Harvard and elsewhere. They are: Drs. James Luther
Adams, Robert Freed Bales, Kenneth D. Benne, Peter
A. Bertocci, Robert Chin, Harvey G. Cox, Paul K.
Deats, Arthur J. Dyck, George W. Goethals, James W.
Fowler, Homer L. Jernigan, Merle R. Jordan, Stanley
H. King, Ralph B. Potter, William R. Rogers, Krister
Stendahl, Orlo Strunk, Robert L. Trease, and others.
I am very grateful for their intellectual stimulation, encouragement, and friendship. My dialogue
with church leaders in this area has been warm and
cordial. I am deeply grateful to them. They are:
Dr. Victor F. Scalise, Dr. Justus J. Fennel, Dr. Joseph C. Williamson, Dr. Oliver Powell, the Rev. Paul
Clayton, the Rev. Richard Dodds, and others. I am
grateful to Dr. Richard C. Cabot for the timely en-
couagement through the award of a modest grant from
the foundation he established. Last but not the
least, I would like to express my great appreciation
to my former professors and those, who have helped
my study, and to my wife and son, who have supported
and encouraged me.

Brookline, Massachusetts   C. K.

NOTES

1. Lewis J. Sherrill, <u>The Struggle of the Soul</u>
    (New York: The Macmillan Co., 1961), p. 1.

2. Antoninna Vallentine, <u>H. G. Wells, Prophet of
    Our Day</u> (New York: The John Day Co., 1950), p.
    14.

CHAPTER

I

QUEST FOR MEANING

"Vanity of vanities, says the Preacher, vanity
of vanities! All is vanity. What does man gain by
all the toil at which he toils under the sun?"[1] Has
life any meaning? What makes it meaningful? Why is
it that life is meaningless? How is life to be lived
and not merely tolerated? How and when to end this
pathetic pronouncement of the Preacher who has gained
support from Schopenhauer and other pessimistic philosophers and countless depressed people of all ages?

Is life meaningless because it is cyclical?
The term "life cycle" is often used by psychologists,
psychiatrists, and philosophers in their discussions
and writings, or by ordinary people in their conversations. How this Hindu-Buddhist notion of time and
history crept into the Western mind is a worthy task
for historians to undertake in their inquiries. However, it was certainly not so strange a concept for
the Preacher, who was keenly aware of the natural
phenomena--"the sun rises and the sun goes down, and
hastens to the place where it rises. The wind blows
to the south, and goes to the north; round and round
goes the wind, and on its circuits the wind returns."[2]
The repeated, static, and cyclical features of natural
phenomena make one feel that life is a "treadmill,"
apathetic, stagnated, and extremely boring. But,
on the other hand, it provides a sense of security
and dependability of nature. Is life a cycle? Does
one go back to the womb from which he or she is born?
Is life just a striving after wind? Does it go nowhere after all? Or is it going somewhere?

Perhaps in different ways we experience the
emptiness of life, and cry out like the Preacher,
"Vanity of vanities! All is vanity." "All things are
full of weariness." History repeats itself, and "there
is nothing new under the sun." Every day we eat the

1

same food, run the same route, meet the same people, and perform the same duties like a cog in a machine. Is life only an unbearable treadmill?

The human organism is purposeful, and life is a pilgrimage. Once in a while during the quiet hours of night, when life becomes stagnated and monotonous, we are likely to ask, "Who am I? Why am I here? And where am I going from here?" Human purposefulness makes us move forward and strive toward a destination; it breaks the monotony of life and cracks the nutshell of cyclic enslavement to repetitious existence and a stagnated state of mind; it opens up the door for a new journey. Even the Hindu-Buddhists want to be emancipated from the cycle of rebirth (samsara) for the nirvana. Life is not just a cycle. It is intrinsically so equipped to strive for progress toward a goal, a destination, a shrine. This progress is not necessarily physical or spatial. Life is meaningless when it becomes merely a self-closed circle; life becomes stagnated when there is no progress toward something. This progress can be spiritual, and it is to find meaningful life.

After the 1977 Ingersoll Lecture about life after death given by Prof. John Hick of England at Harvard, a student questioned the assumption of progress as a myth. Whether human progress is a "myth" in the sense that it is unreal, or in a technical sense that it is a religious symbol, the human organism is striving forward and purposeful. This is basic to evolution. American optimism, or utopianism of any kind, is bound to have roots in this purposefulness of human organism, which wants to grow and mature. In fact, the term "life cycle" is used to signify the course of developmental changes through which an organism passes from its inception as a fertilized zygote to the mature state in which another zygote may be produced, a progression through a series of different stages of development. Human life is a process of development; it is a process moving toward a destination. Life is an adventure; Life is technologically conceived as "human development." When life is purposeful, it is meaningful.

In A Psalm of Life, American poet Longfellow

2

expresses this sentiment:

> Life is real! Life is earnest!
> And the grave is not life's goal.

If the grave is not life's goal, then what is? There must be something beyond physical death, for life goes on aiming at something which transcends the physical body and cannot be expressed in purely physiological terms. The life's goal is not just physical growth, although that is indeed an essential part of it. Life involves the growth of human personality and the development of moral character. In the classical sense, life is a spiritual pilgrimage trying to reach the City of God, as John Bunyan tried to teach in his novel Pilgrim's Progress.

In Analects, Confucius made an autobiographical statement saying, "At the age of fifteen, my mind was set on learning. At thirty I knew my character had been formed. At forty I had no more perplexities. At fifty I knew the Mandate of Heaven. At sixty I was at ease with whatever I heard. At seventy I could follow my heart's desire without transgressing the moral principles." For him, life was a process of self-cultivation, and its goal was to reach a stage of mature living.

The cultural crisis today is that life is understood only in physical terms. Value is measured only in terms of dollars and cents. For many people the grave is life's goal. Life is just a game, the point of playing the game is expressed in terms of material wealth and prosperity. "If you do not, you are stupid." This candid warning was considered to be the best advice one could give to a good friend starting a career. Under such circumstances, it is essential to examine the process of human growth and maturity, the qualities of a healthy, mature person, and how such qualities are developed and integrated one with the other in the process of maturation. This will show that, indeed, the grave is not life's goal.

Having studied the concept of maturity in psychology, Christian theology, and Chinese philosophy

3

in the context of East-West encounter, I felt the
need to supplement such conceptual work with something concrete from the personal interviews and biographical (or autobiographical) studies. With the
help of several social scientists and church leaders
in the Boston area, I interviewed about one hundred
persons, asking two open-ended questions--1) "What
is maturity?" 2) "What are the significant factors
in your growth toward maturity?" The follow-up questions varied from person to person. The procedures
were also different depending on the person's background and the situation, largely on what was available to begin a conversation. The interviews were
designed to get more specific at certain points. Confidentiality was assured, and the interviews were
tape-recorded. Those who kindly participated in the
personal interviews were recommended by others as
"mature" persons or chosen by virtue of public recognition manifested in the leadership they assumed in the
community and their professions with a few exceptions
for the sake of comparison. They were from various
professions, age groups, religious backgrounds, and
levels of education. In the personal interviews, I
was given the privilege of going to the sacred altar
and of reading the hitherto undisclosed texts of some
people who had kept their inner holy of holies un-
touched. I listened with attentive ears and a responsive mind. In one's memories, there are particular
excitements and disappointments, joys and sorrows,
successes and failures. For this privilege, I am
deeply grateful.

Life is full of complexities. Its variables
are countless. No one can fully comprehend their
meanings and measure what is by nature unmeasurable.
The psychodynamic correlations among them can be in-
ferred and hypothesized, but are often subtle, elusive,
and beyond human captivity. Only the fame seeking
pseudo-scientist can proudly proclaim total victory
in this area. In a summary article about a conference
on life history research in psychopathology, Prof.
David F. Ricks of Columbia University concluded: "The
complexity of this model for schizophrenic development,
with genetic, biologic, familial, school, and community factors all involved in the production of the
disorder, suggests that there is not likely to be any

4

dramatic new development that will suddenly indicate one
'cure' for schizophrenia."[3] In search of significant
factors in growth toward maturity, I also found this
complexity manifested differently, but positively,
in each person's life. In view of this complexity,
I can only hope that the findings of these interviews
and biographical studies be used merely as some significant illustrative indications rather than as something definitive. In order to consolidate the validity
of the conclusion, I went a step further in reflecting
on the findings in reference to a few related theories
and other appropriate statistical and empirical studies. The reader may see here and there certain implications for the present society and for oneself.

    In presenting the relevant data from personal
interviews and biographical studies as illustrations,
I have edited the materials so that the confidentiality
of personal identities would be safeguarded, as I
promised in the beginning. So, whenever a personal
name is given, take it as a fictional creation by the
author rather than as authentic and original. However,
in an effort to provide a contextual framework for
comprehending the true meanings of what was said in
the interviews, I have briefly described the person's
profession, age, geographical locality, religion, etc.
whenever it was appropriate and available. Naturally,
the reader may be tempted to conjecture who the person
was. But this speculation should be limited to knowing the situational context rather than the true identity of the person. It would be more helpful to ponder
about one's own life experiences and to compare them
with what is being said and concluded in this study,
and then to visualize one's future growth and the kind
of life one is going to live.

    There may be some proud behaviorists who consider
their quantitative empirical approach the only path to
truth, and would try to disqualify other methods. They
may consider biographical studies unreliable and inaccurate because the biographers tend to select their
materials to suit their purposes and preconceived ideas,
and interpret them according to their subjective
prejudices. But this cannot become the basis for rejecting biographical studies as a means of understanding human maturation. It has been done by several

5

eminent psychologists such as Gordon W. Allport, Erik
H. Erikson, Robert W. White, and others. Furthermore,
the selection of materials is an inevitable feature
of human perception. With no exception, scientists
also formulate their hypotheses and select data and
areas of their studies in accordance with their pre-
determined interests and scope. Their problems are
sharply defined and strictly limited. It is impossible
to deal with all variables, and one has to define the
nature and methodologies of one's study. In defining,
one is subjectively bound. There is "a prior personal
subjective choice" of purpose and values in any scientific endeavor, as pointed out by Carl R. Rogers.[4]
Subjectivity is inevitable in any human activity.

Increasingly, quantitative method is considered
to be superior to humanistic method in academic circles.
Indeed, it has its value and strengths, but there are
certain subtleties of meaning in human behavior, which
cannot be accurately expressed quantitatively. The
same expression may have a slightly different meaning,
intensity of emotion, and connotation to different
people. In view of this fact, the findings are not
treated statistically but are synthesized by the author
in reference to those established theories in related
fields in order to comprehend the facts of human growth.
My attention was focused particularly on the frequency
and intensity of impact of certain types of experience
on the lives of the subjects according to their recol-
lections and biographical accounts.

Some memories may lose accuracy as time goes on,
but traumatic ones often remain vivid. For some
behaviorists, the retrospective method through personal
interviews and biographical studies is unreliable,
because one may manipulate his or her memories to suit
one's emotional needs instead of being accurate. For
them, information about one's childhood and adolescence
cannot be truly drawn through personal interviews.
"Retrospective information is widely used, and interpreted with cheerful dogmatism by persons attached to
a variety of different dogmas," said Dr. Merrill Roff
of the University of Minnesota in his discussion of
some of the problems in life history research.[5] There
is a point to his somewhat sacarstic remark. However,
it seems to me that every person has a unique set of

dogma related to one's perceptual set and emotional needs. One's dogma is comparable to the scientist's hypotheses in guiding the interpretation of life experiences; if one allows a possibility for change or modification, dogma is just another form of hypothesis. This indicates that subjectivity is indispensible to our interpretation of natural phenomena and life experiences. Furthermore, concerning past experiences and their impact on one's growth toward maturity, no one knows better than the person himself or herself. Because of this subjective dimension in human understanding, there is a justifiable basis for the retrospective approach being utilized in this book.

Recent memories are usually more accessible to our recollection than earlier ones, unless we are senile. For a person in mid-life to recall something from childhood or adolescence with great excitement and vividness must indicate its great intensity or enormity of impact on his or her personal life. The trivial may disappear, but the most crucial remains in our minds, and constantly exercises considerable influence on our decision making and way of life, whether we are consciously aware of it or not. From this point of view, recollective personal interviews are appropriate to understanding some of the significant factors in growth toward maturity, although it is not the only method. In order to safeguard my findings from the subjective distortion of memories, I have determined them reflectively in reference to some relevant empirical and behavioral studies whose variables are highly controlled and limited.

This book is divided into three parts: the first part provides some concrete examples of growing experiences and contexts drawn from my personal interviews and biographical studies; the second deals with the basic principles and stages of human growth; and the third discusses the major themes of maturity.

If life is compared to a journey, this book is intended to show the major stations on the way, what can be expected at each stage of the journey, what problems can be worked out from one stage to another, what ideal goals can be achieved, and what kind of

experiences and qualities are particularly remembered
by those who have gone through most of their lives so
far. This book is intended as a guide with depth and
perceptive insight for life's journey, showing the
major highways and interconnected networks among them.
It is rather eclectic, but integrated with a little
cross-cultural flavor, and life's basic principles.

I have looked for a book to guide teaching and
learning, but so far have not found one I really liked.
There are many books on human growth. Some are childrearing manuals, centering on hows and techniques;
others are youth guidance books on marriage and sex,
but again centering on technicalities, social skills
and physiological details; and a few are purely en-
tertaining and challenge one's dormant desire for
pleasure and stimulation by offering rare cases. Some
academic treatments of human growth are limited to
the author's special areas of expertise and their particular schools of ideas. The secular books on the
whole rule out the religious dimension of life, and
barely touch the surface of the philosophical problems
of living. On the other hand, philosopher's treatments are inclined to be short of the actuality of
day-to-day living. The following pages may be a little
different in that I have attempted to integrate the
secular and the sacred, the theoretical and the practical, and various dimensions of human growth. Thus,
one may see the totality of human growth, the partic-
ularities at each stage, and some practical implications for actual living.

Today's family, school, and church are three
institutions in grave trouble. They are the most
vulnerable institutions, as sociologist Robert Bellah
of the University of California at Berkeley has pointed
out. But having listened to personal interviews and
studied a number of biographies, I cannot help but
acknowledge the indispensibility of these institutions
to human growth toward maturity. We cannot live without
them in our lives. Sometimes they are regarded as un-
necessary and outmoded, because they are not keeping
up to what they should be. The following pages show
some of the positive influences of these institutions
on human growth. Naturally there are also negative
influences, but their significance for human grwoth

will be great according to the experiences of those whom I have interviewed. They are important contexts for human growth.

Life is a journey. Each task of our life is a part of it. The reading of this book may be a significant venture. If so, it may become another important context for growth, as some of the interviewees experienced.

NOTES

1. Eccles. 1:2-3. (R.S.V.)

2. _Ibid._, 1:5-6.

3. David F. Ricks, "Life History Research in Psychopathology: Retrospect and Prospect," in David F. Ricks and Merrill Roff (eds), Life History Research in Psychopathology (Minneapolis: The University of Minnesota Press, 1970), p. 304.

4. Carl R. Rogers, On Becoming a Person (Boston: Houghton Mifflin Co., 1961), pp. 391-396. See also Jerome Kagan's comments on the issue. He writes, "Students of human development find it almost impossible to avoid taking sides with respect to the criteria of adaptation, and the history of psychology is littered with their choices--sensory, acuity, . . ." Jerome Kagan, The Growth of the Child (New York: W. W. Norton & Company, Inc., 1978), p. 78.

5. Merrill Roff, "Some Problems in Life History Research," Ricks and Roff, Life History Research, p. 10.

PART ONE: CONTEXTS

CHAPTER

II

CONTEXTS, EVENTS, AND PERSONS

Before we examine what I call "triune dynamism"
in human maturation and the major themes which constitute maturity, we need to begin with concrete,
actual, and personal experiences and examine some
of the data from personal interviews and biographical studies. In my personal interviews, I asked
two open-ended questions--1) "What is maturity?"
2) "What are the significant factors in your growth
toward maturity?" This chapter will be focused on
the answers to both questions. Some people were
more capable of remembering and articulating their
past experiences, while others were less able to do
so. Nonetheless, each person had something to say.
Excerpts of their answers have been organized
according to the contextual significance of growing
experience as follows: 1) family context, 2) educational context, 3) church context, and 4) other contexts.

1. Family Context

In family context, my question was: "Who were
the significant family members who shaped your growth
toward maturity, and in what way?" Unlike rebellious
adolescents who consider their parents outmoded,
ignorant, hypocritical, or untrustworthy, most of
the people I interviewed had had positive images of
their parents, and regarded them as the most influen-
tial persons in their lives. Occasionally there
were negative comments, but in no way did they ridi-
cule their parents. Generally they commented on the
mature qualities of their fathers or mothers respec-
tively, and how such qualities were manifested in
their childhood and later life. The following excerpts are significant examples.

13

An eminent social scientist described the mature qualities of his parents by saying, "My father was fifty-six years older than I. I had an understanding father. The thing I valued in my father was that he listened to what I had to say, and wanted to know what I had in mind before he responded. He was mild, but strong. My mother was much more self-centered. I am more on my father's side because for him community and other people came first. My parents enjoyed reading." On another occasion, a retired Confucian scholar and historian said, "My father was a learned Confucianist. He died when I was eighteen years old. I had been greatly influenced by him. He was a loving father." Likewise, an outstanding church leader said, "I was fortunate enough to have a Scottish father and mother. They were people with deep religious convictions. They became my constant environment. It was a very pervasive thing. It created the atmosphere in which I grew up. It has reached very deep in my life, and I have never ceased to be grateful for what they did for me." It seems that the mature qualities they perceived and appreciated had great impact on their choice of professions and image of personal becoming.

Among those I interviewed were two counseling professors. In giving a mental portrait of their parents, one said, "My mother was a very bright, capable and steady person, eager to sacrifice for me, while my father was a person of responsibility, allowing me to criticize and disagree with him. I owe a great deal to my father. He was a great repairman, and I am a repairman too." Similarly, the other said, "I had well-adjusted parents who loved me and trusted me. Because they trusted me, I was given a lot of independence. When I said, I would be home by eleven o'clock, they would believe me, and I was always be home by then. They would take my word for it. Other kids were comfortable at my home. My parents had strong faith." Love and trust, freedom and responsibility, the down-to-earth skills as well as spirituality were significant factors in shaping their maturity and maturation.

Today we find traditional Puritan work ethics

eroding from the moral fiber of a new generation of people; they want to spend money before they earn it; and their major concern is enjoyment here and now. However, hard work still had a positive impact on many people. It did not sound as bad as the recently coined term "workaholic" would suggest. A housewife and head of a nursery emphatically said, "My parents were mature people, hard-working people. My father worked in a paper mill, and my mother in a shoe shop." But hard work was not enough. There were other things--freedom, trust, intelligence, etc. "My brother and I were the only children, but I felt as if I were the only child. My folks gave me freedom, but not . . . careless freedom. They always had confidence in me so that I could handle my own things. Not many people went to college then. I wanted to go to college, and they let me go. They were very mature. . . . They were good parents. They did not restrict me."

In the same manner, a business manager said, "My father was in the construction business. He took me as his partner. He was always honest and well respected by others. I would say that my father was the most influencial person in my life. He was always a hard working man." This shows a correlation with the findings of A. L. Baldwin and others that the most growth-facilitating pattern of parent-child relationships is that of "acceptant-democratic."[1] Besides the value of hard work, the pattern of parent-child relationships was an important factor.

A mature person is able to work and to love deeply. The following case also shows this combination in the family. A female biologist said, "I had loving parents and we did things together. Puritan ethics, working hard. It was just so hard to be relaxed. At an automobile accident, my father was calm and able to deal with the situation. He was a community leader. Although he did not hold public office, he was looked upon as a trusted person. People came and discussed about their problems with him. Our dinner table was always open, not fancy food, but all were welcomed. We children were not kept away from adults. My mother was also a trusted person."

15

Not only were the personal qualities of hard work and equanimity of parents important but also the pattern of their relationships with the people in the community. A federal employee said, "My parents were devoted to each other. My father was particularly outgoing; he was a buyer in a department store; he saw the best in people and got along with them very well. If someone could not get along with others, the next door neighbor would say to him, 'Go and see Mr. so and so.' My mother was dependent on my father."

Similarly, what a retired employee of a mental health institution said about his parents is also noteworthy: "My parents came to this country from Ireland. I cannot say anything bad about my parents. They were so good. They did not allow me to discriminate against others. If anyone was in trouble, sick or anything, they would go all the way to help them. There was a neighbor who had five children. The husband died, and my mother used to ask me to bring milk to them for five years or so, and gave them vegetables from our garden until their children grew up."

A physician's wife was very appreciative of her parents' encouragements to make her own decisions from early childhood. She remembered being asked by her parents to say what she would like to eat at mealtime, and at other times selecting clothes to wear. When she grew older, she experienced a difficult decision one summer. Her mother wanted her to take a well-paid job at a bank, but she was more inclined to take a counseling job working with poor children and disadvantaged teens. In the end, she was allowed to do what she really wanted.

The best encouragement is parents' trust. A college professor remembered his father's trust in asking him to do responsible things. "At the end of the month, my father used to hand me bills and said, 'Check them,' and gave me the total amount of money to pay them. Sometimes, he let me handle one hundred dollar bills, and later on he let me sign the check. He trusted me!" His father's encouragement and trust were appreciated, because they

16

were so significant to his maturation.

Moral character and religious faith are often mentioned as highly influencial in shaping one's growth as a child. A retired teacher said, "My mother had a strong Christian faith, and influenced me more than I could think of. She was very gentle and loving. My father was a Scotsman, severe, and authoritarian, but he was really a kind person." Another retired teacher said, "My parents influenced me most. My father was very conscientious and honest. He had a strong sense of what was right and what was wrong. I have been greatly influenced by my father. After my father died, my grandfather was one of those highlight people in my life. He was the kind of person I consider to be mature. His maturity was his fairness and his understanding of how other people felt, and we lived our lives guided by my grandfather's sermonettes, such as, 'The money you give to the Lord, you never miss,' or 'What you have, belongs to the Lord, and you should give it to Him.' 'Your standard should be high so that other people would look at you and respect you.'"

Actual involvement in church activities is significant in the eyes of a growing child. In this way, parents set an example. A middle-aged man said, "I have inherited from my parents the heritage of hard work, stubbornness in overcoming difficulty, . . . integrity, and a sense of history. Both were active in the church, and my mother was much more a theologian, a Sunday School teacher. They placed great value on education and family." Another middle aged man said, "My father rose to the professional status by his own effort as a physician of considerable stature. My mother had some college education. Both of them had close relationship with the church. My father wanted to become a minister at one point. He had love and affection. My father was particularly good at serving the church." Perhaps it is because of the combined impact of his father's being a physician and unfulfilled wish of becoming a minister that the man became a minister and clinician of considerable distinction.

In commenting on her parents' maturity, a

17

Roman Catholic nun said, "My parents were both prac-
ticing Christians, and had strong faith. When I
told them that I was going to become a nun, they said,
'If it is what you want and will make you happy, we
will be happy. But we will miss you.' My father was
a very perceptive man. After his visit, he wrote to
me, 'Your smile could not fool me. I realized that
you were having a tough time. I want to make two
things clear--1) You are more than welcome to come home
if you know that you do not belong there, 2) It is
a good idea that you have tried. If you feel you
belong and feel tough, then I want to say to you,
'In my life and experience, it is tough no matter
what you choose. Whatever you choose, we believe in
you." Her father's perception of reality was the
key to the ability to handle her crisis. His appeal
to her autonomy and sense of responsibility was significant; his appeal was based on the reality principle rather than pleasure principle. This is a
sign of maturity, and has helped her becoming a mature person in her own profession as a professor.

One may consider the following cases as an
example of permissiveness, but it was a positive
experience for a middle age professional. When he
reflected on his youth, he said, "I had good balanced
parents. . . . The beautiful thing about my father
was his quiet way of love. He let me be myself. In
high school, I was to fight with two boys. My father
drove by and held one of them, while I fought with
the other. He let me struggle through and worked it
out. My mother was a mystical person, a perfection-
ist in keeping the house, although I did not like it."
One may also question his father's fairness to the
situation by allowing him continue to fight instead
of stopping it. But the positive aspect of the incident was to let him be himself and work it out. Likewise a middle-aged woman said, "My mother strongly
upheld the notion that I went to church because I
wanted to. This was in high school. I was free to
go or not to go." Another interviewee simply said,
"He helped me do what I chose to do." These comments
express similar appreciation of parent's respect for
the child's ability to work things out, when appropriate.

18

On another occasion, a parent's firm "No" was
appreciated by another middle-aged professional. He
failed all courses at a private prep school and deeply
discouraged. He wanted to leave the school so badly
that he called his father. He told his father how
miserable he was, but his father told him in a firm
yet sympathetic voice, "No, you are going to stay
there. I know it is hard, but you will make it."
He stayed and succeeded. Before long, he began to
like the school. This became his turning point, and
he was ever grateful to his father's firmness. Had
his father yielded to his request, he would have become a different person. He would not have been
elected an "Outstanding Young Man of America" later.

Some people lost a parent when they were small.
A minister said, "My father died before I was born.
Being fatherless created a great problem for me. Later
I felt cheated. He died of tuberculosis. My mother
was a nurse and looked after him. Since my father
passed away, my mother devoted herself particularly
to the care of TB patients. Her self-giving became
part of me." Another minister said, "My mother died
when I was six weeks of age. My step-mother was warm
and loving. She provided stability for the family,
and I did not develop mistrust in life. My aunt and
grandfather were very warm and affectionate people.
They showed interest in what I was doing. We had
meals together and sang together around the piano."
He became a warm and mature professional assuming
national leadership in his field.

For other people, maturation seems uneventful,
and there is nothing spectacular to talk about. "My
parents came from Scotland. Being immigrants, they
were considered to be inferior at first. After school,
I went to my father's bakery instead of coming home.
By this I learned early to give in to certain people
and had a better understanding of human nature. My
mother was more outgoing. I am a bit on my father's
side, quiet. They were perfectionists and successful
in business," said a retired teacher.

In almost all the biographies and autobiographies I studied, there is an unmistakable sign of

parental influence. Senator Edward M. Kennedy told
his biographer he was "fortunate to have had a father
who was such a forceful personality, and a mother who
was not only strong but believed in some basic but
pretty sensible virtues that work." They believed in
implanting in their children a love of God, a respect
for the country and its institutions, and self-reliance.
He "was also fortunate to have had the guidance and
example of my brothers and sisters."[2] Furthermore,
in his early childhood he enjoyed a warm and beautiful
relationship with his grandfather, an old politician,
who took him by the hand and hiked all over Boston
with him.

For a Chinese woman, the influence of her grandfather was more decisive than that of her father and
mother. In an autobiography, she wrote about her
self-understanding and identity formation in the context of the extended family in which her grandfather
was the chief authority. When she thought about herself, "there was a little 'I' or 'me' about it."[3] One
day this little "me" was nicknamed by the grandfather
as "Little Fairy Fair," because she constantly insisted
on dividing things fairly. She wanted to boss everyone in school and hated to be bossed by anybody. Eventually her will-power grew and she wanted to break the
traditional engagement arranged by her parents. In
her struggle, her grandfather came to her rescue and
sanctioned her independence in pursuing her own life's
career in medicine. With a deep appreciation for her
enlightened grandfather's intervention in her struggle
with parental authority, she wrote more about him than
her parents "because he had such a decisive influence
over my formative years."

We can also find parental influence in the lives
of great artists, architects, historians, and other
professionals, as a series of NBC interviews has shown.
Frank Lloyd Wright was asked about his choice of profession, and he succinctly answered, "Well, fortunately
I never had to decide. It was decided for me before
I was born. My mother was a teacher and she wanted
an architect for a son." Quite naturally, he became
an architect. "I was conditioned by her," he said.
"The room in which I was born was hung with the wood
engravings of the English cathedrals made by Timothy

Cole."[4] It seemed that he was born into architecture, and there was no choice for him. And yet, he has become one of the radical architectural innovators of the century.

In the same series, Arnold Toynbee was interviewed. He too was very much conditioned by his mother, a historian herself. "I grew up assuming that I was going to be one, too, because of her." When he was small, his mother used to tell him the history of England in bits of about a year, until they had gone through it all. Furthermore, he had great uncle Harry, a ship captain, who put the world on a map.[5] In due time all these experiences came together to make him a great historian.

In a different way, Pablo Casals was grateful to his mother. When he was young, his family was poverty stricken. They lived in France. He played in a vaudeville theatre as second cellist for four francs a week. He had to run a long distance every day for rehearsal and became chronically ill. Everyday his mother went out as usual and brought home work to be done. One day she came home without a hair on her head, because she had sold it to support the family. In response to Pablo's question, "Mother, what have you done?" she replied, "This has no importance, my child, no importance. Don't talk any more about that."[6] His illness continued, and the family returned to Barcelona. But when he returned to Paris in 1899, life was quite different. He made his debut and became a well-known cellist. His mother's great love was very significant in the making of him.

Ralph Ellison is one of those giants whose short biographies constitute a volume entitled Master Minds. He has authored Invisible Man, one of the best selling novels in America. His father died when he was three years old. While he was still young, he wanted to excel at everything he tried. His mother had a sense of the value of excellence: "She often said that she didn't care what I became as long as I tried to become one of the best."[7] His father gave him a significant name, Ralph Waldo. He concluded that his father destined him to be a writer like Ralph Waldo Emerson. Indeed, he achieved the goal that his father had originally envisioned when he was born. The value of excellence is a significant factor in human growth.

A parent's moral values, religious beliefs, and philosophy of life are often communicated to children in a way seldom noticed at the time. The mother of President Dwight David Eisenhower was considered to be a highly religious person. She taught him to believe in a "higher being." Her favorite recreation was solitaire. Out of this and her religious faith, she formulated an epigram, "The Lord deals the cards; you play them."[8] It was reported that she used to repeat it to him with a twinkle in her eyes, when he was young. President Eisenhower often thought about this epigram while he was dealing with the national and international affairs.

A. Scott Crossfield had been an unyieldingly ambitious aviator and rocket testing pilot. He made up his mind to fly while still a child. Shortly afterwards he was struck down by a disease that kept him bed-ridden for almost five years. He was told he would never fly, but he was determined, and stubbornly plotted to make it eventually. Somehow by "sheer will power and the help of God," he found himself gaining strength. In explaining his unusual recovery, he said, "I think my father's example--his refusal to display physical or emotional weakness influenced me tremendously in this regard." "I must have inherited a broad stubborn streak."[9] He emulated his father, took positive command of himself in times of crisis, and did what he considered to be right. He seemed to be a "no emotion" type in coping with stress, as we will see later in part Three, and like his father, he had the positive attitude, persistence, and determination to have "always another dawn," as he called it. The strong tie he had with his father can be seen from his experience on the last day of his father's life. Knowing the closeness of his father's death, he was reluctant to leave for a flight, but his father encouraged him to go. He asked, "Would you wait for me?" and the answer was "Yes." He went. The moment he touched the ground was the exact time his father died.

22

Bertrand Russell's notorious unconventionality
was by no means accidental. In retrospect he realized
the powerful influence of his grandmother on his life.
Her fearlessness, her public spirit, her contempt for
convention, and her indifference to the opinion of
the majority were what he could appreciate. In fact,
these qualities were part of him. In tracing her
influence, he recalled that his grandmother gave him
a Bible with her favorite text on the flyleaf: "Thou
shalt not follow a multitude to do evil." This had
something to do with his determination not to be
afraid of belonging to small minorities.[10] Obviously
there were other things which contributed to his unconventionality and uniqueness.

The maternal influence was very crucial in the
life of Thomas Edison. Early in life he learned that
there was inexplicable cruelty in this world. Out
of curiosity he set a little fire inside the barn
just to see what it would do. As a result he was
punished by his father. The school was repulsive,
and he ran home. He was removed from school, and
his mother, who had been a schoolteacher before her
marriage, taught him at home. His schoolteacher did
not understand him, but his mother did. She encouraged
him to go on teaching himself by experiments with his
own hands, and testing for himself. As he looked
back at these traumatic years, Edison said, "My mother
was the making of me; she understood me; she let me
follow my best."[11] Other boys might be playing in
the fields or fishing in the pond, but Edison buried
himself in his cellar laboratory.

Albert Einstein's father was a man of perpetual
good nature and high hopes, but his goodness had been
exploited and his small business destroyed. Nothing
in Albert's early life suggested any genius. On the
contrary, he seemed somewhat retarded; even at the
age of nine, he was not verbally fluent. His parents
feared that he might be abnormal. When his father
asked the school headmaster what profession young
Albert should adopt, the headmaster replied, "It
doesn't matter; he will never make a success of anything." However, his parents brought two significant
influences on his later life. When Albert Einstein
was ill in bed at the age of five, his father showed

23

him a pocket compass, whose iron needle constantly
pointed in the same direction no matter how it was
turned. This impressed him very much and tapped his
interests and talents in exploring the mysteries of
the universe. Another influence came unexpectedly
from his uncle Jakob, who taught him that algebra
was a merry science, saying "We go hunting for a
little animal whose name we don't know, so we call
it X."[12] The impact of such timely stimulation is
indeed significant. At the age of forty, Einstein
wrote to his uncle saying "You have always been my
best-loved uncle. You have always been one of the
few who have warmed my heart whenever I thought of
you, and when I was younger, your visit was always
a great occasion." On one visit, his uncle brought
him an engine model which further kindled his interests in physics. It was to his uncle that he first
revealed an outline of the imaginative ideas later
developed into the Special Theory of Relativity.

        Paul Villiard wrote about his growing pain as
a son of immigrants from Europe.[13] His father never
adjusted even though he had been naturalized in the
United States for years. His father was very strict,
and had a strong sense of justice, but no humor. It
was easier for his father to ignore than to rear his
children. As the title of Villiard's autobiography
Growing Pains indicates, he had great pains in the
process of growing up. He got into trouble again
and again--he delayed a train, he blew up the house,
he burned down a forest, and he made his teacher sick
with poison ivy. But he was grateful to his father
for one thing--his father finally threw him out of
the family at the age of fourteen. "I was forced
to go out into the world on my own. Willy-nilly, I
became self-reliant and able to earn my living." His
curiosity about the things around him never diminished.
He learned that the more one knew about everything,
the more easily one could find work and make a living.
He felt that he owed his father a debt of gratitude
because what his father did to him at the age of
fourteen was just. Parental firmness is important
to a child's growth. Such firmness is not just an
indication of strong will or stubbornness, it is an
expression of parental transcendence from possessiveness, and a parental sense of justice.

The family is the earliest and most persistently infuencial context for the child for whom the parents are the source of love, authority, and role models. All subsequent experiences are perceived, understood, and reacted to largely in accordance with what has been learned in one's childhood, although one continues to learn new things through life. Later learning will no doubt modify the influence of the family, but the early core experiences can hardly be eradicated. As the eminent sociologist Talcott Parsons and social psychologist Robert Freed Bales have pointed out, high divorce rates and even the high incidence of marital conflicts do not indicate a diminishing importance of the family. The old saying "like father, like son" is still relevant.[14]

The life of Richard Leakey was briefly treated in a Time magazine essay recently. His father's influence on him was evident to those who had worked with both. Since he was six months old, he had been involved in the anthropological expeditions with his parents in Africa. His father's gifts were passed on to him, and he made his own name in his own way and at his own place of digging. But "Richard's just like the old man," said a colleague who knew them both, "You could talk to either one of them and know he was in another world thinking about some theory and not hearing a word you said."[15] Like his father, Richard Leakey is capable of working on "ten different things at the same time," ambitious, persistent in "following through an idea to the point where they were proved either right or wrong," and highly stimulating to others.

Perhaps we may ponder the family context in which we have been raised, and the family context in which we are going to raise our own children now or in the years ahead. If so, it may be well for us to consider the fact that the parents of children who have strong achievement motivation tend to have high standards of achievements; that they are likely to be warm and encourage excellence, but do not dominate; and that they tend to be consistent in their determination and self-driving, and are unanimously respected by their children, because they are generally decisive, confident, and loving.[16]

25

2. Educational Context

In addition to parents, school teachers and college professors are generally considered to be influencial in one's growth toward maturity. They are "significant individuals," who have left an indelible impact on their students. Most of the people I interviewed talked about their teachers and college professors with considerable enthusiasm, a sense of gratitude, and affectionate nostalgia. Apparently they were aware of the impact they had received in schools and colleges. Perhaps such impacts were unnoticed at the time and generally taken for granted. The things they talked most were the teacher's interests in students, timely encouragements, competence, enthusiasm, friendliness, personal care, commitment, etc.[17] The following excerpts are some of the memories which have survived the vicisitudes of life by virtue of the intensity of their emotional impact and the depth of meaning. No one can really judge except those who were personally involved.

"In the sixth grade, I had an outstanding teacher who gave me good preparation for junior high. She was an amazing person, challenging me to go ahead in doing something. Before that, I was content with what I was. My high school principal was an amazing person too. He gave us side-lectures on life experiences: He is still living and still comes to our reunion, . . . The things they had in common were their concern for me as an individual. Both of them challenged me. Their common characteristic was their ability to challenge. They made an impact on me; they were mature individuals; they had concern for me. . . . The mature teacher ought to have the ability to communicate the subject matters he teaches." This is a reflection of a retired teacher, which is focused on the teacher's ability to challenge the student, and the teacher's personal concern for the student as an individual.

A similar comment was given by a woman in her early forties. "In high school, I loved my math teacher. She was outstanding, very understanding, friendly with all children, and yet still our teacher. I thought this way too about my English teacher. When we put on a pageant for the graduation, he was one of our advisors. I thought I could not go on. But he shook my shoulder and said to me, 'You can do it! You can do it!' He is now retired, and I think very highly of him. I remember Dr. E. in college. During World War II, he wrote a letter to students and made us feel important. He did not talk down: He encouraged them. He would not hurt anyone's feelings. If he did not know something, well, perpahs next time he would."

The significant point in this comment is the teacher's maturity, manifested in the ability to maintain a dialectical tension between the effort to become friendly with the students and the need to act as an authority figure representing society and disciplining the students if necessary. To become friendly with the students means to be integrated with them, and to be the teacher means to be differentiated and transcendent from the students. The teacher's maturity is manifested in the dynamics of the three basic principles in human growth--1) differentiation, 2) integration, and 3) transcendence, which will be discussed in part Two. Some teachers become friendly with the students but cease to be the teacher. However, the mature teacher can balance the polarities, and is able to challenge students and to be a friend at the same time: "Very friendly . . . and yet . . ."

In describing influencial teachers in high school, another woman said, "A gym teacher and German teacher seemed to get the best out of me . . . . Influencial teacher? A math teacher, she was excellent because she knew her materials well. She was really interested in students. We knew her as a person, not just a teacher. She was firm and gentle. If someone worked hard, she would do all she could to help him." In this case, the dialectical nature of maturity is expressed in the phrase "firm and gentle." Furthermore, firmness is expressed in the teacher's challenge, and gentleness is an expression of love, care, and concern. In his study of American education, Harvard sociologist David Riesman has pointed out that "young people miss something if they are not called on for

27

any sacrifice or challenge."[18]

However, such a challenge needs to be communicated to the students in a way that makes them feel the teacher's respect for their ability to make the right choice in accordance with self-interest. A head nurse seemed to convey the challenge nicely, "One of my head nurses was very influencial when I was in training at the age of nineteen or so. After I graduated, I dreaded the responsibility. I was very upset and completely torn apart. It was the first time I was away from home, . . . terribly home sick. She said to me, 'Why don't you finish your probation period and then go into the area you would be interested.' But I did not run away. I have stayed on the job till now." The nurse is now close to retirement, and works in a large prestigeous hospital. It seems that the head nurse's firm challenge was cushioned by gentleness.

Sometimes a challenge may be just straightforward request or suggestion. A university professor said, "The most significant change took place in my college years. A teacher asked me to do things which seemed impossible to me then, namely, to write an essay about the measurement of social interaction. I was so unique in my approach that my peers considered me going in the wrong direction. . . . Two professors were particularly close to me. One of them said, 'If you want to research something, you don't have to go far away. It is right in your backyard! That was very significant." He has become one of the giants in his field.

At other times, a challenge may be indirect. Another university professor said that he did well in high school. In each stage of life, he seemed to have a particular hero--a teacher, a minister, a politician. But the most significant challenge took place in high school. It was customary for each graduating student to have a "year book" and collect signatures from teachers and friends. He went to the registrar, who wrote, "Paul, you would be a success, if you are able to think about others first." This was a turning point. He has become a champion for social justice and a strong supporter of the downtrodden.

28

A teacher's encouragement is often remembered.
When Richard was transfered to a private school, he
found himself at the bottom of the class. In order
to catch up with others, he studied very hard. What
meant most was that, when he passed the Latin test,
the dean of the school said to him, "From now on,
you will be O.K." His self-confidence was restored.
Before long, his name appeared on the Dean's list.
In response to the question "What are the common
characteristics of those who have influenced you
most in school?" he answered, "Those people were
entirely wrapped up in their teaching. For instance,
a Slavic professor was amazing. He was totally devoted, and made us feel that the language was alive
because he was so enthusiastic." In those who had
been influencial to him were their ability to establish a rapport with other people, their giving
of extra time and care, and their sense of wholeness.

Similarly a business executive remembered this
significant event in high school. A teacher took
him and another boy to a play, his first exposure to
the cultural programs of the city. It was such an
exciting experience that he went alone later. He
said, "She did not know how much it had meant to me."
This cultural exposure seemed to open his eyes and
tap his potential for artistic creativity and community involvement. Likewise, a retired French
teacher appreciated the kindneness of her teacher
in taking her for a trip. The relationships had
developed in such a way that she became a friend of
the family. The trip seemed to have stimulated her
interests in traveling. A little friendly gesture
may turn out to be a significant experience for the
student.

A number of interviewees considered their
teachers' total commitment and devotion to teaching
highly influencial and significant in their growth
toward maturity. These teachers were extremely interested in what they taught. "Three teachers stood
out. They were very stimulating and challenging.
A nun. . .teaching history. . . was in love with the
subject. She was so excited about the subject that
we became interested too. I worked for what I got."
"In college, an anthropology professor. . . his

commitment to his tasks, nothing else, made him
communicate so well to students. He was really committed. . .completely dedicated. These were the
common characteristics of those who had influenced
me." "There were two really good teachers--one in
seventh grade and the other in eighth grade. . . .
They were interested in what they taught and had
gone beyond their responsibilities." "In eighth grade,
I (son of a missionary) was sent to school back in
the United States. I had an influencial teacher,
very sensitive, very committed, and interested in
his subjects and made them come alive. He took
special interests in students, and became our family
friend. He was instrumental in my transitory period
of living in American culture." Likewise, a history
professor was acclaimed by a minister who said, "He
lectured in the way you would feel the presence of
St. Francis of Assisi. He made me feel these great
men being part of me."

Teachers were remembered because they had expressed an interest in their students, showed warmth
and compassion, and had confidence in them. "The
common ways these people have influenced me? One of
the common ways was that I had no doubt that they
liked me. I was an important person in their eyes;
they trusted me; the decisions I made, the ways I
behaved, were O.K. to them. I developed confidence
in myself because they had confidence in me. They
were sensible, gentle, and ready to confront antagonistic attitudes," said a middle age counselor.[19]

Sometimes, fellow students and friends can be
very influencial in one's growth toward maturity.
A college administrator said, "No particular teacher.
A Lutheran student worker was influencial because he
was able to say things I would like to identify with.
He was a graduate student." Another young adult said,
"In college I had a close friend whose husband had
suddenly died last summer. We were always seen together as two. . . it was, . . . mostly friendships,
the chance of becoming independent and of assuming
responsibilities. . ." that she found significant.

Likewise, we can find similar factors in biographies or autobiographies. The educational context

is important in human growth, and the teacher's professional competence, commitment and devotion to the subject matters, personal interest in and care for students, and the ability to communicate and challenge them is significant. In John Dewey's biography, we find that Professor George Sylvester Morris at Johns Hopkins University deeply impressed his students. He believed wholeheartedly in what he taught, and presented his ideas with force and sincerity. "My chief impression of Professor Morris as a teacher, vivid after the lapse of years," wrote Dewey in 1915, "is one of intellectual ardor, of an ardor for ideas which amounted to spiritual ardor."[20] The problems which troubled Dewey at the time seemed to be solved, and he became converted from his previous "intuitionist philosophy" to Neo-Hegelianism.

Thomas Merton was deeply impressed by Professor Mark Van Doren of Columbia University who was remarkable in his supreme simplicity, absolute sincerity, and heroic humility. In his autobiography, Merton wrote, "I thought to myself, who is this excellent man Van Doren. . . who really loves what he has to teach." He did "not secretly detest all literature," nor did he "abhor poetry, while pretending to be a professor of it." "Most of the time he asked questions. His questions were very good."[21] He seemed to bring out the best in his students with his questions, in a way unnoticed at the time but realized later. Being questioned, his students would say excellent things which they did not realize they were capable of saying. By questioning, he "educed" the best from his students. No doubt, Thomas Merton was deeply appreciative of Van Doren's sober and sincere intellect, his manner of dealing with his subject matter with perfect honesty and objectivity. Van Doren's maturity can be found in Merton's description of him, and the power of his teaching seems to reside in his challenge by questioning.

A woman autobiographer specified two teachers who had been influencial in her life. One was a woman teacher who had great pride and demanded her pupils have pride also. The group of children in her school was a highly select group. Her rules and regulations were strange and archaic, judged by

31

present educational standards and philosophy, but
many of her methods were more effective than some
modern ones. The sense of pride her teacher expressed and demanded was a challenge to seek greater
excellence and higher ideals. This teacher was a
good singer, and whenever she was going to sing at
a particular church, she would let her pupils know
so that they might follow her and share her sense of
pride and excellence in singing. Another significant
teacher was in the public school which she attended
later on. When she was transfered to the public
school, she was not happy at first. One day a man
came and gave a show at which several canaries performed tricks. Pupils were asked to write an essay
about it afterward. Her essay was chosen by the
teacher and applauded in front of other pupils. "The
sudden recognition did something for me," she said,
"from then on I felt better about going to public
school."[22] Teachers who encourage pupils to seek
excellence are often remembered and appreciated. On
the other hand, the teacher needs to give the pupils
good chance of achieving excellence.

Helen Keller is another case. Unable to see
or hear, she did not have much chance in life. But
she was fortunate enough to have a teacher who really
cared--Anne Sullivan. Patiently and understandingly,
Sullivan taught Keller a sign language through which
Keller began to understand what her teacher said.
Eventually, she learned to speak, and later she went
to Radcliffe College, took her examinations, and became a world figure, writing, lecturing, and appear-
ing in films and television. Nothing was more influencial in her like than her teacher.[23]

Genevieve Caufield was blind. When she was
young, she felt ashamed of the unjust treatment of
the Japanese in the United States and decided to be
a peace maker by bringing good will to the people of
Japan. Step by step she prepared herself for the
mission, gathering necessary knowledge about Japan
and its culture, making personal contacts with people who might be of help to her in achieving her
objectives, and actual planning. First she went to
Overbrook School for the Blind in Philadelphia. The
principal of the school was "a remarkable man." In

her autobiography she wrote, "His pervasive personality and his unshakable confidence in our ability
to live full lives in spite of our handicap fired
all of us with courage and enthusiasm."[24] The principal instilled in them "the desire to live like
other people, to be independent and to contribute
something to the world instead of just asking the
world to take care of" them. She was also impressed
by a teacher who was totally blind. He shared the
principal's fervent conviction that they should be
urged to involve themselves as much as possible in
the world outside. "The power of decision lies
within yourselves," he said. "If you are determined
to do it, you can do it." Again this shows that the
teacher is often remembered for challenging, confidence, enthusiasm, and encouragement.

A physician appreciated the firm attitude of
the Academic Dean who challenged him to either do
well in his study or leave the Medical School, because his study had been severely affected by his
interest in women. In his autobiography, he wrote
"He certainly convinced me, I began paying more
attention to my classes."[25]

One of the most significant of growing experiences is being treated with due respect and
personal interest. In her autobiography, a Chinese
woman expressed her appreciation of her physics
teacher for treating his students as adults, not
small children.[26] And in Robert W. White's study
on growing experiences, Hartley Hale, one of his
subjects, said "Some people I admired most were my
teacher of physics in high school and my teacher of
biology in junior college, both of whom were men
and both of whom were very inspiring teachers. Both
were intensely interested in the subjects that they
taught and both were intensely interested in individuals, which is a rare quality in a teacher, and I
did well in those subjects because I liked both
teachers so much."[27] In the autobiography of Williard Uphause, two college professors were remembered
for their friendly invitation to join them in sports
and other activities--the roar from an upstair window
of Dr. J.'s office, "What about a game of croquet?"
or helping with the haying on another professor's

small farm. They shaped "my mind and heart, calling forth feelings and powers from me that I didn't know were there." "That was a man!" said Williard Uphause.[28]

Unfortunately what happens in school is not always appreciated and educationally constructive. The Gymanasium which Albert Einstein attended seemed to have a negative impact on him.[29] Its discipline created in him a deep suspicion of authority. In his speech at the seventy-second Convocation of the State University of New York, he talked about his school experiences in his boyhood: "The teachers in the elementary school appeared to me like sergeants and in the Gymnasium the teachers were like lieutenants." This method of teaching was based on fear, force, and arbitrary authority; the discipline was ruthless, and had a "near paranoia" affect on him. The boyhood hardships symbolized what was the worst in the German character so much so that he could not develop real friendships among the German-born. "No friendship for any real German," said he. "Max von Lane was the closest to me." However, one teacher there stood out positively. He tried to make his pupils think for themselves while most of his colleagues did little more than academic drilling.

Malcolm X seemed to have had a good attitude toward his teachers until something happened in school one day. In his autobiography, he says that he did well in English and the teacher liked him. Once this English teacher said to him, "Malcolm, you ought to be thinking about a career. Have you been giving it thought?" Actually he had never thought about it. But he answered, "Well, yes sir, I have been thinking. I'd like to be a lawyer." The town had neither a black lawyer nor physician. All he really knew for certain was that a lawyer didn't wash dishes. He was sick and tired of washing dishes. The English teacher looked surprised and said, "Malcolm, one of life's first needs is for us to be realistic. . . . A lawyer--that's not realistic goal for a nigger."[30] The teacher suggested carpentry. It was then that Malcolm X began to change inside--he drew away from white people. The teacher might have had good intensions, but he lost Malcolm X.

34

3. Church Context

In the personal interviews and biographical studies I have had, religious institutions appear to be another significant context for growth toward maturity. Naturally, there were exceptions. Negative comments about religious institutions were mostly due to experiences of power struggles and factionalism, prejudice and narrow-mindedness, irrational and superstitious religiosity, and archaic tradition and practices. Without referring to particular individuals, a counselor jokingly said, "You know? There are some sick people in the church." He seemed to suggest that he was deeply disappointed and surprised. In response to the question of whether he had found any support from his church in coping with his divorce, a business executive said "No, I did not." The man who had had an affair with the executive's wife was also a member of the church. "What was helpful to me then was the basic philosophy I learned from my father in childhood--'Do your best.'" He remarried, and his second wife was also a member of the same church. It was her first marriage. So he was neither hostile nor bitter toward the church.

On another occasion an engineer said, "I am an agnostic. No religion has influenced me." Similarly another engineer said, "I am not a religious person. Back in China, Buddhism was superstitious. I went to the church when I first came to the United States. It was mostly social. But I do not go to church now." A retired professor said, "I wanted to go into the ministry and went to a seminary. In my senior year, I attended the Annual Conference for the first time as an observer and had a glimpse of its power struggle . . . ." From his point of view, it was "utterly unethical." That was his first and last attendance of a denominational meeting. Another retired professor said, "My father organized a union of farmers to cut cost. . . . We went to a rural church, and we sometimes talked about the church. One day I said to my father, 'You know? The farmer's union is more Christian than the church--more co-operative.' And my father said, 'I feel the same way too.' (laugh)." In describing her church life, a biologist said, "My

mother was a Catholic, and my father was a Protestant.
I did not feel accepted by the church. . . . So, I
had no root in the church. Neither of my parents
participated actively."

However, the majority of those I interviewed
have had positive experiences with religious institutions. This corresponds with the study of "good
neighbors" in America by sociologist Pitirim A.
Sorokin.[31] He found that American good neighbors
appeared to be predominantly religious groups, although there were a minority who had no affiliation
with any of the institutional religions. However,
such an "irreligious" altruism or purely ethical
religion was possible only for some 2 to 8% of his
sample, but the majority of good neighbors were religious altruists. This indicates the positive significance of religious institutions in human growth toward
maturity.

A young psychiatrist came to the United States
not long ago. He was an active member of an evangelical church; he was converted by an American missionary who taught at a mission school in Manila. With
great excitement and a positive view of the church,
he said "I was very much influenced by the church.
I was very active, singing in the choir, talking to
people, doing evangelical work, etc. During my high
school years, I became a Christian. That was my happiest experience."

Likewise, a physician's wife had a positive
experience with the church. When she had a crisis
in her mid-adulthood, she moved to the town where
she used to live. She worked and supported her husband going through Medical School, but her husband
left her for his student nurse. In search of support,
she turned to the church. "In 1969 I came to this
town. I looked for church affiliation. I went to
. . . church and liked it. The minister preached
in non-magical terms. He preached Jesus as a human
being, trying to help people in the way he helped me.
For the first time I felt the appeal."

Recently, preaching seems to have lost some of
its centrality and power in the Christian ministry.

The minister's study becomes just an office. However, there are individuals who consider preaching as an effective way in which the church made significant impacts on them. There were particular sermons which they deeply appreciated. A retired professional said, "Our ministers were good. I went to hear . . . in Boston. I remember one of his sermons. One Sunday evening, he said 'We need three things to be happy-- physical wellbeing, being needed by someone, a worthwhile job." A seminary professor specified a sermon preached by a German-born theologian who was superb in his communication. On a day when the whole seminary community was busy cleaning its environment, he did not use manuscript, but a small piece of paper, on which, were written three phrases--"unused muscles," "unseen corners," and "unwanted tasks." A housewife said that one of the sermons she heard at a college was very significant and influencial in changing her attitude. It was entitled "The Seven Sins," and the sin of pride meant the most to her at the time.

A graduate student from Hong Kong greatly admired his bishop saying, "He was not a popular preacher, but his sermons were very 'touching.' They met the people's spiritual needs. His sermons were something which came out of himself, his own inner life in a very simple way. It appealed to man's needs for self-denial and aroused a sense of hunger for justice. It appealed for a higher level of living." He went on describing the youth conference he attended one summer. The most inspiring experience during the conference was the candle light service in the evening on the last day. Some of the things he heard made a great impact on him. "Above all, the speaker talked about his own weakness during the period of adolescence. His personal experience made me realize the problems I had to struggle with as a third generation Christian," said he. In answering the question "Who is your hero?" a man close to his retirement recalled his teenage years and young adulthood, saying, "Hero? The pastor of the church was my hero. He was the greatest preacher I have ever known. . . . When he preached, it was perfect. He became my model. . . . He was willing to stick his neck out."

The right words at the right time can be very

significant for those who struggle with a particular
problem. They often find new insights about themselves and the problem, and can then set things in
a proper perspective. A bereaved widow greatly appreciated the right words of her minister who said, "You
do not have to work yourself to heaven." His words
gave her a better understanding of herself--"That
struck me. Somebody said it, and I was ready to hear
it." A minister lost his father when he was approxi-
mately fourteen. He tried to recapture what happened
to him and said, "The church was very sympathetic at
that time. The minister who was older than my father
gave me warm support emotionally. His recognition of
my presence at the church and participation in its
program helped me affirm my self-esteem and personhood. I felt that 'I am somebody.'"

   In describing his pastor, a graduate student
said, "My pastor was influencial. The kind of thing
and the way he did it influenced me. It might be
because he and my father were quite different persons.
When there was an important decision to be made, my
father was a person who would pray and fast for days,
and then he would say, 'This is the will of God.'
But being trained in science, I was not happy with
him. I appreciated the way my pastor solved important problems--he would pray, but he would also do
things rationally." This helped the graduate student
resolve inner conflicts.

   A retired minister recalled the influence of
a Sunday School teacher. When he was a youngster,
he was popular and active in the church. "A Sunday
School teacher was very significant. . . . She was
one of the kindest and most open persons I have known.
She taught me that she was a servant of God to serve
everybody. She had no children, just her husband.
I learned later that her husband was a drunkard. And
yet she poured herself out for others. Once she
invited us children to her home. Her husband came
back very drunk. She felt ashamed. This opened our
eyes to see her problems and made us realize why she
seemed to have something to cover up. Although I
was only a boy, I could sense how much she had to
put up with." She was very sacrificial in loving

children in spite of the fact that she had her own problems. She seemed to leave an indelible impression on him as a boy.

For a business man, the Bible plays an important role in his religious life and growth. He said, "My religious beliefs certainly have something to do with honesty. . . . I do not worry about what will be my next job or when it will come. But it always comes. I can go to the church and do not listen to the sermon. But I cannot stay home without going to the church. I feel I should be there. I like to do my share. Frankly, I do not enjoy . . . meetings. But I feel I am expected to be there. 'The fear of the Lord is the beginning of knowledge,' but I do not think 'fear' is the right word. I read the Bible every night." For him, the Bible seemed to be the key channel for his growth.

Above all, the minister is the influencial person in a church context. "When I am with church groups, I feel secure," a teacher said, "I am a Christian, and I like to help other people live the kind of life I do value. Church is always an important part of my life. Our minister in my childhood was a grandfather figure. This old man made young people feel close to him. He was the one who taught me and arranged for me to attend conferences and learn how the church operated and how to take responsibilities. Then, my attitude changed from being a receiver to that of giver, and I began to teach Sunday School. I find our present minister very helpful. He always draws me into conversation or gets me involved in something. Whatever I say or do will be responded to by him." Without the help of the outgoing minister she might have become withdrawn and isolated. She acknowledged that she was a shy person. Acceptance, encouragement, and challenge are important in human growth toward maturity.

Church is a place where acceptance of another person seems most conducive. For an administrator of a church-related institution, the significant event was his adventure of leaving his familiar small town for an entirely new environment in a metropolitan city. "It opened up experiences in the urban scene, and we joined . . . church. The youth worker was a graduate student, who opened up my sensitivity. His intense concern about me as a person and willingness to share with me his inner problems meant a great deal to me. I was twenty-two years of age at that time. His acceptance of me prepared my turning point."

It was reported by a minister that when a new bishop met with the people under his care, the atmosphere was tense at first; being sensitive to the barrier between him and the audience, the prelate talked tactfully about his own problems, and before long the atmosphere began to change and the ice melted. By talking about his problems, the bishop extended an invitation to his people to share something meaningful and deep within him. What was behind the invitation was his acceptance of them as persons with problems. Such acceptance is powerful in transforming personality structure, and it is essential for that transference to take place.

Life crises are often the best opportunities for the church to play an influencial role in helping people undergoing stress and strain. A government employee said, "I have a great admiration for Dr. L. He helped us when my sister was killed in an accident. He helped my mother when my father died. He always took interest in people." But this does not mean that growth can only take place at a time of crisis. An unmarried career woman said, "Since I was a child, I haven't had the problem of believing in God. The doubts other people had did not upset me. I might not have the answer, but they did not upset me. I believe in God's love for me. Somehow I was born with a desire to do good for others. I want others to know how much God loves them. If God loves them, I have to reach out in tangible ways. If I have to die, there will be good life before me." Gradual conversion may be the norm for those whose life seems without any major crisis.

For an immigrant family, the crisis was not so obvious, but the timely help of the minister of the nearby church was a significant contribution to the growth of its children. In retrospect, a college

40

professor said, "We were the only Chinese family in the community. I went to the church more for the sake of socialization than for religious reasons. . . . The minister was always kind and helpful. He was very concerned about our social adjustment. Our parents did not allow us children go out in the evening. I was thirteen. The minister came to our home consecutively for two weeks talking to my father in to letting us go out. Eventually he convinced my father that it was safe to do so. That was the first real contact we had with the outside world." It was no surprise that he had found a career in social psychology.

Church is not only significant for the growth of the laity, but also for the clergy. Just as professors often acknowledge their indebtedness to their students, ministers often express their appreciation for support from congregations. They have served, but they were also served at one time or another. An outstanding churchman said, "When I had my first parish. . . during the Great Depression, I discovered that the people with whom I was associated did more things for me than I did for them. They were mature people. I was the one who received. . . . Their courage and wisdom helped me." Another churchman said, "During my pastorate in West Virginia, I found a layman significant in my growth. He was 'down to earth.'" A chief church executive expressed his indebtedness to a layman saying, "I am thinking of a man of sixty-six years of age, a banker. . . . He is a kind of 'seasoning.' I often go out of my way to spend an hour or two just to listen to him because I value his judgements, although he is no longer a member of our church board. He is very candid and also very warm in relating to me. He is objective in judging my decisions." For him, this banker was a model of a mature person.

From biographies or autobiographies, we can also find religious impacts on human growth both positive and negative. H. G. Wells' mother tried to pass on to him her own simple faith in an almighty God, a faith that had been shaken by the death of her little girl but later reasserted itself all the

41

more strongly. At first Wells did not have doubts, but later he was filled with indignation against the God who watched out for human weakness and punished backsliders with hell-fire. This struck him as unfair and cruel. Outwardly he was confirmed as an Anglican, but he never quite forgave himself for the bitter humiliation he felt as he knelt at the altar rails on the day he was confirmed. His resentment against the church endured to the end of his life. He hated compromise and never bargained with his conscience.[32] One may suggest that his uncompromising spirit is indeed the most religious, and that what caused his resentment against the church might be traced to his mother's imposition and the theology of his time. In fact, his protest could be considered an inevitable part of maturation.

Bertrand Russell's parents were radicals. His father was a free-thinker and lost his seat in the Parliament for advocating birth-control. Bertrand was only two years old, when his mother died. Shortly after that, his father died also. His father's will gave custody of young Russell to two atheists. His father wished his two sons to be protected from the "evils" of religion. Nevertheless, Bertrand Russell was not as completely irreligious as he professed to be or is acclaimed to be. In the spring of 1952, when he visited Greece, he found what he saw there exceedingly interesting. After being impressed by the great achievements of the past, he found himself in a little church belonging to the days of the Byzantine Empire. To his astonishment, he felt more at home in this little church than he felt in the Pantheon or in any of the Greek buildings of pagan times.[33] He realized then that the Christian outlook had a firmer hold on him than he had known. The hold was much deeper than cognitive understanding or reasoning; it was at the feeling level. It was a moment of self-understanding and self-discovery.

In the biography of Bill Lear, a successful technologist, we can find that the significance of the church in his growth toward maturity was mainly that of socialization.[34] At the Moody Institute, he learned grammar, speech, and social skills. He remembered that when he was shaking hands for the

first time, he was chided, "Look, don't give me a
cold fish! Look at me straight in the eyes and give
me a firm hand." This helped him significantly, and
the church became the channel by which he made contacts with the world. Unfortunately, his experiences
at the church were not all positive. He made an
innocent remark about a girl friend who missed the
Sunday School picnic because of illness. His teacher
misinterpreted what he said about his girl friend,
and he lost her. He became sour, and ever since the
church saw very little of him. Perhaps such a misunderstanding was not very serious but its impact on
him could not be ignored by the teacher.

In an autobiography, a journalist disclosed a
different kind of negative impact. On one Easter
Sunday in his childhood, the church was packed with
fathers and mothers. During the service, he was
called up to the pulpit, patted on the head by the
aging minister, and awarded a prize for memorizing
Bible verses. To his great disappointment, he found
that what he received was totally useless to him.
"It was a full-rigged ship! A ship in the desert,
a ship with no sea to sail it on," he said angrily.
He carried it home, put it carefully away in the
woodshed, and forever thereafter refrained from anything religious.[35]

On the other hand, we can also find that the
church sometimes has a positive impact quite unexpectedly at a critical time. This happened to an
English clergyman who wrote an autobiography entitled
Determined to Live describing his struggle with cancer,
which struck him while he was travelling in the United
States. He received a letter while he was in the
hospital in Los Angeles from a woman whose name he
could hardly remember. She wrote, "I used to be a
member of your St. Margaret's Church in London. I
thought I would write to you as it will be twenty-
one years ago on the 26th July that God used you to
help me. I very nearly did not come into that meeting that night. I shall never forget walking up and
down Lee High Road trying to decide whether to go or
not to go in. . . . Finally I decided to go, just
this once, and make it the last. How different were
my feelings when the meeting was over."[36] The church

meeting that night could not be very different from
other meetings, nor did the minister know of her
coming. But it became a turning point in her life.

There is a dimension to such an incident which
transcends and passes human understanding. There
are wonders in life which we cannot really antici-
pate. We may be albe to study the details of such
experiences scientifically, but nobody can really
predict the exact outcome of any simulation or dupli-
cation of the experiences, because the dynamic forces
behind the visible phenomena are not entirely under
our controls. At best, we can acknowledge partial
success of human controls, because we are not the
master of these forces in and outside of ourselves.
Sometimes, we do not even know what is working in
us. We are in the midst of the interplay of differentiation, integration, and transcendence.

4. Other Contexts

In the United States, we emphasize individual
independence and achievements so much that it is
difficult to accept the fact that human growth is
not entirely dependent on our own efforts and planning.
Our growth depends on our openness and receptivity
as well as on external stimulation and nurturance.
In a sense we are what we have received and internalized. Whoever is prevented from experiencing
external stimulation and nurturance is bound to be
crippled. The evil of so-called "discrimination"
is to prevent particular groups of people from experiencing particular things based on race, sex, and
creed. So far, we have discussed significant stimulation and nurturance from parents, teachers, professors, youth workers, ministers, and Sunday School
teachers, etc. in the contexts of family, school,
and church. There are other significant sources of
stimulation and nurturance in human growth, and they
may come from people of genuine good will who are
eager to help, like the Good Samaritan in the Bible,
from professional mentors, from books, or from nature
itself.

Johnny was always in trouble. He tried not to
fail, but failed all the time. In an utter despair,
he cried out "What am I gonna do? If I play with
the big kids, they get me in trouble. If I play with
the little kids, I get them in trouble. What am I
gonna do?" Fortunately, a Good Samaritan came to
his aid. Mr. O'Brien helped him and loved him sincerely. Being impelled by conflicting drives within
himself and besieged by conflicting influences outside, Johnny was perplexed and unhappy. However,
there were times Johnny was able to restrain himself.
What was the source of his power of restraint? He
said to Mr. O'Brien, "I did not steal because I
thought of you."[37] This was highly significant in
his growth. The altruistic love of his counselor
became a source of inner strength. Since Johnny was
an orphan, it was arranged that he should stay at
Mrs. Baker's home, and there were further changes in
his personality and patterns of behavior for the
better, because she was "a very loving, affectionate
woman." If Johnny had not met Mr. O'Brien, Mrs.
Baker, and others who genuinely loved him, he might
not have changed.

William James was fortunate enough to have a
truly gifted man, Charles W. Eliot as his teacher at
the Lawrence Scientific School Chemistry Laboratory.
Eliot later became the President of Harvard University
and made it a distinguished institution. It was Eliot
who offered James his first academic position and who
took great pleasure and satisfaction throughout suc-
ceeding years in watching him rise to world eminence,
first in psychology and then in philosophy.[38] Likewise, when Henry Thoreau had a hard time getting
what he wanted in teaching after graduating from
Harvard College, he was fortunate in that Ralph Waldo
Emerson provided a living place for him, made his
personal collection available to him, and stimulated
his thinking by the exchange of ideas. In the fall
of 1848, Emerson did his best to persuade James
Clark to invite Thoreau to give a lecture in Boston.
But Clark ignored Emerson's suggestion. Emerson
did not give up, and before long, Thoreau delivered
a lecture in Salem on November 23 of that year. The
lecture, on "Student Life in New England, Its Economy,"
was a great success.[39]

Reinhold Niebuhr has often been considered one of the master minds of America and a giant in modern Protestantism. Sherwood Eddy became his prime professional benefactor. Attracted to Niebuhr's creative ministry among the industrial workers in Detroit and by several articles in <u>Atlantic Monthly</u> and <u>The Christian Century</u>, Eddy provided Niebuhr an assistant minister so that he could have more time to write and lecture. Eddy recommended him to the newly created Chair in Christian Ethics at Union Theological Seminary in New York City in 1928. Consequently Niebuhr was able to dialogue with students, and produced numerous contributions to modern Protestant thought. In addition to Eddy's help, we may trace Niebuhr's growth to the influence of his father, a Lutheran evangelical minister, to his re-reading of the Bible and St. Augustine, and to the impacts of his pastoral experience.[40]

The mentor can be very significant in one's professional as well as personal growth. In describing his mentor, an electrical engineer in Boston said, "He was a great man. His maturity was multidimensional. He was sensitive to the feelings of his subordinates. When he did anything that hurt them, he rectified it the next day. Everybody admired him and he had personal concern for us. He was able to bring us together and maintained harmony among us all." This electrical engineer had succeeded his mentor as the director of his research lab, and operated it almost in the same way. On another occasion, a former official of a penal institution described his superior by saying, "K. was a great man. If I could see him today, I would embrace him like a big brother. What I discovered in him was a man who above all respected honesty and morality. I learned that he was one of the rare executives who refused to remain distant and aloof from us. His decency was absolutely inspirational." These two professionals spoke of their superiors with an affection, understanding, and respect no less than one would have for parents, or teachers, or ministers.

The influencial person can be one's own spouse. It does not mean domination by one's spouse, but

rather meaningful change through the relationship
established between the couple. This was evident
in the life of an artist who came to the United
States as an immigrant. Leaving his home in Austria,
he felt unsettled and uprooted. He rented a small
room in Greenwich Village and later took over a barn
studio in Connecticut. He furnished it in order to
settle down there. But "a stranger in a new country
will always be a stranger," he confided in his diary,
"until he falls in love with--and his love is recipro-
cated by--a woman of that country."[41] The significant
person for him was the woman with whom he fell in
love. Although he painted and cooked lavish meals
for himself, the tranquil life he dreamed of seemed
far away. His lover dispelled his sense of alienation in this new land. He settled down and became
identified with the adopted country.

Significant individuals in one's life can be
colleagues or career partners. In each stage of life,
we may have different significant persons who make
influencial impacts on our lives. Sigmund Freud had
Josef Breuer, a scientist and one of the most respected family physicians in Vienna. Breuer was a
"man of striking intelligence" and had produced several works of lasting value on the physiology of
breathing and other medical subjects. In spite of
the age difference (Breuer was fourteen years older
than Freud), they became intimate friends and helpers
in difficult circumstances, and shared their scientific interests with one another.[42] At each stage
of life, one needs a close companion. When H. G.
Wells was young, he was discouraged because of the
harsh review of his biology textbook. But he was
fortunate to find a friend and partner in Walter
Low, whose experience was just the opposite of Wells.
From Low he learned a great deal, because Low had a
broader outlook and a more general cultural upbringing resulting from the prosperity of his family in
childhood.[43] Somehow, each Freud has his Breuer,
and each Wells has his Low. Mutual stimulation among
colleagues is important in human growth toward maturity.

In a variety of ways life is changed, and in
each significant event, there is at least one signifi-

cant person involved so as to make it happen. For
one immigrant, the Good Samaritan was a woman lawyer
who supported his graduate study and the subsequent
settling down of his family in the United States.
For a cancer patient, the most influencial person
was the physician who was willing to take a chance
on him and challenged his determination to live. For
a sixteen-year-old girl, it was someone who put in
a good word for her first interview. Informed of
the positive response from the employer, she was overwhelmed with joy and said, "Thanks, thanks a lot.
Everyone was so kind to me that I went to the ladies
room and cried."

Reading can be significant to growth, although
learning is more than accumulation of facts and knowledge. Among those I interviewed, there were individuals who considered the atmosphere of avid reading by
parents, brothers, and sisters at home or the stimulation and encouragement for avid reading by friends
at school highly significant in their early mastery
of basic knowledge. "Our Christmas gifts were books,"
said one proudly. "My friends in high school were
all avid readers," said another. This was also true
for Edison. After he lost his hearing, he drove himself to more reading and experiments. The public
library in Detroit became a refuge during lay overs,
while he worked for a railroad company. He became
a member of the library by paying the substantial
fee of two dollars for a card. He said, "I didn't
read a few books. I read the library."[44] He got a
collection of The Penny Library Encyclopedia and read
it through. He read Burton's Anatomy of Melancholy,
heavy reading for a fifteen year old boy. George
Washington upheld the notion that "a knowledge of
books" is "the basis upon which other knowledge is
to be built."[45] Acknowledging that education did
transcend book learning, he admonished his officers
to read books. He worked hard to equal those of his
contemporaries who had had a formal education. In
high school, John Dewey sought the company of books.
The reading of Plato's Republic had a great impact on
the life and thought of H. G. Wells during his visit
to Up Park and thereafter.[46] For an undergraduate,
the crucial thing in the student's life was the reading of James Joyce's A Portrait of the Artist as a

For others nature can be significant. As a young man, William O. Douglas left town before dusk one day, and climbed the barren ridge west of Sela Gap. The historic memories of the region filled his mind and unfolded before him. He sensed that man is indeed insignificant, and that man should not fight against nature but to seek "health and strength and courage" from it. Then he felt at peace with himself and the universe. In his autobiography, he wrote "That night, I think, there came to me the germ of a philosophy of life."[48] This can also be found in the life of Yuichiro Miura who skied down Everest. Standing on the rim on top of Mount Fuji one day, staring at the straight and deadly run below, he momentarily experienced a clarity of spirit. He said that only when he was posed on the edge of life and death did he fully appreciate the wonder of human experience, the beauty of humanity and the spontaneous pleasure of his inner self. Only with the threat of loss did he fully cherish what he had.[49]

Young people are often encouraged by educators to wander through the forest, play in the lakes, climb mountains, and sail across the seas. Thus, they would have the opportunity to try their strength against the uncompromising hand of nature, and through testing their own potentials they can come to know who they are and what they can do. And only with that self-knowledge can they begin to co-operate with their friends and society at large, and live in harmony with the earth. This is well-illustrated by Siao Yu's Mao Tse-Tung and I Were Beggars. They tested their strength by choosing the hard route around the province one summer when they were young friends.[50] By living in harmony with the earth, they draw strength and inspiration from it. This has been the basic Taoistic attitude.

Confucius said, "The wise delight in water; the good delight in mountains. The wise move, the good stay. The wise are happy; the good endure."[51] In the world there are good people and happy people-- the good people love mountains and the happy people love the sea. The good people are steady, trustful,

and principled just as the mountain is steady, un-
moveable, and calm, unless it is a volcano: The
happy people are energetic, changeful, and dynamic
just as the sea is challenging, changeful, and
dynamic. Nature provides mountains as well as seas
to meet the needs of both good people and happy
people. The good people are not always happy, and
the happy people are not always good. But nature
can meet the needs of both and is a significant context in which all may grow.

In brief, maturation takes place largely in
the contexts of family, school, church, and other
situations which can be philanthropic, literary, or
nature itself. In each growing event, there are
significant factors which can be personal "thou" or
impersonal "it" and in each growing experience, there
are concrete manifestations of differentiation (such
as challenge and encouragement to become an individual person), integration (such as love, trust, care),
and transcendence (such as spiritual renewal, a sense
justice, and value of excellence) which constitute
paradoxcial and yet unified dynamism.

NOTES

1. A. L. Baldwin et al., "Patterns of Parent Behavior," Psychological Monographs, 58 (268) (1945),
   pp. 1-75.

2. Lester David, Ted Kennedy: Triumphs and Trage-
   dies (New York: Grossett & Dunlap, 1972), pp.
   234-235. Cp. James MacGregor Burns, Edward
   Kennedy and the Camelot Legacy (New York: W. W.
   Norton & Co., 1976), p. 71.

3. Bu-wei Chao, The Autobiography of a Chinese Woman
   (New York: The John Day Co., 1947), pp. 45-80.

4. James Nelson, ed., Wisdom (New York: W. W. Norton & Co., 1958), p. 193.

5. Ibid., p. 204.

6. Ibid., p,7.

7. Richard Kostelanetz, Master Minds (New York: The Macmillan Co., 1969), pp. 36-37.

8. Augustus Cardinal Bea et al., What I Have Learned (New York: Simon and Schuster, 1968), p. 65.

9. A. Scott Crossfield, Always Another Dawn: The Story of Rocket Pilot (New York: The World Publishing Co., 1960), pp. 23, 61, 66, 89-98.

10. Bertrand Russell, The Autobiography of Bertrand Russell (Boston: Little, Brown and Co., 1969), p. 18.

11. Matthew Josephson, Edison (New York: McGraw-Hill Book Co., 1959), pp. 12-40.

12. Ronald W. Clark, Einstein: The Life and Times (New York: The World Publishing Co., 1971), pp. 9-12.

13. Paul Villiard, Growing Pains: The Autobiography of a Young Boy (New York: Funk and Wagnalls, 1970), passim.

14. Talcott Parsons and Robert Freed Bales, Family, Socialization and Interaction Process (Glencoe, Ill: Free Press, 1955), passim. See also, Robert Freed Bales , Personality and Interpersonal Behavior (New York: Holt, Rinehart and Winston, 1970), pp. 197-198.

15. "Puzzling Out Man's Ascent," Time, November 7, 1977, pp. 64-67, 69, 77-78.

16. David McClelland, The Roots of Consciousness (New York: D. Van Nostrand, 1964), pp. 39-44.

17. Cp. The qualities of the effective psycho-therapiest are: 1) empathy, 2) genuineness, 3) regard and liking of the client by the therapist, 4) unconditional accetpance. See, Carl

R. Rogers, <u>On Becoming a Person</u> (Boston: Houghton Mifflin Co., 1961), p. 265.

18. David Riesman, <u>Constraint and Variety in American Education</u> (Lincoln, NE.: The University of Nebraska Press, 1956), p. 151.

19. Cp. Richard Shikiar, "Student and Faculty Perceptions of Teacher Characteristics," <u>Journal of Psychology</u>, 92 (1976), pp. 215-218.

20. George Dykuizen, <u>The Life and Mind of John Dewey</u> (Carbondale, Ill: Southern Illinois University Press, 1973), pp. 31-33.

21. Thomas Merton, <u>The Seven Storey Mountains</u> (New York: Harcourt, Brace and World, 1948), pp. 138-140.

22. Septimer Poinsette Clark, <u>Echo in My Soul</u> (New York: E. P. Dutton & Co., 1962), pp. 18-19.

23. Helen A. Keller, <u>The Story of My Life</u> (Garden City, N.Y.: Doubleday & Co., 1955).

24. Genevieve Caufield, <u>The Kingdom Within</u> (New York: Harper & Row, 1960), pp. 24-26.

25. Morris Fishbein, M.D., <u>An Autobiography</u> (New York: Doubleday & Co., 1966), p. 16.

26. Han Suyin, A Mortal Flower (New York: G. P. Putman's Sons, 1965), p. 272.

27. Robert W. White, <u>Lives in Progress</u> (New York: Holt, Rinehart, and Winston, 1966), p. 46.

28. Williard Uphause, <u>Commitment</u> (New York: Holt, Rinehart, and Winston, 1966), pp. 17-18, 29.

29. Clark, <u>Einstein: The Life and Times</u>, pp. 12-14.

30. Malcolm X and A. Haley, <u>The Autobiography of Malcolm X</u> (New York: Glove, 1965), p. 35.

31. P. A. Sorokin, <u>Altruistic Love</u> (Boston: Beason Press, 1950), pp. 41-48

32. Antonnia Vallentine, H. G. Wells, Prophet of Our Day (New York: The John Day Co., 1950), pp. 1-37.

33. Bertrand Russell, The Autobiography of Bertrand Russell, 1872-1914 (Boston: Little, Brown and Co., 1969), pp. 8-10; The Autobiography of Bertrand Russell, 1914-1969 (New York: Simon and Schuster, 1969), p. 83.

34. Victor Boesen, They Said It Couldn't Be Done: The Incredible Story of Bill Lear (New York: Doubleday & Co., 1971), p. 11.

35. Owen Payne White, The Autobiography of a Durable Sinner (New York: G. P. Putman's Sons, 1943), p. 45.

36. Brian Hession, Determined to Live (New York: Doubleday & Co., 1957), p. 109.

37. Jean Evans, Three Men (New York: Alfred A. Knopf, Inc., 1954), p. 29-39. Also in the Grant Study at Harvard, it was found that what appeared to help Godfrey Minot Camille, M.D., mature was "a sustained relationship with loving people." See, George E. Vaillant, Adaptation to Life (Boston: Little, Brown and Co., 1977), p. 251.

38. Gay Wilson Allen, William James: A Biography (New York: Simon and Schuster, 1969), pp. 75-76.

39. Walter Harding, The Days of Henry Thoreau (New York: Alfred A. Knopf, Inc., 1965), p. 236.

40. Kostelanetz, Master Minds, pp. 238-244.

41. C. L. Sulzberger, Unconquered Souls: The Resistantialists (New York: The Overlook Press, 1963), p. 43.

42. Sigmund Freud, An Autobiographical Study, Vol. 26 of The Complete Psychological Works of Sigmund Freud ed. by Ernest Jones (London: Hogarth Press, 1935), p. 32.

43. Vallentine, <u>H. G. Wells</u>, p. 92.

44. Josephson, <u>Edison</u>, p. 33.

45. Richard B. Morris, <u>Seven Who Shaped Our Destiny</u> (New York: Harper & Row, Publishers, Inc., 1973), pp. 36-37.

46. Vallentine, <u>H. G. Wells</u>, pp. 37-42.

47. George W. Goethals and D. Klos, <u>Experiencing Youth</u> (Boston: Little, Brown and Co., 1971), pp. 31-42.

48. William O. Douglas, <u>Go East, Young Man</u> (New York: Random House, 1974), p. 38.

49. Yuichiro Miura and Eric Perlman, <u>The Man Who Skied Down Everest</u> (New York: Harper & Row, Publishers, Inc., 1978).

50. Siao Yu, <u>Mao Tse-tung and I Were Beggars</u> (Syracuse, N.Y.: Syracuse University Press, 1959).

51. Fung Yu-lan, <u>A Short History of Chinese Philosophy</u> (New York: The Free Press, 1966), pp. 25-27.

PART TWO: MATURATION

CHAPTER

III

MATURATION (I)

Most of us reading this book are no longer
children. We have gone through several stages of
life's journey, and it is no longer alien to us.
There are things we can depend on in our understanding of each stage, because we have experienced them
and are personally involved. They are no longer just
sign posts in a distant and untrodden land, because
we have already seen them somewhere. A complete
description of each stage is hardly obtainable, as
each person has his or her unique experiences and
potentialities. Nonetheless, we have enough common
experiences to make some generalizations without
ignoring the unique features of each person.

The direction of our maturation is determined
by two major interacting sets of factors--1) the prenatal potentialities we have inherited from our parents, and 2) the postnatal factors we have encountered
within the environment. A person's hereditary potentialities are fixed at the moment of conception. Even
the tiny zygote is already a unique individual. Our
genes are the direct vehicles for hereditary trans-
mission from one generation to another, but it is now
recognized that the genes within a species are constantly subject to mutation and changes in structure,
and thus produce new versions of old traits. We human
beings are more plastic than other animals, and yet
our hereditary potentialities can reach fulfillment
only within proper environments. The direction and
extent of human growth is by no means fixed by our
biological inheritance. Our growth is largely conditioned by personal experiences. So, a person is
a combination of inherited potentialities and postnatal experiences, i.e., the people and events one
has and will encounter in the course of growing up.
We are unique individuals. On the other hand, we
are, through the genes we have inherited from our

parents, linked with other members of the human species of the present and the collective humanity of all ages. We are not alone.

1. Basic Principles in Maturation

Maturation needs to be seen on three levels-- 1) on the biological level, we are organisms, 2) on the psychological level, we are persons, and 3) on the spiritual level, we are transcendent beings. These three levels also constitute three vertical dimensions which interact one another and affect one another. Furthermore, maturation follows three basic principles which constitute "three-in-one" "one-in-three" triune dynamism. They are:

1) Differentiation. Our maturation involves the process of differentiation. Human organisms are differentiated from the simple to become complex, from the homogenous to become heterogenous, and from the One to become many. The birth of an infant is an act of differentiation from the mother, and bodily growth implies multiple differentiation of cells and organs. Psychologically, the emergence of an individual personality is an outcome of differentiation from the parents who provide primary support. Cognitively, differentiation is manifested in analytical thinking and oriented to the left hemisphere of the brain. The appearance of human spirituality is also a sign of differentiation which leads to a transcendence of the self from oneself and the world, seeking the ultimate in and beyond this world. Differentiation creates diversity and plurality, and at the same time threatens unity and harmony. But differentiation does not constitute the whole process of human maturation.

2) Integration. Our maturation also involves the process of integration. What is differentiated must be integrated. Otherwise, there will be disintegration of our body, personality, and spirituality. The differentiated multiple cells must be integrated to become an organ, and all organs must be integrated to constitute a fully functioning body. Psychologically the differentiated individual personality must be

58

reunited with the parents as an independent person when adulthood is reached. The Prodigal Son must come home after he has achieved his independence. Cognitively, integration is manifested in holistic thinking and oriented to the right hemisphere of the brain. Spiritually, the transcended person must reenter into the world, i.e., the physical and the social realm from which one has transcended, when the mature stage is reached. Integration brings about unity, harmony, balance, and homeostasis. But again integration alone does not represent the whole process of human maturation.

3) Transcendence. Furthermore, our maturation involves the process of transcendence. It intermingles with the processes of differentiation and integration in making particular highlights of growth at certain parts and times. Biologically, this is expressed in the inequality of growth of different parts of the body, e. g., the new life's placental structures come first during the germinal period, and the reproductive organs take the lead during the adolescent period. Psychologically, transcendence is manifested in the fact that there are major problems, tasks, and crises in each stage of life; transcendence is also manifested in the hierarchy of human needs, values, self-images, roles, and meaning. Perceptually, transcendence is seen in the differentiation and articulation of figure from background. Cognitively, transcendence is manifested in the theological thinking which is both analytical and integrative, natural and supernatural, and oriented to both the right and left hemispheres of the brain and also beyond our human brain. Spiritually, transcendence is expressed in our liberation from egocentricity and self-objectification, beginning to "ask about asking itself, and think about thinking itself," and to "leap" for the Ultimate.[1] It makes us aware of the ideal, the excellent, the perfect, and the divine. Transcendence may create inner tension and restlessness, and brings about inequality, inbalance, and ultimately a hierarchical integration and differentiation, which leads to different levels of spirtuality and religious experiences.

Psychologists often ignore transcendence. This

is understandable. As pointed out by Swiss psychiatrist Paul Tournier, "science has to set transcendence aside because all scientific curiosity disappears as soon as the cause of any phenomenon is attributed to God."[2] Although the principle of transcendence has been set aside by many psychologists in their discussion of human maturation, it does not disappear from our experience. We can see it manifested in various ways in individual life, as it will be discussed in this and the next chapters.

These three basic principles may give us better understanding of the findings of established theorists from a new perspective.

2. Infancy and Paradise

We now turn to the stages of human maturation. They are dealt with differently by various psychologists. Each tends to emphasize particular aspects of it using particular terms. Freud focuses on the child's psycho-sexual aspect; Erikson and Sullivan, the psycho-social; Piaget, the cognitive; Kohlberg, the moral; and Fowler, the recently emerging "faith development." Each contributes to our understanding of human maturation with a particular emphasis. But we need to see them as a whole. All aspects of human life are interrelated and interact one with the other as each human being attempts to achieve internal equilibrium and engages in the process of adaptation.

When does human life begin? Is it at the time of birth or conception? Is human life so different from animal life? Is a new born baby just a piece of meat? Answers to these questions would have great significance to the issue of abortion which is not only a matter of religious beliefs or moral conviction, but also a political issue. The developmental perspective may be of value, but the more fundamental question is, "What is life?"

Life is the source of human action; a quality manifested in functions such as metabolism, growth, response to stimulation, and reproduction; a quality which distinguishes the human organism from inanimate matter; and only derivatively "life" means human activities, relationships, and interests collectively. Basically life is a dynamic source of vitality. Therefore, an infant is not merely a piece of meat which weighs seven pounds and measures twenty inches; an infant is a human being, which must be in a proper environment, or will die. Leaving the passive vegetable existence in the womb, the baby curls like kitten, spraws like an eagle, and roots with the mouth in search of a nipple like a puppy. The baby is active and full of vitality. Soon the patterns of behavior become clearly inner-directed and purposeful.

It seems to me that the child's birth is not the beginning of life. The newborn baby has prepared himself or herself in the mother's womb for nine months prior to the first debut on the stage of life. The baby is a living organism grown from the union of two germ cells, a sperm and an ovum, in which life exists. The life's feature can be detected through the microscope. The spermatoza are free-swimming cells with whip-like tails. The living force makes the sperm swim by lashing their tails, and it signifies a kind of life which is prehuman.

The infant is a full-fledged human being. All the potential which exists in a newborn baby are to be developed. Life begins to evolve from the helpless state of infancy. In order for the baby to grow, baby and mother constitute a symbiotic unit during the first year or so. The infant can suckle and move about, but needs to be cared for more than fed, washed, changed, played with, carried, etc. After a few weeks of perceptual learning and maturation, the infant becomes intimately attached to the mother and practically becomes one with her. This symbiotic relationship becomes the behavioral and experiential basis for future personality development.[3] The infant's perception develops rapidly, and it is primarily through oral experience that the foundation for a construction of external reality is laid. The mouth is the first and the most efficient center for testing one's adaptation and mastery,

so much so that Freud calls the first phase "oral."
The mouth is the only feeding organ and the major
source and zone for pleasure and satisfaction.

We see differentiation in the act of birth;
integration in the union of two germ cells, a sperm
and an ovum and in the symbiotic relationship between
the child and the mother; and transcendence in the
success of the sperm which excels other sperms in
achieving its goal. Likewise, we see transcendence
in the primacy of the oral zone in the child's psycho-
sexual development. The child's mouth supercedes
other areas of the body in sensing pleasure and
gratification. We may also note that transcendence
implies differentiation and integration in each
situation.

The first eighteen to twenty-four months constitute the initial stage in cognitive development
centered on the sensory-motor experiences of the
child. This stage is primarily prelogical. The
mouth is a self-contained sensory-motor system ready
to be engaged in activities related to the external
world. It acts as a center for making differentiations and for setting boundaries between the internal
and the external. The lips can be used to admit and
to exclude things and such oral experiences form the
basis for an early discrimination between internal
and external reality. The mouth is a richly endowed
receptor as well as rejector. Inside it are sense
organs sensitive to pain and pleasure, pressure and
temperature. The tip of the tongue is often considered to have the finest touch discrimination of
the body. Moreover, the muscles of lips, tongue,
and cheeks contain kinesthetic sense organs which
provide a constant source of feedback through muscle
movements. So, oral testing becomes a major basis
for reality-testing. After a little experience, the
hungry crying baby begins to quiet down when he or
she is placed in a nursing position. This oral anticipation introduces the experience of delay and
moderate frustration. Such experience is essential
to the development of the human personality. In this
the unitary need-satisfaction sequence is exchanged
by a more flexible need-delay-satisfaction sequence.
Here we see the process of integration following, or

rather developing simultaneously along with, the process of differentiation and transcendence.

The central nervous system is peculiarly fitted to retain the effects of its own patterned activity coming from oral perception and imagery. The non-nutritive use of sucking without the help of others is the prototype of future self-sufficiency. Each retention of imagery is accompanied by emotional and feeling components. Subsequent experiences consolidate and elaborate mental representations in new functional patterns of the central nervous systems. Thus, temporary experiences can bring about enduring changes and become internalized. Orality persists throughout life--we never cease to function as an oral being. Tasting, eating, drinking, kissing, and smoking are ways of orality.

Next in importance to the mouth in early childhood development are the eyes, ears, and hands. They are other sensory-motor organs, which may be sequentially secondary as perceptual channels. Organization of the visual system is developed later, and it matures rather slowly over a considerable period of time. In the beginning, what the infant sees seems to be independent--even though it is the child's own hand, the child merely stares at it as if it were something emerging out of the void.[4] Visual pursuit and search is done without reference to any oral or manual action. What the hands grasp is not subjected to the oral examination. Such independent development of sensory-motor organs is an expression of differentiation, which is to be followed by the integration of them.

Only the auditory system appears to be tied with visual movements almost from the beginning.[5] This constitutes the prototype of future orientation in space. It is during about the second month when the infant begins to fixate on a moving object by moving with it visually. By the third month, the infant has completed the maturing task in coordinating head movements, which help the eyes to fix on moving things; and thus, the child begins to gain control over the world and extends reality testing in space and time.

From the second month on, the child's hands become more systematically adaptive through repeated movements of fingering, touching, scratching, grasping, pulling, and letting go. In time, the hand searching becomes guided not only by manual perception but also by visual aids. By commonly "registering" in the brain organization, the hands and eyes which used to function separately, now work together cooperatively. Here again we see differentiation and integration.

Whatever the eyes and ears take in becomes assimilated in the central nervous system in turn becomes "food" for the visual and auditory organizations of the child's mental life.[6] What originates outside of the body brings about changes in the mental organization. What is internalized and incorporated does not necessarily represent the experiences, because the human organism selects and eliminates. What is taken in bears some relation to the perceptual organizations which have already been in existence internally. On the other hand, the taking in of new perceptions always makes some impact on the existing mental organization of the brain.

Although oral experience is superior during the first few weeks, it loses its superiority as time goes on, while visual and auditory experiences grow in importance. The eyes and ears can "receive" things from afar, whereas the mouth cannot. Gradually, visual and auditory incorporation supercedes oral in perception, organizing a space-time world. They become the major channels for gaining information from the external world.

The mouth and ears cooperatively develop human language, which is the supreme achievement of and expression of communication by the human beings. The child's visual function is particularly important at the moment he or she is able to read. As time passes, the hands become more and more adept in exploraing the surroundings, and contribute to perceptual development. The hands are flexible to feel, touch, grasp, and to enclose things in the external world and then incorporate them perceptually. Thus the child's

manipulation by the hands contributes to the construction of reality and testing, and in due time
will become superior to oral manipulation in exploring the body and external reality. Generally eye-
hand coordination is achieved sometime between the
fourth and sixth month.

Now the hand can test the form which one sees
or remembers visually. The eyes can guide the hands
toward the things which they see, or act as scanners.
Each infant must go through the process of acquiring
the intercoordination between the visual and manual
fields. With the passage of time, the functions of
mouth, eyes, ears, and hands become fully integrated
with one another.[7] In this integration, we also see
transcendence, namely, growth.

Psychosocially, Erik Erikson points out that
during the period of infancy, the child develops
attitudes of basic trust or mistrust. What the outcome will be depends on the way the child's physical
and emotional needs are met.[8] Infancy is characterized by the child's dependency on others, and in no
other period of life is a person so transformed
physically and emotionally. The child needs to be
fed physically and loved emotionally. A shortage
of warm and caring experience may lead to undesirable
consequences. The pleasant feeding experiences
nourish the baby's body, mind, and spirit. The process of satisfying the child's physical needs has
emotional and spiritual meanings. The quality of
the parents' touch convey a sense of emotional well-
being, security, and affection. It tells the child
that the world, and the people in it, can be trusted.
The parents' ill handling of the child may frighten
the feeble "soul" by its lack of love and affection,
which comes from the compassionate, tender, and yet
firm and self-assured loving parents. Basic trust
is an expression of the child's integration with the
parents, and love is an expression of the parents'
integration with the child.

There is no single way of loving a child, but
parents' love must be genuine and reliable. A child
needs a healthy emotional climate in which he or she

can experience the variety as well as the stability
of becoming a secure and confident person. The
mutuality between parents and child is important.
By enjoying playful interactions with the child and
by their care and sensitivity to their child's needs,
the parents may create an emotional climate for
healthy growth. Thus, it is safe to say that the
first developmental task is acquiring basic trust
in others and the world, and eventually in oneself
and the Ultimate Being.

The child is not only an organism, but also
a person. Parents' singing and nodding is needed
in eliciting a child's response. Early in this
century a pediatrician's study showed that the incidence of deaths among institutionalized infants was
high in spite of adequate nourishment and clean
surroundings, while the incidence among those being
adopted early and brought up by foster parents was
relatively low.[9]

It seems to me that integration is needed for
differentiation. This can be seen from the fact that
the loving symbiosis between the child and the parent
is needed for the healthy growth of the child.

The newborn child's mental world is undifferentiated and "global." There is no awareness of one's
own experience because the child cannot distinguish
what is "me" and what is the rest of the world. Moreover, the infant is not aware of having a body. The
world is a diffused field with objects coming and
going without boundaries, and there is no fixed frame
of reference or mental organization in the infant's
mind.

At first, the mother acts like the infant's
ego, defending and protecting the baby. For the
infant everything is related to his or her immediate
needs, wants, and experiences. There is simply hunger
and wetness, and there is no "I am hungry" or "I am
wet." The "me" (selfhood) emerges gradually from
experiences with others, particularly the parents,
and other significant individuals. This occurs as
a result of reality testing in perceptual responses
and differentiations. Throughout the period of

infancy only those objects, and particularly only those aspects, which have meanings can become differentiated.

The meaning of an object for a child is defined first by what it can do to him or her. The meaning always precedes the object itself in perception and is modified later if necessary. When previously undifferentiated aspects of reality are made functionally meaningful, these aspects are said to be differentiated and perceived. For instance, the stairway may be meaningless and essentially non-existent to the six-month-old baby, but it becomes meaningful for the toddler who can climb it.[10] The perceived world grows out of the child's emotional involvement, because the child's behaviors are motivated emotionally.

Through meaningful experiences, the child begins to develop a rudimentary frame of reference and has better ideas of what to expect, what objects and behaviors are needed for gratification. The formation of the frame of reference is indicative not only in the growing awareness of the **permanency** and stability of the perceptual world, but also in the birth of selfhood with its emerging ego boundaries. In this way the child is becoming human. A sign of this development is awareness that the child's body is his or her own and a sense of fear in the presence of strangers.

What accounts for the diffused state of undifferentiation in the child's perception is the primary identification with the mother, which constitutes the infantile symbiosis. Perceptually, the infant is incapable of making a distinction between oneself and the mother, because there is no ego boundary. The infant is in a state which we experience while dreaming, and there is a kaleidoscopic shifting of imagery. This is because the child and the mother are one. The child participates in what the mother does without knowing it through the unitary emotional tie. As the child encounters delay, frustration, and conflicts, the conscious ego system becomes more differentiated from the unconscious dreaming state and develops a more complex series of

67

defense mechanism, and a system of adaptation and mastery later in life.

In the undifferentiated state of being, the child's experiences are wrapped up in the present, because there is no concept of time at least during the first six months and probably well into toddlerhood. The child's future is "present future" and his or her past is "present past."

Due to the mother-child symbiosis, the child is likely to incorporate certain aspects of the mother's behavior and personhood and, to a lesser degree, of the father's, siblings' and other significant individuals'. The content of this internalization may contribute to the kind of person one is going to become. The mother-child symbiosis disolves gradually in the process of becoming an individual person. Paradoxically, the child's successful dissolution of the symbiosis with the mother comes from experiencing oneness with the mother. In this we see the paradoxical nature of integration and differentiation--integration (symbiosis) is needed for differentiation (birth of the self) in human growth.

The phenomenon of mother-child symbiosis is cross-cultural. All children, whether they were raised at home or at a day-care center, whether they were Chinese or Caucasian, go to their mothers for comfort when they are tired, bored, or apprehensive because of some unexpected provocation from the external world. This can be seen from the behavioral study of children in Boston by Prof. Jerome Kagan of Harvard University and from the study of children in Israel by Nathan Fox.[11]

Perhaps it is due to the greater intensity of mother-child symbiosis that the first-born is likely to excel in those characteristics valued by the family. If the parents' standards emphasize obedience, the first-born will be more obedient; if the parents value academic excellence, the first-born will get better grades; if the parents promote religious attitudes, the first-born will be more committed to the family's religion.[12] First-born children are more inclined to adopt idealistic philosophical positions and the

68

unifying basic principles in morality and science.[13]

Furthermore, the intensity of mother-child symbiosis may contribute to the formation of a stronger sense of selfhood among the first-born. This may explain in part the fact that eight of the nine Presidents of the United States during the periods of social crisis (during or just before wars) were first-born or only sons.[14]

Now we may wonder whether infancy has any religious signficance. What is the spiritual dimension of infancy? Has this mother-child symbiosis any religious meaning? We may answer these questions with three observations largely from the Christian point of view.

1. Paradise is a symbolic expression of the mother-child symbiosis in religious terms. It represents what we aspire to regain, namely, the unity, oneness, and cohesiveness with the source of our being. The Garden of Eden is a symbolic place in which the first man and woman in the Creation Story lived. It is a blissful state of symbiosis between the creature and the Creator, the human and the divine, and between the human and the nature. Everything is one and in harmony with one another.

The mother-child symbiosis represents the undifferentiated state of oneness expressed in the teaching of Jesus--"Abide in me, and I in you."[15] In the life of Jesus, He is believed to have experienced identification with God the Father. The purpose of his coming to this world is to restore oneness between God and man and between man and man. Without this restoration of oneness, there will be no real peace and harmony. Mysticism is powerful, because it is an experience of oneness with the divine. Paul the Apostle experienced this mystical oneness saying "I have been crucified with Christ; it is no longer I who live, but Christ who lives in me."

Today, some people try to achieve mother-child symbiosis in communal living of various kinds, such as the Communist classless society, aimed at undifferentiated oneness, unity, and cohesiveness. We can find such yearning for the mother-child symbiosis in cult groups which deliberately destroy human individuality and autonomy, whose leaders assume the authority of parental figure demanding dependency from group members, and the structures of which do not allow freedom of choice by individual members. A yearning for mother-child symbiosis is very powerful because it is the most fundamental experience of human beings after leaving the mother's womb.

In Chinese thought, yearning for undifferentiated oneness may be seen in the teaching of sacrificing the "small self" for the "larger self" of the family, the community, and ultimately, the state. It can also be seen in classical Taoistic oneness with Tao and Nature.

Freud's "oceanic" feelings may make us trace our religious aspirations to the state in the mother's womb. Our yearning for God may stem from the prenatal experience of oneness with the universe: It is a yearning for support from the infinite.

Socially, a yearning for undifferentiated oneness is expressed in the American ideals of "equality," "non-discrimination" and, to some extent, in the myth of "melting pot." Such ideals are important to American civil religion. They carry the power and authority of religious beliefs and symbolize American Paradise on earth, and their underlying principle is integration.

2. The mother-child symbiosis is crucial to the development of religious faith and moral character later in life. In discussing the religious dimensions of infancy and childhood, Prof. Lewis J. Sherrill of Union Theological Seminary says, "When the infant encounters love he encounters God."[16] In receiving parental love, the child receives God's love; in experiencing human love, the child experiences divine love. To a great extent, the quality of the emotional life of the child determines the kind of religious faith he or she will respond to in the future.

The major task of the child's psychosocial

development in infancy is basic trust. The mother-child symbiosis is the context in which basic trust is nurtured and developed. The basic trust which the infant experiences in the symbiotic relationship with the mother is an essential ingredient for future development, leading to happy adulthood and mature faith. There are people who have difficulties believing in God, because their experiences with their parents have not been good. They feel repulsed by religious phrases, such as "Our Father who art in Heaven," "God the Father," and "Holy Mother." The parent's love and the child's religious faith are inextricably related. Love and religion are the most emotionally charged spheres of life. Consequently, many people associate them in their minds. If a person is afraid of losing love, he or she is afraid of losing faith as well. If one has faith in love, he or she is likely to have faith in faith.[17] It is significant that during the Reformation, Martin Luther emphasized "sola fide" (faith alone) in contrast to the Roman system of his time. For him, the relationship to God is personal "I-thou" relationship of trust, love, and unconditional acceptance, which he called "faith." This relational aspect of faith is rooted in the mother-child symbiosis which is based on the principle of integration, and any religious breakthrough must touch the affective aspect of life.

3. Paradise may turn out to be Hell. There are two kinds of oneness, unity, and undifferentiation which the mother-child symbiosis represents. One is positive, while the other negative; one encourages the emergence of new selfhood of the child, while the other denies it. The former is Paradise, whereas the latter is Hell.

Religious symbols are hardly neutral; they are either male or female, gods or goddesses, in accordance with their roles fulfilling the human yearning for support, oneness, and harmony with the universe. A detailed discussion on the formation of religious symbols is beyond our scope, but we may note one relevant question: the feminist attack on the fact that the Judeo-Christian heritage has been male oriented and that God is believed to be He, and not She.

71

This question is complex, but it is possible that male-orientation in the formation of Judeo-Christian religious symbols might have been to protect the emergence of selfhood in the mother-dominated symbiosis. Being human, mother's love has its positive as well as negative aspects. Generally, the mother is inclined to affirm the child's independent existence as a human being in spite of the child's total dependence on her. Her affirmation of the child makes the emergence of new selfhood in the child possible. But there is also a negative tendency in the mother's love, characterized by possessiveness and denial of the child's independence. This negative aspect of motherhood may be what "Mom" implies, as pointed out by Erikson.[18]

In order to safeguard the emergence of new selfhood, God was conceived by believers as Father who could protect the child from a domineering and possessive mother, and socially the system of patriarchy came into being. On the other hand, God was conceived to have attributes of the positive aspect of maternal love in the mother-child symbiosis: God is loving and forgiving.

3. Toddlerhood and The Fall

Integration leads to differentiation. The mother-child symbiosis comes to an end, and the child becomes a toddler. The toddler's world is a world of action; the child trots and runs from place to place, moves and explores things, big and small, closes the door when it is open and opens the door when it is closed, climbs, jumps, and falls. The toddler is now becoming aware of oneself as a separate person with growing sensitivities and capacities; the child wants to experience his or her new abilities with no help, hindrance, or coercion from other people and expresses "No!" defiantly; the child wants to be differentiated from the parents and needs ample opportunity to test things on his or her own. Sometimes the support the child needs is a minimum of necessary prohibitions; he or she vacillates between dependence and independence. In the transition from integration to differ-

72

entiation, there is transcendence, namely, growth.

Psychosexually Freud calls this period "sadistic-anal."[19] As a sign of growth, the focus of the child's gratification and concern has shifted from the mouth to the anus and lower digestive tract. In contrast to taking in and absorbing in the oral stage, the child may now deliberately withhold or expel his or her wastes as an expression of resentment against his or her parents. The conflicts which arise from toilet training are believed by the Freudians to have significant impacts on later development.

The phase of self-assertion and sphincter control begins with the dissolution of the symbiotic mother-child unit. The child strives for independence as a separate individual, but still within the context of the family. Generally, the child succeeds, but there is a danger that he or she may become overly self-assertive. The danger resides in the paradox between integration and differentiation. If the child is frustrated too much, he or she may become either chronically angry or submissive, and lack the normal initiatives. There is a danger in abusing freedom. Although the child functions more and more as an individual person in his or her own right, every now and then, he or she may run back to mother's arms, thus momentarily re-establishing the old mother-child symbiosis. Normally parents and siblings encourage and support a child's efforts to differentiate from the mother as a separate person.

Bowel control is a new step toward maturity, a pleasurable accomplishment which parents and siblings appreciate. However, if the child arouses anger, tension, and rage in the parents by non-compliance in toilet training, the child may become incapable of having a movement. Sometimes, as a result of over differentiation, children become unreasonably obstinate, parsimonious, and constricted, frustrating and controlling others by invoking arbitrary laws and regulations, just as parents once arbitarily frustrated and controlled the child. On the other hand, as a result of over integration, the child may insist on routines, rituals, order, or cleanliness. In the contest of wills at this level,

73

the child may finally accept defeat and become excessively compliant. If this is the case, the child
becomes intimidated, and compulsively conforming later
in life. In toilet training is not only a function
of differentiation but also integration.

The central theme at this stage is "autonomy
vs. shame and doubt" in Erikson's term.[20] Autonomy
grows out of the child's basic faith in existence,
and central to autonomy is the toddler's growing self-
awareness. The child is encouraged to stand on one's
own feet, and psychosocially he or she needs "the
gradual and well-guided experience of the autonomy
of free choice." In infancy the child is symbioti-
cally united with the mother, but now he or she is
so differentiated from the mother that there is a
sense of being a separate individual. However, the
child is still not sure where the boundaries are and
may laugh because someone nearby laughs. The child
seems to experience indirectly the way the environment echoes his or her behavior. An over emphasis
on toilet-training is likely to expose the child
to shame and doubt. The child sees him or herself
through the eyes of the world, because the principle
of differentiation is also functioning side by side
with the principle of integration.

A certain amount of negative experience will
not damage a child. Only in a climate of constant
criticism, reproach, and taboo does a child's experience of self become fixed in morbid self-consciousness, a sense of shame and doubt. If the child is not
well-guided, the child may turn against him or herself
all urges to discriminate and manipulate. Consequently
there will be overmanipulation of self and the development of a precocious conscience, which makes the child
overly self-conscious and shamed. Feeling shameful,
the child wants to destroy the eyes of the world, as
Erikson points out.[21] This negative growth is due to
distorted differentiation which is qualitatively different from healthy differentiation.

A sense of shame and doubt in early childhood
leads to an adult concern for losing face. However,
in Chinese culture one must be concerned about losing
face, because a sense shame is a moral virtue which

74

has little to do with toilet training; a sense of
shame is an important quality of maturity. On the
other hand, a sense of autonomy fostered in childhood and developed later in life provides a basis
for a sense of justice in economic and political
life, and a sense of legitimate human dignity and
independence among adults, which in turn gives the
child confidence and safeguards the child against
undue doubt and shame. Psychosocially, the child's
differentiation from the mother is necessary for
internal integration manifested in autonomy, and in
integrity in adult life.

Another dimension in the development of autonomy is the learning of language. As the child
acquired names for things, actions, and relationships,
he or she controls the world in a new way. Once en-
closed in the immediate situation, now the child can
talk about it, think about, even when it is outside
the experience of sensory perception. Language gives
the child a new power to communicate feelings and
desires; without language, the child is limited to
physical expression. When the child grasps the categories expressed in adult language, he or she gets
more in touch with the world and at the same time is
liberated from it mentally through linguistic sym-
bolization of reality. In this linguistic symboliza-
tion, we find the principle of transcendence, making
the child gradually stand above the physical world
mentally.

The learning of language takes place in actual
settings, and the child needs to differentiate language from the facial expression, voice and gesture
of the speaker. Probably the earliest words the
child learns are those that always accompany an obvious action, and in time evoke the action when they
are used alone. Speaking lags slightly behind understanding. A foreign language is easier to learn to
read than to speak. The first active words are usually
names of people, things, and actions--"milk," "baby,"
"eat." The child sees the world in a new way, as
though names were able to fix and stabilize experience, and make it really one's own. Furthermore, the
objects seem to take on a new existence when fitted
into the frame of language. Three basic principles

are all needed in learning language. Differentiation is not enough.

     With language, the child can communicate,
criticize, and commands oneself. Gradually, speech
moves away from feeling and action to the exchange
of facts. In factual communication, the child shifts
from one-word sentences to two-word sentences, to
three-word sentences, and so on. The child's earliest utterances always refer to the immediate situation and are in the present tense. Later the child
refers to the future, and then to the past. But the
child's future is still the present-future, and his
or her past, the present-past, refering to where the
child is now headed or has just been. The child
learns names for other people before learning his or
her own name; the child learns "dada" before he or
she learns "mama"; the toddler uses "no" long before
he or she uses "yes." There is some variation in
which words are learned first. The toddler's language has not yet become abstract and general yet.
Transcendence is needed for abstract conception; integration is needed for general conception.

     In learning language the child, not only learns
to communicate verbally, but also assimilates a cultural system of meanings and ways of thinking and
reasoning. More than the speed and fluency of linguistic development is involved; the child must
develop a trust in the use of verbal communication
and thereby in the value of rationality. Eventually
the child learns meaning because parents consistently
respond to a word in the same way. Words gradually
gain discrete and sharpened meanings and become symbols designating the identity of an object seen from
different perspectives and in different situations.
Moreover, the same word can denote categorized objects
with the same essential attributes.

     Through language, the child internalizes the
environment symbolically, imaginatively manipulating
the world. Knowing a name actually bestows a new
power on the child, and it is significant that the
moment Helen Keller learned that objects have names
constituted the turning point in her life. Likewise
the learning of language constitutes a turning point

in the life of the child. Such a turning point is an indication of human transcendence, a sign of growth.

Now we turn to the religious dimension of toddlerhood. Emerging self-awareness and self-assertion has great significance in our understanding of the Creation story in the Bible, particularly the Fall in the third chapter of Genesis. After the climax of symbiotic identification with the Creator, Adam and Eve are believed to have broken their blessed relationships with God. They broke God's commandments; they wanted to become independent from God and differentiated from Him, to be like God and equal with Him, not in character, but in power. Adam and Eve submitted to the temptation of Satan, and became alienated from God because of their defiance. They were not merely differentiated from God; they rebelled against God. Reinhold Niebuhr interprets sin in terms of human rebellion against God. Sin seems to be a religious expression of the toddler's "No!" It is the fall from the state of grace; it is distorted differentiation.

In an interview with a young mother, I was bombarded with her toddler's defiance. Looking at her three children (aged 3, 2, and four months), she was both angry and amazed. As she had observed, "children are born to be egocentric." Soon the eldest began to beat the youngest in the crib. The mother shouted, "Stop it!" but he would not. She seemed frustrated and vulnerable, and wondered what she could do. Finally, she gave him a new toy and asked him to say, "Thank you!" but the toddler defiantly said, "No!" Without even looking at his mother, he played with the toy and enjoyed it enormously. Erikson describes the central theme of toddlerhood as "autonomy vs. shame and doubt," but one wonders whether such defiance could be properly called "autonomy." It may well be called "the Fall." This question will be discussed later in the chapter on autonomy and independence.

In the Fall, Adam's disobedience lead to ex-

pulsion from the Garden of Eden and a return to the
ground out of which he was made: death. Death is
inevitable, the final consequence of our alienation
from God. Because of our defiance and rebellion,
differentiation becomes alienation; the nakedness
we hitherto were not ashamed of becomes an intolerable
indecency; and sex is accompanied by shame and guilt.
This is the human predicament which Swiss psychiatrist Paul Tournier describes in terms of "Paradise
Lost" complex, "an anguished feeling experienced by
all men, that they have lost support they needed in
order to live."[22] It seems to me that rebellious
egocentricity is held by all, and all share its curse
and are cheated by it.

        Distorted differentiation has made the poten-
tial purposiveness of the human organism into self-
assertive defiance. Traditionally, sin is believed
to be hereditary, and a child is born with "original
sin." Since St. Augustine, sex has been considered
unclean and sinful because sin is transmitted from
generation to generation through the process of reproduction. For believers, the "original sin" is
interpreted in terms of the solidarity of human beings and the inevitability of social conditioning
in committing sins. But "original sin" could be
interpreted in terms of our innate purposiveness and
propensity of creating an independent telic center
in conflict with the larger telic center of the universe, namely, God. This relentless rebellion and
defiance of human beings is a prodigal act. The
symbiotic mother-child relationship is often exploited
by the child, strengthening his or her egocentricity.
But we can keep our telic center in harmony with the
larger telic center. This is socialization, very
important later in childhood.

        Near the end of toddlerhood, the child may be-
lieve like a three-year-old Roger whose egocentricity
was manifested in his fantasy that he was God, making
his friends and everybody else do what he wanted them
to do, as child psychologist Selma Fraiberg describes
in The Magic Years.[23] He believed in his own omni-
potence and wished to be all powerfull in a world of
his own. He dreamed of creating an independent telic

center of his own totally differentiated from the
telic center of his family, proclaiming the desire
that he would be his own boss. He wanted to command
others, like a powerful dictator. This is common
among toddlers. It is significant that the Ten
Commandments forbid the people of Israel to have no
other gods, except Yahaweh.[24] The propensity of creating an independent telic center as a god is inherent
in every human being. Often dictators are motivated
by their childhood dreams, which become an inspiration to them and their followers. The prohibition
against making any human being a god curtails egocentricity. It challenges the "I am God" fantasies
of early childhood. As the child grows older, he
or she begins to make some observations, which cast
doubt on childish magical powers, and gradually the
child realizes that such fantasy is wrong. The
little boy realizes that he is not the cause of all
things; the objects outside himself can exist inde-
pendently of him; he is not omnipotent.

     Parents must oppose the "I am God" fantasies
of their children, but they will not be effective
unless they offer genuine love and affection. The
teaching of God's sovereignty and human depravity
can be misused and create undue degradation of self-
esteem among believers, but it can also be a positive force, destroying the childish fantasy of "I
am God," if it is accompanied with "God is love."
Thus, it may contribute to growth toward reality-
oriented living, a sign of maturation. Parents must
represent what is real and try to help the child
differentiate reality from fantasy.

     The myth of the Garden of Eden is still rele-
vant. As infants, we are one with the mother and
the rest of the world, blissfully ignorant of the
human predicament and fate, but as we differentiate
from the mother, we are bound to feel self-conscious,
like Adam and Eve who ate the "apple." We are no
longer in the blissful state, ignorant of shame and
doubt like other animals. The fundamental paradox
of "autonomy vs. shame and doubt" remains with us
always. This is the predicament of being human, and
it begins as early as childhood. The Fall is ours.
It is the core of our religious dimension.

79

4. Early Childhood and
Anthropomorphic Faith

Around the age of three, the child grows into
another stage. As a toddler, the child is a member
of the family primarily, but now the child is engaged
in the long-term process of finding one's place in
the world at large. Increasingly, the child is seen
as an individual, and there is greater spontaneity
and openness among children of this stage. Sometimes
the child has striking insights into his or her world
as well as the world of adults. The child is still
very dependent, yet eager to become independent. At
one moment the child may appear to be "mature" but
at the next moment may be extremely babyish. Sometimes the child appears affectionate, at other times,
antisocial. Day-dreams are still egocentric, but
also social.

Psychosexually, the child begins to develop a
new and acute awareness of his or her body and learns
to be a boy or a girl. Throughout the preschool
years, sex differences in growth rate are not very
striking, although boys and girls have already begun
to follow somewhat divergent paths of psychosocial
development. Until the time of Freud, it had been
customery to describe small children as asexual.
Puberty was marked as the first flowering of human
sexuality. Freud described the child's sexuality
in relation to the Oedipus legend and Shakespeare's
Hamlet.[25] He rejected the notion of asexual childhood, and made ancient legends of unconscious incest
relevant to contemporary experiences of childhood as
a real drama. Sometimes, between the ages of three
and four, a child falls deeply in love with the parent of the opposite sex, and at the same time develops
jealousy toward the other as a competitor. Freud
believed that the investment of sexualized energy
(libido) shifted from the anal zone to the penis in
the boy and to the clitoris in the girl, and called
this period "phallic." If children are not too inhibited, they openly express the desire to marry the
parent of the opposite sex when they grow up.

The Oedipus Complex is controversial, but it

80

has some truth. In a conversation, a Chinese medical technician reported that his four-years-old daughter said to him, "Daddy, I love you. I love. . . ." Not knowing the oedipal phase of his daughter's development, he was annoyed. It was a simple child-love for the parent, but somehow it was not so simple. Likewise a friend of mine from the Pescadores said that his daughter always wanted his companionship while she took baths as a little girl, but he felt somewhat uncomfortable. Some scholars may insist that the phenomenon of the Oedipus Complex belongs to Western culture, but it seems to me that it is cross-cultural, although sexual inhibition differs from one culture to another.

The normal outcome of going through the Oedipus Complex would be a new stage of growth. When a boy falls in love with his mother and turns against his father as a rival for her affection, an intense spontaneous anxiety emerges inside him, and makes him fearful of bodily injury or loss of his genitals or other forms of retaliation from his father (castration anxiety). In the resolution of this conflict, the boy has to repress his unacceptable desire for his mother, and aligns and identifies with his father. But the task is not easy. Children are ambivalent about their parents; they experience both love and hate; they blend or alternate hostility with affection. On one level, a boy identifies with his father, whom he admires and love, but on another level, his identification with his father increases guilt he feels over his revengeful fantasies about his father and over his wish to displace his father and possess his mother. A girl follows roughly the same sequence --she identifies with her mother but hates her also, in the relationships of both attachment and hostility (Electra Complex). In the process of resolving the Oedipus Complex, the boy buries his symbiotic over-attachment to his mother, and replaces his hostility toward his father with a strong identification, and the girl does similarly in replacing her hostility toward her mother with a strong identification. As a result, certain aspects of the parents' character become internalized, and the child's conscience (super-ego) emerges. A healthy and complete resolution of the Oedipus Complex makes the child incorporate parental love and dependability as well as threat.

The conflicts of the Oedipus Complex can be seen as an expression of the paradox of two polarities and between differentiation and integration. Guilt is integration incompleted as much as differentiation aborted. Identification is a function of integration, and its power is love. The opposite polarity is differentiation, and its power is hostility. In the process of resolution, the two polarities are united, reversed, and transcended; integration is turned to differentiation, and differentiation, integration.

In the process of resolving the Oedipus Complex excessive threats by parents may produce guilt feelings in the child, causing various disturbances, including constriction of spontaneity and initiative. It is important to establish close ties of affection between the parents and the child, and not competitors of sexual love. Because it is a humiliating experience for the oedipal child to realize that his or her wishes are not going to be fulfilled, that these wishes have been based on a grand illusion, and that children are to be treated as children, not as little men or as little women, parents should do everything possible to understand and love the child, because the source of oedipal resolution comes from a parental ability to maintain the paradox of differentiation and integration.

With the help of parents' understanding and love, the hard lesson of grand disillusionment can be learned. Now the boy's love for his mother excludes its sexual aspect, as does the girl's love for her father. The child who successfully resolves the Oedipal Complex will be ready for rapid and realistic growth, maintaining the functional boundaries between the pleasure oriented id and the reality oriented ego. Gradually the child will be able to perceive internal and external reality without too much distortion, and to tap inner resources of self-control, self-esteem, and ego-ideals. In the resolution of oedipal conflicts, the child increases his or her ability of self-transcendence, i.e., the superego.

82

Here we may note a parallelism between the triune dynamism of differentiation, integration, and transcendence and Freud's understanding of human personality composed by three psychic forces, the id, the ego, and the superego. The id is like a chaotic caldron full of the seething energy of the instincts; the ego synthesizes, organizes, combines, and unifies our mental processes; and the superego functions within each person as a moral agent of the society and exercises its power in discriminating what is right and what is wrong, like a hidden judge enthroned within us. The id is oriented to differentiation; the ego is based on integration; and the superego is linked to transcendence.

During the preschool years, a child's social horizon slowly broadens to includes people outside of the family, although the child still likes to have familiar adults around. By the end of this period, the child has learned primary socialization. In going to nursery school the child has to go through a period of transition, shifting trust from mother to teacher. As the children get together, their imitation of each other becomes more pronounced, and they begin to do things in bunches--"associative play." However, their communication is a "collective monologue."[26] In conversation, a child may say something which has no connection with what another child has said, because differentiation and integration is still primitive, but developing. In interpreting the formation of the superego, Freudian psychoanalysts focus on the Oedipus Complex, but sociologists such as George Herbert Mead, Talcott Parsons, and others see the importance of interaction with "significant individuals" such as teachers as well.

Other social aspects, which begin to appear during the preschool years are, sympathy, aggression, and leadership.[27] We may see a child pause in play to stare at another child in distress; the child may begin to console the other who has been hurt. The child's motives may not be pure sympathy, containing elements of superiority, guilt, hostility or other feelings. Sympathy and leadership go hand-in-hand. Some children show leadership traits in various ways--by being bossy, or by sheer force of

of muscle or character. Aggression and leadership
are obviously related, but the correlation between
sympathy and aggressiveness is by no means perfect.
For the young child, aggressive behavior may be more
of an exploration than an act of hostility. Children
will become increasingly combative up to the age of
five when they quickly become self-contained. From
the point of view of triune dynamism, sympathy is an
expression of integration; agression is tied to differentiation; and leadership manifests transcendence.
They go hand-in-hand, just as leadership implies sympathy as well as aggression.

Preschool children have two ways of getting
to know the world--1) by interacting with it, and
2) by identifying with other people and things or
role playing, as they become less egocentric. At
first, the central theme of preschool children's
dramatic play is domesticity, but later, they will
go on to the more societal. In block play, the three-
year-old is more concerned with the problems of balance, size, and ways of combining blocks than with
building anything; the four-year-old builds, but the
structures are usually amorphous or loosely hung together; the five-year-old builds highly integrated
and balanced block structures. In general the five-
year-old is able to initiate a chain of activities,
whereas the younger child is discontinuously impulsive. Growth implies the increased ability to dif-
fernetiate and to integrate.

In the preschool child's experiences, facts
and fantasies are likely to be interchangeable. The
child's growing insistence on realism in play indicates that the child is becoming more aware of the
difference between what is real and what is pretended.
Being more sensitive to adult standards of reality,
older children may be reluctant to talk about fantasies. As the child becomes psychologically more
differentiated from the mother and the surroundings,
the awareness of self and the environment will be
increased. But awareness of other people precedes
awareness of self; the child is aware of other people's capacity to gratify or harm before knowing
that he or she is there to be gratified or harmed.
It seems that objective awareness precedes subjec-

tive awareness. But the child's objective awareness is nonetheless egocentric rather than object-centered.

By the age of five, the child often has a fairly specific sense of the harm one can suffer and may become fearful of death, but this fear of death is not rooted in recognition of human finitude and mortality. People do die, and something may happen to the child; the child is not afraid of dying eventually, but of dying now. Told that death is like a long sleep, the child may suddenly become relunctant to go to bed at night. Children of this period will benefit if they are given as many facts as they can understand.

In addition to being aware of self, the preschool child is also aware of the transitory nature of experience--birthdays come and go. On the other hand, the child is growing in power, and independence brings about responsibilities and loneliness. Ups and downs are a part of normal growth, and the child is ambivalent about growing up to some degree. Greater independence brings insecurity, which is an extension of separation anxiety. But the child's emerging awareness of self does not mean a constant self-image. It can shift dramatically under emotionally charged circumstances, as in a dramatic play. The identity of other people is also perceived as unstable and lose. Although the preschool child is aware of self and others, he or she seems seldom able to maintain both simultaneously. If a child draws a picture of his or her family, he or she is not likely to appear in it; asked if he or has a brother, the answer will be "Yes." But if he or she is asked whether his or her brother has a brother, the answer is "No," as Piaget well observed.[28] The child has not yet noticed that the word "brother" denotes a reciprocal relationship. This indicates a deficiency in the child's ability to differentiate and integrate.

In cognitive development, preschool children acquire sizable vocabularies and master essential syntax. They gradually become freed from the tangible sensori-motor schemata and concrete present and are ready for the development of imagination and fantasy (which need not be referred back to reality)

through internalized visual signs and verbal symbols.
For a time, this capacity to manipulate symbols
imaginatively may interfere with problem-solving,
because it is simpler to solve problems in fantasy
than in reality. As is often observed, preschool
children cannot differentiate fully between reality
and fantasy. It takes some time before they can
sort out facts from fantasies, and realize that fantasies do not change reality. At best fantasy can
be a prelude to coping with reality. It is not until
a child is six or seven years of age that they have
learned enough to abstract from tangible image, form
superordinate and subordinate categories, and begin
to think logically.

Preschool children do comparatively little
thinking for themselves about the nature of the world
because they rely on the authority of their elders.
Through sorting experiences as to what satisfies and
what frustrates, the child begins to grow cognitively.
The "preoperational stage" (from 2 or 2.5 to 6 or 7)
is a prolonged transition from the sensori-motor to
concrete operational intelligence, in which conceptual
thinking begins and retains marked residues of sensori-
motor behavior. Preschool reasoning is loose; the
use of "because" is rare. The child lacks adequate
categorization, reference systems, and differentiation between the subjective and the objective; he or
she is apt to center on one aspect of the object,
neglects other attributes, and consequently distorts
reasoning. Thinking tends to be static because it is
impossible for the child to take into account the
transformation from one state to another. It is
impossible to maintain an original premise while reasoning; the child cannot remember the image with which
one has started and which one needs for comparison
with the end result. There is an imbalance between
assimilation and accommodation during this period,
manifested in the child's imitation and symbolic play.
In imitation, accommodation prevails over assimilation,
whereas in symbolic play, assimilation prevails over
accommodation. In cognitive development, differentiation needs to be accompanied by integration. Imbalance
is due to a lack of integration, and the two polarities need to be maintained simultaneously.

Concrete concepts become "true concepts" when children can do something with them, compare them, combine them, and talk about their attributes. In the early part of this period, preschool children can generally deal with the difference between two concepts, but hardly single out their similarities. Only sometime later in the school years, can children deal simultaneously with similarities and differences, and recombine concepts into higher categories, such as "dogs and cats are animals." Preschool children develop the ability to differentiate, but their ability to integrate comes later.

Naturally there are exceptional cases. One of the interesting stories about children I heard of was told by my brother Sam living in Long Island. His son Stephen was at a nearby nursery. One day his teacher drew four chickens on the blackboard and asked the children to tell her how many there were. Everyone said "Four chickens" except Stephen. He kept quiet for a while, and then said, "Three chickens." The teacher asked him to count, and he said, "One chicken, two chicken, three chicken," and stopped. The teacher said, "But there is another chicken." He said, "No, that's not a chicken. A chicken has two legs, but it has only one leg. It is not a chicken." The teacher looked at the picture and quickly solved the embarrassing situation. Stephen's ability to differentiate things and categorize them was superior to that of his friends.

Adults and preschool children often do not communicate as well as they might, because they use the same words for different meanings. Children are more impressed by concrete than essential features, they cannot always distinguish their own feelings and outside events, so they can live comfortably with inconsistency and contradiction. But adults cannot, because they have more ability to differentiate things and integrate them into categories.

Adults have fewer barriers to abstract thinking than preschool children. The fundamental barrier is the weight of emotional significance in some words. Emotional attachment is the basic difficulty in dealing with prejudice, whereas emotional detachment is important to abstract thinking. The emotional meaning of a word is primary for preschool children, even where it appears to be incidental to adults, so much so that the emotional overtone may make the mentally detachable properties (like big, thin, good) of objects appear absolute and embedded in the objects themselves. Increasingly these detachable attributes become relative, allowing for comparisons.

Time and space are other important aspects of cognitive development. At the end of the preschool period, there is still no overall consistent framework of time; the child's time is fluid and personal; the concept of time is an uncoordinated patchwork. The child learns time through personal experience and events--eating, sleeping, seeing the sun rising and setting, birthdays. In our development of spatial concepts, there are five major types.[29] They are:

1) Action space is based on children's awareness of the location to which their movements are anchored, and of the region in which they move.

2) Body space is based on children's awareness of direction and distance in relation to their bodies.

3) Object space is based on awareness of the location of an object in relation to other objects in terms of direction and distance.

4) Map space is based on awareness of "mental maps," dependent on systems of coordinates and directions applicable to concrete spatial experiences. It is both concrete and abstract.

5) Abstract space is based on the definite visualization dealing with the mapping or navigation problems, geographical or astronomical ideas, and so on, at the most abstract level.

Preschool children have developed the concept of action space, and are able to move easily in familiar locations. Now, they are beginning to learn body space, up and down, near and far, in front of and behind. An object can be beside another, but for most preschool children, it cannot be behind

88

or in front of it. However, the object can be on
or under, above or below, inside or around another
object. In the later years of this period overall
coordination of familiar spatial regions begins to
emerge. Preschool children have scarcely any deal-
ings with map space or abstract space. In the development of spatial concepts, differentiation and
integration are also in operation as well as transcendence.

By the age of five, preschool children are
able to count objects in small series. But mathematical abstraction is beyond their ability. The
ordinal numbers develop only crudely during this
period. "Me first!" appears initially, and it takes
sometime before "last" appears. A four-year-old
child cannot simultaneously takes into account different dimensions. Consequently, he or she sees a
pint of water in a tall and thin jar as more than
a pint of water in a short and squat jar. Preschool
children seldom question the causes; in their ram-
bling style of narration, words indicating causal
sequence never appear. They require no lengthy
causal explanations of why things are as they are,
although children of this stage are curious about
their world.[30]

It is some time later that children learn the
general principles against which they can probe into
causal relationships of unusual phenomena, and move
away from the unquestioning assumption that human
or human-like agencies cause all events. Meanwhile,
preschool children are fragmentary in their construction of experience, anthropomorphic in making the
familiar human sphere of the self and other people
as the prototype of all action and phenomena in the
world. They are intuitive and magical in tolerating
inconsistencies and contradictions. Preschool children can recite but not paraphrase or summarize.
Their cognitive development is very much the product
of tutelage, and not an automatic process.

The two-year-old child does not have a system
of built-in controls, which we call "conscience,"
but around the age of four or five, there are signs
of self-control. However, the child's morality is

basically heteronomous. Preschool children do not
have the moral principles of right and wrong; their
moral behavior is based on rewards and punishments.
Parental authority is its cornerstone, and obedience
is essential. Parents' disapproval means their
withdrawal of love and affection, and the child is
afraid of losing parental love. Wise and sensitive
parents do not abuse their children's need for love
and affection, and create abnormal fear and guilt
feelings by unusually severe disapproval or punishments, which may prevent normal development of conscience and curiosity. On the other hand, parents
should express their disapproval when the child mis-
behaves. When the parent's punishment is beyond
the capacity of the child's understanding, he or
she may feel mistreated, hostile, and revengeful.
As children's conscience develops, they will find
themselves more able to control their own sadistic
impulses.

The renown Harvard behaviorist B.F. Skinner
wrote about his first memorable experience of moral
training at his grandmother's house: "In whatever
way it was accomplished, my ethical and moral training was effective and long standing."[31] In order to
make him never tell a lie, his grandmother vividly
described punishing hell fire by showing him the
coal fire in the heating stove, and told him that
children who told lies were thrown in a place like
that after they died. Later, when he told a lie,
he suffered torments.

What is the religious dimension of preschool
childhood? Certainly it is related to the psychosocial and cognitive development of the child. During preschool childhood, God is only conceived in
physical and anthropomorphic terms: unpredictable
and vindictive to the disobedient and naughty, and
in possession of magical powers. A seminary professor described his daughter's concept of God with
what he heard one afternoon when she was swinging.
Imagining that God was somewhere in the sky above
and near, she said cheerfully "Hi, God! Hi, God!
Hi, God!"

As pointed out by British religious psychologist and educator Ronald Goldman, the beginning of real insight in religious thinking does not occur until sometime in adolescence, and the child must spend considerable time "experiencing and understanding the data of life upon which religious thinking is based." In toddlerhood, egocentrism is manifested in the child's defiant "No," but in early childhood egocentrism is transformed into pre-anthropomorphic animism and anthropomorphic concepts of God. The child's religious faith at this stage is "intuitive-projective"; he or she intuitively accepts the images and beliefs from the parents and significant individuals and projects his or her own experiences and fantasies in religious terms. God is conceived to have both non-human and human qualities, as shown by Dr. Fowler's study of faith development and Klink's <u>Your Child and Religion</u>.[32]

In his interview with a 4.5-year-old girl called Debbie, Fowler found not only her mother's influence but also egocentrism in her concept of God. In their dialogue, she said that in addition to bringing a mask along to scare the darkness away, "somebody with a fuzzy coat on" could be helpful, and this somebody was not an animal but her mother--"My mamma has a fuzzy coat on." In response to the question of "What do you think God might look like?" she said without hesitation, "Air. You know why? (Why?) He's everywhere." "But not in your hands." Being puzzled, Fowler asked, "Not in your hands?" She responded "My mum said not in your hands." Being pushed further, she repeated the same phrase, "No, not in your hands. Not in your hands. And also she said, 'When you love God, He's in your heart,' and I love God." The second part of the interview was centered on probing egocentrism by way of the emotionally charged phrase, "not in your hands." The phrase was associated with her frightening dream one night. In describing the dream, she said "I was really scared! . . . And closer and closer! I had my eyes over my--my hands over my eyes." This was something nobody could see except her. Although God is like air everywhere, He is "not in your hands." Here lies her egocentrism, or rather the subjective dimension of religious faith, which is always integrated with the objective, "My mum."

91

Likewise, Klink gives us several interesting cases: A boy aged three said, "I have seen God. It's a lady." Another boy of age five said, "If God is everywhere, is he in this vitamin tablet as well? He must be awfully crushed up!" A five-year-old girl said, "You always say God and he, but I say she." A child once asked her father if God ever had a birthday. The father replied, "God never has a birthday." The child left the room deeply disappointed, but came back later full of enthusiasm and cried out, "Mummy says that God has a birthday every day." Another girl of age five said, "It isn't raining and I just got a drop on my nose. God must have been washing the window." A five-year-old girl prayed, "God, our Father, when will you send the sun through the clouds? I do so want to play outside." A six-year-old girl prayed, "Later on I am going to marry God, then I can go and live in heaven and then I will have a fine view." It is not only the girls who try to link human experiences with their conception of God; boys do the same. A boy aged six said, "I wish I could be God for once, then I could pinch out of all the sugar bowls." Another boy aged seven said, "Hasn't God got a wife? Oh, no. he wouldn't have much use for one, because he hasn't got a body." These sayings indicate children's anthropomorphism and egocentrism.

Anthropomorphic egocentrism is better than the defiant egocentrism of toddlerhood, but it needs to be developed. The danger of anthropomorphism is idolatry, making God in human terms and in the image of us. The Christian faith affirms that God has created us in His own image, and that God transcends from all He has created. Anthropomorphism is immature because it lacks transcendence and differentiation. The divine and the human are to be differentiated, although God is immanent. The identification of the human with the divine in anthropomorphism may be an expression of integration, but there is no paradoxical differentiation and transcendence. It is dominated by egocentrism.

Likewise the "God is on our side" mentality is egocentric and childish. In every neurosis there is a reversal of values, and the neurotic puts ultimate

on his or her own feelings, thoughts, and problems.
As Prof. Ann Ulanov of Union Theological Seminary
points out, the neurotic "wants to have everything
without paying for anything--to get love without
making himself lovable; to be forgiven without any
repentence on his part or change of behavior."[33] The
nation is plagued by best sellers that concentrate
persistently, if not feverishly, "upon one's thoughts,
feelings, wishes, worries--bordering on, if not embracing, solipsism: the self as the only or main
form of (existential) reality." So, "the end of con-
sensus" may be indeed near, if this continues, as[34]
Prof. Robert Coles of Harvard alarmingly states.
The Christian affirmation that the God of love is
also the judge of all may help us grow out of the
anthropomorphic, childish, and even neurotic egocentrism.

5. Middle and Late Childhood and Socializing Faith

This stage is another mile stone in life's
journey. The developmental tasks during this period
cover the learning of physical skills, attitudes,
concepts, moral values, social roles and skills, and
the basic skills necessary for reading, writing,
arithmatics, and for the preparation of everyday living and economic independence.[35] During this period,
affiliation with age-mates becomes very important;
the significance of the peer group cannot be over-
emphasized. Through peer groups, the child learns
social skills, competition, cooperation, group loy-
alty, discipline, leadership, followership, justice,
injustice, and the structure of group organization.
The child must establish a close relationship with
a "chum" or significant adults other than his or her
own parents. Such relationship may save the child
from rejection or other destructive influences at
home.

Children live in two worlds--the adult world
and the world of peers. Analogously, they live in
a no man's land. In the beginning the child is likely
to be a fringe member of the gang, but by the age

of twelve, the child will be competent, and scornful of all things childish. Preschool children focus on family relationships, trying out the roles and activities of grown-ups, but school-age children form a separate subculture with their own games, moral values, rules, and memberships. This subculture has some attributes of primitive cultures, such as oral tradition and rituals. In this way, the processes of differentiation and integration begin to have a collective meaning. In socialization, children are differentiated from parents, and integrated with friends.

The process of becoming an individual person requires the child to join peer groups, although they are transitional and temporary in their function and significance. Previously the child's self-image came from feeling loved and accepted by the family, but now it must come from recognition and acceptance by peers, and from a sense of adequacy and competence. Now children are able to criticize themselves to a great extent, and to see themselves and their achievements through the eyes of others. However, there is a danger of being enslaved by peer groups so much that the child, seeking independence from the family, is now unable to think for him or herself. They move and do things in groups. The children declare independence from their families and defy their parents, but now they are subservient to peer groups for protection against the risks of such defiance. They may jump out of the frying pan, but are caught by the fire in the long run.

The child's independence is strictly limited, and subject to the control of the group. But the group is valuable insofar as it is part of emancipation from the parents and adult authorities. Defiant groups arouse adult authorities to anger so that they can outwit or outrun them, and say "We can stand up to adults and survive." On the other hand, children at this stage need support from home, and will not stop loving their parents suddenly in spite of their insistence on freedom and independence from adults. They need parental backing in facing group pressure; they are not ready for full democratic self-determination. They still need the support, security and

guidance of their parents, and still feel required
to adapt to parental restrictions. Home is a haven,
which provides security and comfort; the child at
this stage is now entering a wider society, not as
a lone wolf, but as a member of a family with which
other children can identify them. The child can
never be as totally free of family as he or she wants
it to be.

The peer group has rigid standards and rules,
which may be quite different from the standards and
rules at home and in schools.[36] Its demand for blind
compliance tends to make those who join the group
look infantile. However, proper demands for conformity are needed for human growth toward maturity,
because freedom must be tailored to meet the needs
of children at different age levels. School-age
children are not ready to make choices and decisions
with complete freedom, and they may sometimes become
impulsive and unpredictable. Therefore, they need
guidance, encouragement, and limitations as well as
freedom.

Once in a while we see spoiled children among
school-age children. They try to dominate others
as they have dominated their parents. The over in-
dulged child tries to dominate other children because
he or she has been accustomed to dominating his or
her parents. Such a child cannot meet peers on an
equal status by peers. Consequently, the child can
never become fully integrated with normal play groups.
The reason is that, due to weak conscience and moral
self-control, the child is abnormally quick to become
jealous, angry, and spiteful when entering into the
community outside the home. This will in turn interfere with acceptance by play groups and make the
child into a lone wolf.

During this period, boys associate more osten-
tatiously with other boys, and girls with other girls,
each group pursuing separate interests and identities
until the arrival of adolescence, when the two sexes
suddenly come together again. The sex cleavage becomes conscious and institutionalized gradually, and
boys and girls shun each other, and speak with ring-
ing contempt of the opposite sex in order to estab-

lish their sexual identities. This task appears to
be more difficult today than decades ago, when the
sex roles were more clearly defined. It is difficult
to generalize at the present time, because there
are unpredictable changes going on in society, particularly in regard to sex roles.

The currently controversial issue of sex differences is beyond the scope of this book. However,
it is generally observed that boys are more aggressive, self-assertive and independent than girls,
and identify with achievers, initiators and leaders,
showing greater interest in power symbols, and empha-
sizing strength, dexterity, adventure and courage;
girls are less violent and boisterous than boys, and
enjoy taking care of little children. Norms for girls
tend to be more consistent and clear-cut. Girls are
commonly found to develop their linguistic skills
earlier than boys and do better in most aspects of
the verbal performance. In contrast, boys are more
proficient in spatial skills than girls, and show
better arithmatical reasoning.[37]

Sex cleavage may be a reaction formation to
keep sexual impulses under control. But it is temporary. The school years are a relatively quiet
interlude between two periods of turbulence--the
oedipal and the pubertal. Both are deeply rooted
in the awareness of sexual drives. The latency period
seems quiet, but before long repressed sexual energies burst out like an explosive volcano.

The resolution of the oedipal conflicts leads
to a readiness for further cognitive and moral
development. Intellectual curiosity among school-
age children is a sublimation of repressed sexual
energies. Their unsublimated sexual desire and
unchanneled aggression may interfere with their
learning. Normal children are likely to replace
most of their oedipal curisoity with general curiosity. Their aggression is channeled into mastering
more knowledge to enrich their experiences and extend the horizons of external reality. They are no
longer dominated by the sexual desire of the oedipal
conflicts, but are still sexually curious and interested in certain amount of sexual experimenting dur-

ing this period. Just as in socialization with peer groups, we see differentiation from the parents and integration with friends; in the sublimation of the sexual desire for intellectual curiosity and moral development we see transcendence of the ego from the id, and the superego from the ego in the same process. But sublimation does not mean "cut-off"; on the contrary, it also implies the integration of the ego with the id, and the superego with the ego, so that both the ego and the superego receive energies and function properly.

Children learn to use their bodies effectively, and develop physical skills in jumping, diving, vaulting, skating, playing ball and so on. Closely related to the new sense of identity is each child's specific competence. The central theme at this stage is "industry vs. inferiority," as Erikson points out.[38] The child "learns to win recognition by producing things" in the world of tools; his or her ego boundaries include tools and skills; the child learns a sense of division of labor and differential opportunity, because further differentiation has taken place in his or her life.

Generally school-age children are gluttonous learners. As Piaget points out, they have reached the concrete operational stage. Learning during the early years in school continues to be largely concrete-and action-oriented. As they grow older, they become more concerned with abstraction and generalization.[39] In contrast to the preschool years, when children are still unable to differentiate symbols from reality, the school years are a period of time in which they begin to understand symbols as representations of reality, and they are very much aware that language is something to be mastered and utilized. They think in terms of cause and effect later, and may become quite fatalistic in outlook.

During the school years, children are likely to be acutely sensitive to moral inconsistencies and contradictions, particularly those which affect them; and one of their outcries is, "It's not fair!" Their moral judgment may become excessively rigorous. It is often said that school-age children pass much harsher judgments than adults. In a highly permissive society, this may not be true. However, it is generally observed that children can be far more stringent than most adults could tolerate. By the end of this period, children's mental structures are essentially the same as those of adults, and like adults, they become experts at rationalization, denial, projection, and other defense mechanisms. Morally, they are concerned more with the letter than with the spirit of rules, and argue legalistically; later in their school years, they relinquish much of their moral absolutism in favor of tolerance, relativism, and flexibility.

What is the religious dimension of children in this stage? The most important aspect of school-age children's religion is socializing faith. The significance of church for boys and girls at this stage, who are in need of friendship and peer groups, is not only religious but also social. Church is more of a socializing agency, preparing them for adult living, than a narrowly defined religious community. In one instance, a church in the Chicago area was remembered by a successful electrical engineer as a place where he learned not to be a "cold fish" in shaking hands, but to look at the person and express enthusiasm and affection. In another incidence, a church in the New York area was remembered by a college professor as a place where he learned social adjustment and the minister was remembered for the success of persuading the father to let the children go to the church in the evening. The fellowship of the church may not be fully understood by children of this age, but they certainly will find it meaningful to their needs for friendship and peer groups.

On another occasion, a young adult graduate student found his sweetheart at Sunday School, and later they were married. Likewise, his wife found her closest friends at Sunday School. It would be narrow-minded to criticize children who go to church for social reasons. As pointed out by a minister of education, who has served two churches in an urban area, the most important thing for children is that

the church is a community and they find supportive
friendships there.

The "I"-oriented differentiation of early
childhood needs to be balanced by the "we"-oriented
integration, and the egocentric anthropomorphic faith
needs to be transformed into the cooperative socializing faith of middle and late childhood, as the child
grows from one stage to another. Religion has been
a strong socializing force for all ages. This reminds
us of Émile Durkheim's analysis of the sociological
function of religion as the preservation of society
and his concept of God as a hypostatization of society;
society, like God, was greater than individual persons
capable of inspiring a sense of duty and altruism.[40]
His analysis has some truth in it; but, it seems to
me, it reflects the socializing faith which is still
anthropomorphic, the religious dimension of middle
and late childhood.

The more advanced child may be able to say that
the Bible tells why and science tells how, as shown
by an interview in Fowler's study of faith development.[41] He has found that a ten-and-a-half-year-old
boy tried to separate what was a myth from what it
symbolized. Although his effort to demythologize
was not as sophisticated as the Biblical scholars,
essentially the purpose was the same. For him, the
devil was just an emotion expressed as a mythical
character. The devil does not have a body; he uses
the human body to do evil. Modes of religious expression during this period have significant correlations with the child's cognitive and moral development.

A minister was deeply intrigued by his niece
Johnnette, who was very talented and doing well in
school. On one visit, she asked him, "How could God
be the Father, Son and Holy Spirit and not three gods?
A friend of mine said, 'only one God.'" He was amazed
and thought for a while, and then replied, "You see,
your father is a scientist, but he is also my brother,
So, he is your father to you, a scientist to his colleagues at the lab, and a brother to me. But he is
just one person, not three. Again, in my family
there are three persons, my wife, my son, and myself.

99

But we are just one family, not three. Right?" "Yeah,
I know," she smiled and replied.

On another visit, she asked him, "How did God
create the world? I asked your son, and he asked me
to ask you." While he was thinking about the best
way to answer her question, she brought a piece of
paper to him asking him what he would like her to
make out of it, "A boat or a ball?" Immediately, he
said, "A boat!" Soon she made a boat and showed it to
him. He said to her, "A while ago, you asked me how
God created the world. Now I ask you, 'How did you
make this boat?'" She answered, "I made it with my
hands." Making use of her personal experience, the
uncle said to the girl, "Just as you made the boat
with your hands, God made the world with His almighty
hands." His niece smiled again and surprisingly said,
"But you cannot see it, because He is God." She may
not be typical of her age, but this illustrates the
religious dimension of middle and late childhood.

Morally children's relationships with God may
be tinged with guilt over specific acts, and they may
still conceive of God as an avenging agent. They
are on the borderline of recognizing the compatibility
of love and justice. In their prayers, there will be
apparent altruism and self-examination. They may show
desires of becoming better persons. This is a sign
of maturation. We can find this level of religious
experience and understanding in the Bible. They often
contain human elements in anthropomorphic terms, and
with God as an avenging agent. The Psalmist says,
"thy eyes behold my unformed substance; in thy book
were written, every one of them. . . O that Thou
wouldst slay the wicked, O God."[42]

Childhood religion becomes irrelevant as one
grows older. Young children may be interested in the
colorful pageantry of religious services, and like to
join singing with a mixture of childhood reverence
and curiosity. But before long, they become critical
of religion, and their interest wanes rapidly as childhood comes to a close. The developmental transition
of childhood religion is, as described by child psychologist E.R. Hurlock, reflected in their prayers.
A preschool child may pray, "Dear God, please give me

100

a new pair of skates"; a six-year-old child may say, "Dear God, please help me to do my arithmetic"; but a ten-year-old child may say, "I don't see why I have to say my prayers. God never answers them."[43] Recently, a young advertising specialist reflected on his developmental transition and disinterest in the church: "When I was in primary school, I went to Sunday School at our church and attended services afterward, but when I grew older, I found what I had been taught was not exactly what I actually heard and saw, and I became disinterested."

When Swiss psychiatrist Paul Tournier was a small boy, he built a "mysterious machine" bristling with gears and springs, which, he believed, would create life through his prayers. Later he found that his daydream concealed a desire to use God for his own glory instead of serving God, and wrote, "This reversal of roles was to become the occasion of my toughest battle."[44] Childhood religion is made of fantasy and egocentrism, and a new faith is needed for the next stage of life.

NOTES

1. Karl Rahner, Foundations of Christian Faith (New York: Seabury Press, 1978), pp. 22-31.

2. Paul Tournier, The Person Reborn (New York: Harper & Row, 1966), p. 24.

3. It seems noteworthy that qualities of therapeutic relationships such as acceptance, empathy, warmth, etc. are found in symbiotic relationships between mother and child, and they are restorative by nature.

4. J. Piaget, Construction of Reality in the Child (New York: Basic Books, 1954); The Origin of Intelligence in Children (New York: International Universities Press, 1952), et al.

5. M. Wertheimer, "Psychomotor Coordination of Auditory and Visual Space at Birth," Science, 134

(1961), p. 1692.

6. Piaget sees six sub-stages in the sensori-motor period--i and ii, reflex exercises and primary circular reactions; iii, the secondary circular reactions; iv, coordination of secondary schemas; v, tertiary circular reactions; vi, the invention of new means through mental combinations. In this, we also see the principle of transcendence in operation, which implies hierarchical development.

7. The early intercoordination of eyes, ears, and hands in infancy may be the most primordial form of integration which brings arts, science, and technology together in modern society. In education, the principle of integration is manifested in democratic education, core curriculum, interdiciplinary programs, work-studies, etc.

8. Erik H. Erikson, Childhood and Society (New York: W. W. Norton & Co., 1963), pp. 247-251.

9. See N. Cameron, Personality Development and Psychopathology (Boston: Houghton Mifflin Co., 1963), p. 53.

10. Cp. E. Becker, The Birth and Death of Meaning (New York: The Free Press, 1971).

11. Jerome Kagan, The Growth of Child (New York: W. W. Norton & Co., 1978), pp. 214-215.

12. A. P. MacDonald, "Birth Order in Religious Affiliation," Developmental Psychology, 1(1969), p. 628.

13. R. Stein, "The Effects of Ordinal Position and Identification on Philosophy of Life, Occupational Choice, and Reflectiveness-Impulsivity," (unpublished honors thesis, Harvard University, 1966).

14. K. Goodall, "Big Brother and the Presidency," Psychology Today, 9 (4) (1972), p. 24.

15. John 15:1-11, 17:1-26, Gal. 2:20. Such biblical passages may be significant from the point
of view of psychotherapy. In psychotherapy
there is a "gestation period" characterized by
"creative symbiosis" prior to the psychological
birth. See, E. K. Hansen, "Symbiosis: An Aspect
of Psychotherapy," Bulletin of the Menninger
Clinic, 42(1978), pp. 191-202.

16. Lewis J. Sherrill, The Struggle of the Soul
(New York: The Macmillan Co., 1961), pp. 40-41.
Also, J. L. Klink, Your Child and Religion
(Richmond, Va: John Knox Press, 1972), pp. 27-
39.

17. Paul Tournier, The Strong and the Weak (Philadelphia: The Westminster Press, 1972), p. 60.
Cp. Paul Tillich, A History of Christian Thought,
ed. by Carl E. Braaten (New York: Harper & Row,
1968), pp. 228-233.

18. Erik H. Erikson, Childhood and Society (New York:
W. W. Norton & Co., 1963), pp. 288 ff.

19. Sigmund Freud, New Introductory Lectures on
Psychoanalysis (New York: W. W. Norton & Co.,
1965), pp. 99, 117-120.

20. Erikson, Ibid., pp. 251-254.

21. Ibid.

22. Paul Tournier, A Place for You: Psychology
and Religion (New York: Harper & Row, 1968),
p. 195. Cp. The Interpreter's Bible, Vol. 1
(Nashville and New York: Abingdon Press, 1952),
pp. 501-515.

23. Selma H. Fraiberg, The Magic Years (New York:
Charles Scribner's Sons, 1959), pp. 184-187.
See also, James W. Fowler and S. Keen, Life
Maps: Conversations on the Journey of Human
Faith (Waco, Texas: Word Books, 1978), pp. 42-
60.

24. Ex. 20: 3.

25. Sigmund Freud, The Interpretation of Dreams, Vol. 4 of The Standard Edition of the Complete Psychological Works of Sigmund Freud (London: Hogard Press, 1956), pp. 257-266. Also, Freud, Three Essays on the Theory of Sexuality, Vol. 7 of The Standard Edition, pp. 135-243.

26. L. Joseph Stone and J. Church, Childhood and Adolescence (New York: Random House, 1957), p. 146. See also, Theodore Lidz, The Person: Stages of Life Cycle (New York: Basic Books, 1976), p. 200.

27. L. J. Stone, "Experiments in Group Play and in Readiness for Destruction," in L.B. Murphy et.al, Personality in Young Children (New York: Basic Books, 1956), pp. 201-263.

28. J. Piaget, Judgment and Reasoning in the Child (Totowa, N.J.: Littlefield, Adams & Co., 1966), pp. 97-113.

29. Stone and Church, Childhood and Adolescence, pp. 184-186.

30. J. Piaget, The Construction of Reality in the Child trans. by Margaret Cook (New York: Basic Books, 1954); Piaget, The Origins of Intelligence trans. by Margaret Cook (New York: International Universities Press, 1956); Ruth M. Beard, An Outline of Piaget's Developmental Psychology (New York: New American Library, 1969),

31. B. F. Skinner, Particulars of My Life (New York: Alfred A. Knopf, Inc., 1976), p. 60.

32. Klink, Your Child and Religion, pp. 30, 43. Cp. Fowler, Life Maps, pp. 42-60. See also, Ronald Goldman, Religious Thinking from Childhood to Adolescence (London: Routledge and Kegan Paul, 1964).

33. Ann and Barry Ulanov, Religion and the Unconscious (Philadelphia: The Westminster Press, 1975), p. 194.

34. Robert Coles, "Civility and Psychology," <u>Daeda-lus</u>, (Summer 1980), p. 137.

35. Robert J. Havighurst, <u>Developmental Tasks and Education</u> (Chicago: The University of Chicago Press, 1972), pp. 19-35.

36. A. Strauss, "The Development of Conceptions of Rules in Children," <u>Child Development</u>, 25(1952), pp. 193-208.

37. R.C. Friedman, ed., <u>Sex Differences in Behavior</u> (New York: John Wiley and Sons, 1974); Richard Green, <u>Sexual Identity Conflict in Children and Adults</u> (New York: Basic Books, 1974); J.T. Spencer and R. L. Helmreich, <u>Masculinity and Femininity</u> (Austin and London: University of Texas Press, 1978); Carol Gilligan, "In a Different Voice," <u>Harvard Educational Review</u>, 47(Fall 1977); E. E. Maccoby, <u>The Development of Sex Differences</u> (Palo Alto, CA: Stanford University Press, 1966), et al.

38. Erikson, <u>Ibid.</u>, pp. 258-261.

39. B. Inhelder and J. Piaget, <u>The Growth of Logical Thinking from Childhood to Adolescence</u> (New York: Basic Books, 1958), chs. 1-3.

40. Emile Durkheim, <u>The Division of Labor in Society</u>, trans. by G. S. Simpson (New York: The Macmillan Co., 1964); Durkheim, <u>The Elementary Forms of the Religious Life</u>, trans. by J. W. Swain (Glencoe, Ill: Free Press, 1954).

41. Fowler, <u>Ibid.</u>

42. Ps. 139:16, 19.

43. E. B. Hurlock, <u>Childhood Development</u> (New York McGraw-Hill Book Co., 1978), p. 435.

44. Tournier, <u>The Person Reborn</u>, p. 3.

CHAPTER

IV

MATURATION (II)

Life is a journey, and it has its stages. But
the transition from one stage to another is not as
distinct as when we travel from station to station
by land, sea, or air. Although we may think that
childhood is over, we may find residues of childhood
in our adolescence and adulthood. On the other hand,
a child may act like an adolescent or an adult long
before other children. There is a certain sequence
of stages which serves as indicators of normality.
However, individuals differ in their rate of development. Sometimes youngsters write to "Dear Abby"
concerning seemingly abnormal physical development
and sexual problems, and receive words of wisdom and
consolation.

Although the transition from one stage to
another is not distinct, there are three distin-
guishable stages--childhood, adolescence, and adulthood. Each new stage represents not only a forward
movement through further differentiation and integration, but also an upward movement through further
transcendence reaching a higher level of existence.
In this age of value-free relativism and the decline
of authority, we tend to be mindful only of horizontal progress and negligent of vertical advancement
in human growth. The term "life cycle" is not sufficient to express the reality of our living, because
this "life cycle" is at the same time a "spiral"
which moves upward, as David Belgum points out by
titling his recent book--"Religion and Personality
in the Spiral of Life."[1] After childhood, we move
up to adolescence, but successful accomplishment of
developmental tasks during adolescence depends partly
on how well we have done in childhood. Our major
task in childhood is centered on the differentiation
from the parents to become an individual person.

What is our major task in adolescence?

1. Adolescence and Doubting Faith

Adolescence is a cultural phenomenon apart from the strictly biological changes of puberty that signals its onset. In primitive societies there is no adolescence as we know. The transition from childhood to adulthood is so smooth and short that there seems to be no adolescence. Adolescence is a "cultural invention."[2] In primitive societies, adolescence is merely ceremony called puberty rites, but in modern society, adolescence lasts from five to ten years, and sometimes even longer. Modern society is complex and differentiated. Aware of these complexities, some psychologists divide adolescence into two substages, early and late, while others prefer dividing adolescence into early-adolescence, mid-adolescence, and late-adolescence. It begins with the pubscent growth spurt and ends with the full development of social maturity; it begins biologically and ends socio-culturally. The beginning of adolescence is not always as distinct as one may think. The physical changes are not enough to explain adolescent turmoil. Pervasive feelings of being out of step, self-consciousness, turbulent and unpredictable behaviors, a sense of futility and inconoclastic rebellion can be attributed to the physiological upheavals associated with puberty as well as to cultural and societal demands. Such upheavals are a sign of further differentiation, desperately in need of integration.

The major task of adolescence is to finish the unfinished task of childhood, and Sherrill describes it in terms of "becoming psychologically weaned from the parents."[3] Adolescence is a stage of further differentiation from parents; it is a period in which one's individuality and identity really take shape. Upheaval at puberty awakens preadolescents to the necessity of becoming individuals in their own right. In this process, youngsters are required to conform with their peers as much as possible in search for freedom to be on their own, to find what they want to be like, and what they can be like. Adolescents cease to be complacent family members, and want to become independent members of a larger society. Internally, adolescents experience a succession of partial disintegration, differentiation, and reintegration, which culminates when they become full-fledged adult members of society.

Adolescents experiment with different social roles in different relationships, trying out what suits them best before they crystallize their personalities into adult forms. After a period of biological and emotional disequilibrium, there will be renewed equilibrium with a growing sense of ego identity. The key to adolescents' feelings is the feeling of being out of step with one's own body, ideals, peers, and the rest of the world. But when the key is turned, there will be a new world, which is hierarchically organized both internally and externally. A person's self-image and feelings and his or her image and feelings about the rest of the world will become integrated.

But a person's self-image is related to bodily growth; if it is too fast or too slow, too soon or too late, it can make the adolescent agonizingly self-conscious. Adolescents are painfully sensitive about their posture, weight, height; and their bodily awareness is closely tied to their sexual feelings. The adolescents' physical growth is an important factor in determining their stand with peers, which in turn will determine self-image. Adolescents' notions about themselves are deeply embedded in their experiences with their bodies. During this period, they are bound to experience the split of self into person-self and body-self; this inner split makes them feel vulnerable, incompetent and even unworthy, and at the same time assert their readiness for full adult status arrogantly.

In this quest for individuality, some adolescents may indulge in perpetual solitary reflection and self-appraisal. They may focus on their failure to meet their own ideals and become unaware of their talents and potential. But as they try on various aspects of selfhood in relation to social expectations, peer groups, leadership roles, or academic requirements, their inner self-image will become crystallized. Gradually, they will be able to narrow down what they want to become after testing role-models provided by society. This narrowing down is a process of internal integration.

The adolescent search for individuality is basically an active attempt to create a personality, and it has both aggressive and the sexual aspects. In this search, the adolescent is first inclined to grasp the externals of role models rather than their essence, and after much weighing of alternatives, the choice will be made to express the innermost self. In this period, the adolescent is dominated by the ideals of his or her peer culture. This indicates a residue of childhood heteronomy. So, in the process of internal integration the objective polarity precedes the subjective polarity.

In pushing for independence, adolescents want more privileges and freedom from parental supervision and restraints; they continue to form their peer groups; and they strive to be like others as much as possible, largely because they feel out of step. On the other hand, individual differences get more distinct. Younger adolescents are concerned with who they are and what they have, but older ones are more concerned with what to do about it with respect to the entire adult world of job, marriage, politics, religion, and economics. This transition signifies the consolidation of subjective polarity which is going to take precedence over objective polarity in young adulthood.

Adolescents' time with parents at home is often characterized by the feelings of frustration, outrage, humiliation, resentment, or dramatic despair on both sides. Adolescents demand privileges, but regard corresponding responsibilities as onerous. They want the privileges of childhood as well as adulthood, but they do not want the responsibilities that are as much a mark of maturity as adult privileges. Because responsibilities are imposed by parents, responsibilities are considered signs of subordination and degradation. Growing older, the adolescent begins to see the essential linkage between privilege and responsibility, but fears that he or she may not be able to fulfil responsibility. In maturity the paradox of the polarities which "privilege" (subjective) and "responsibility" (objective) signify are maintained.

Moreover, our adolescents are in a state of ambiguity and ambivalence; they are conscious of growing in diverse directions and of contradictions within and without. Failure is unthinkable, and they are not sure of their inner voices, nor are they capable of controlling the new forces in their lives. Consequently, they feel secret relief when their parents exercise their authority. They feel neglected if their parents do not interfere. On the other hand, they feel dominated and resentful if their parents do. No matter how well parents treat them, they are bound to rebel, and speak of their parents as out-of-date. Adolescence often begins with rejecting parents, and ends with reconciliation on an equal footing. The child is no longer a child, because he or she has learned that restrictions of freedom are inevitable and that reciprocity binds everyone in all aspects of life.

With the onset of puberty comes a reactivation of preoedipal and oedipal urges and conflicts. At this stage, fathers are likely to draw away from daughters, fearing their sexual feelings for their daughters. As a result, a daughter may feel that her father no longer loves her, or that he is repelled by her. Similar oedipal components can be found in mother-son relationships during the pubescent period. An insight into such phenomena can be significant to psychotherapy, as Prof. Theodore Lidz of Yale University points out.[4] Sometimes a woman in intensive psychotherapy is astounded to learn that her father's withdrawal was a reaction to sexual stimulation rather than to disappointment in her appearance. If a father is separated from the mother due to marital disharmony at the time when the daughter becomes an adolescent, the oedipal situation is intensified. It requires considerable tact and understanding for a father to convey his true feelings about his daughter's attractiveness, and the necessity of keeping a proper distance. Thus, in dealing with the adolescent sons and daughters, parents need to maintain the paradox of the two polarities as well.

Furthermore, adolescent crisis often occurs when parents are going through a critical period in their midlife. Awareness of their child's sexual attractiveness comes when the parents' physical powers are fading. The decline of the child's admiration comes when parents become aware that they have reached a climax in their lives, and must come to terms with their declining abilities. The adolescent becomes impatient with the limitations that parents and adult society impose on him or her at a time when parents themselves most clearly see the limitations of being human.

To parents, adolescent rebellion may appear ungrateful, callous, and senseless; it is an irrational, heartless desertion, and a betrayal of confidence and love. However, adolescents usually become fully reconciled with their parents usually after they have established new relationships outside the home, and have found a place in the adult world. Needless to say, some remain forever in chronic rebellion, whereas others never succeed in emancipating themselves from their parents' control and domination. Finding satisfactory identifications and love objects outside home is essential. In order to be integrated with the adult world, adolescents must differentiate from their parents; and to reintegrate with their parents, adolescents must transcend previous levels of dependency. Such transcendence comes from further internal integration, manifested in the formation of ego identity and individuality. Differentiation precedes integration again, and integration precedes transcendence; yet they constitute "three-in-one" and "one-in-three" dynamism.

Like school-age children, adolescents live in two worlds. They shuttle back and forth between the adult world and the world of peers. In early

adolescence, boys and girls form groups primarily
with those of their own sex, but as teenagers grow
toward young adulthood, they intermingle and pair
off forming deeper heterosexual relationships. They
still feel safer doing things in groups, and hang
around in neighborhoods or classroom corners. Most
average adolescents find emtoional support and understanding in peer groups; they discover that others
are in the same boat, have the same problems with
parents, have the same feelings of resentment, loneliness, and anxiety, and have a need for independence
and recognition as individuals; they share feelings
of aloofness from their elders and feelings of belonging together; they commonly admire certain adults
and hate others, and share various strategies for
handling their mutual problems.

Homosexual groups in early adolescence tend
to be characterized by strong loyalties and group
identifications, which may affect adolescents' future
interaction and love as adults. These groups are
often exclusive and antagonistic toward other peer
groups. On the other hand, such groups are unstable;
their affections shift, and components change. Before
long their contempt for the oppostie sex is forsaken,
although some people carry their contempt for the
opposite sex for the rest of their lives. The culture
which perpetuates contempt for the opposite sex is
an outcome of fixation at this stage. A developmental
perspective may be useful for seeing the issue of
homosexuality properly.

Friendship groups usually form within the
boundaries of certain personality types, basic orientations toward the future, and ethnicity. The seri-
ously-minded and intellectual types may seek each
other out; others may be drawn together because of
common goals, tastes, interests, or socio-economic
backgrounds. Adolescents are keenly aware of the
overall hierarchy of popularity in school; they are
more slavishly tied to peer group values and judgments than school-age children.

However, adolescents do not face the problem
of belonging in general, but the problem of belong-

113

ing to the adult world. Rigid conformity is the rule, because adolescent self-images are highly dependent on peers' opinions. Excommunication from peer groups may have a drastic effect. Adolescents' dependency on their peers is sometimes so great that it may be called "popularity neurosis." They measure themselves not against ideals of their own, but against what they think will make them popular. Without a strong self-image, adolescents cannot be satisfied with what they are or do; they cannot judge their own worth; they seek appreciation and approval of others, with-- out knowing that their peers, too, seek approval. To parents, every adolescent looks like a potential bad influence on their children. In this way, peer groups facilitate the transition between the two polarities and maintain the paradox between them in the growing experience of adolescents.

Patterns of adolescent peer groups in lower classes may be quite different from that in the middle class. Lower class youngsters are discriminated against and excluded by those of the middle class in general, although the situation may be improving in some communities. If lower class adolescents are remarkable, they are sometimes accepted as equals. Class identification varies not only with family background, but within the community in which one happens to live. Lower class parents are more willing to accept adolescents as adults. Minority adolescents form groups with strong group identification.

Boys and girls commonly form gangs, but they are not necessarily delinquent, although their aggression, assertion and ambitiousness may be manifested in different anti-social behaviors. Middle class gangs are less likely to become delinquent, because they experience less frustration than lower class gangs, have better training in self-control, and are better-equipped with resources. Anti-social violence of delinquent gangs is directed toward both adults in authority and other adolescents, namely, those who are more fortunate, those of other gangs, and those of other backgrounds or national origins. Competition in gangs may lead to crime, but the gang tends to disappear as its members establish themselves in the adult world. The normal trend is progressive transi-

114

tion. In this transition, middle class adolescents
are more capable of maintaining the paradox of the
two polarities.

Adolescent sexuality is complex. At the age
of about eight in girls and ten in boys, there is
a speed-up in physical growth. Growth levels off
generally at the age of seventeen in girls and
nineteen in boys. Pubescence is the beginning of
adult genitality, and the central task during this
period is to inhibit, control, direct sexual energies
toward mature love, and to sublimate sexual energies
into productive work. There is wide difference among
individuals, but it is generally acknowledged that,
for girls, love takes precedence over sexuality,
whereas for boys sexual gratification is primary,
and love and marriage secondary. Love is often expressed in a desire to surrender. In love, we see
integration with others; in sublimation of sexual
energy, we see transcendence; in sexual differences
between boys and girls, we see differentiation.

Dating patterns differ as cultures change. However, normally early dating is motivated not so much
by sexual desire as by curiosity and peer pressure.
An interesting part of the transitional phase comes
when a pair of close friends of the same sex become
attached to the same person of the opposite sex. This
is more common among girls than boys. The boy to
whom the girl feels attracted is usually older and
stronger than she is. This seems to be a protective
feature in the pattern of relating to the opposite
sex just as is double dating. Like peer groups,
double dating is a crutch adolescents use while making the transition of polarities and in maintaining
the paradox of subjectivity and objectivity, "I" and
"thou." This transitional phase is partly an effort
to find identifications and love objects outside the
family which may take the place of the once-idealized
parents without fear of oedipal guilt. There are
four categories of adolescents in the heterosexual
relationships--1) those who relate easily to many
persons of the opposite sex, 2) those who relate only
to the same sex, 3) those who have few friends of the
same or the opposite sex, and 4) those unable to
relate to anyone, the affect-hungry.[5]

The sublimation of sexual drive in the adolescent may take the form of idealism, diffused love of nature, or of the world, in which expression and fulfillment is very vague. A thread of idealism runs through much of adolescents' behavior. Adolescents may seek to lose themselves in nature or to give themselves to the service of the whole of humanity. Poetry may bubble in their minds and flow from their lips, or be recorded in their diaries. Some adolescents may give up their old illusions, but they build new ones, and at the same time become convinced of the futility of all illusions, old or new. When this happens, adolescents plunge into cynicism or despair. They seek an ideal world, but their idealism is contradictory to their own true selfhood which carries its own weakness and limitations; they demand perfect sincerity and absolute honesty among friends, and expect utter frankness about all things from all people, but they do not get what they want. The adolescent's crisis comes when the dynamism of human growth is unusually disturbed, and the paradox of polarities lost. Idealism is a preoccupation with transcendence; cynicism, a preoccupation with differentiation and subjectivity.

Sometimes adolescents like to take a solitary walks or write melancholic prose or poems. At other times they toy with the idea of suicide or become identified with the plight of the downtrodden and the oppressed, and wonder why people do not think about and care about injustice, but they refuse to take chances most of the time. They float above the world and secretly glorify the beauty of nature, fall in love with love, or dream of future greatness. Some adolescents are attracted by the political or religious appeals and join crusades. In both political and religious movements, there is a touch of youthful fanaticism.

Idealistic youths rebel against their parents' values, ideals, and standards, but in the end they often do not have much to add, and eventually they adjust themselves to the very things they have rebelled against so strongly. Regardless of what the adolescents think consciously, they retain much of their earlier identification with their parents' values and ideals. Radical children from the con-

116

servative homes may return to conservatism in the
end, and even when they do not, basic elements of
their new ideology may well be derived from their
parents' standards and values. Interestingly, social
trends in the United States seems to follow this
pattern collectively. The trend in the 1950s was
considered to be conservative; the trend in the 1960s
and 1970s, liberal and radical; and the trend in the
1980s seems to swing back to the conservative. The
equilibrium of dynamism needs to be restored.

Asceticism is another means of controlling
sexual and aggressive impulses by the adolescent.
It is a defense to ward off threatening inner realities. After a period of maturation, adolescents will
channel their sexual energies into intellectual, abstract thinking, and gain new knowledge and mastery
of the world. Then they will reconcile their idealism
beyond adolescence and find expression in various ways.
This can be found among some college professors, political and religious leaders. They may be too much
oriented to transcendence and integration.

In late adolescence the crucial issue is not
sex but love. Gradually adolescents become less
self-centered and narcissistic in meeting their sexual and affectional needs. They may become involved
in love relationships in which the major concern is
the welfare and satisfaction of the partner. This
is possible only when the two persons involved come
to terms with who they are, and have fairly well-
defined self-images. When they have this level of
maturity, they often fall in love in a serious way.
The meaning and intensity of intimacy varies from
person to person. They now realize that life is
meaningful only because it is meaningful to others.
Thus, striving for intimacy and identity are two sides
of the same coin, for much of identity comes from being needed and wanted. The meaning of identity comes
when an individual is capable of both giving and receiving. Identity formation is a major task in adolescence, and will be discussed in greater detail in
the chapter on Identity and Ego-ideal. It is a dynamic process which involves differentiation, integration, and transcendence.

117

What is the religious dimension of adolescence? A traditional understanding of the question is no longer adequate. Due to tremendous social and cultural change, the religious experiences of youth have been drastically altered. There has been a decline of conversion experience and other dramatic experiences related to the so-called "storm and stress" of youth, as youth specialist Merton Strommen points out.[6] After a prolonged study of over fifteen hundred youths in the United States, Joseph Adelson says that American youths are on the whole not deeply involved in ideology, nor are they prepared to do much individual thinking on any value issue of a general kind.[7] The adolescent's society is a conformist society, as mentioned previously, and youngsters conform to the judgment and tastes of peers rather than form their own independent choices as autonomous persons.[8] However, such phenomenon is temporary.

There are three phases in adolescence relevant to the understanding of religious development in youth: 1) cognitive development, 2) identity formation, and 3) orientation and practice for future social roles. They are interrelated.

According to a study of more than fifteen hundred adolescents by Piaget and Inhelder, the cognitive development of youngsters tends to change from the ages of eleven to fifteen, and the nature of the change is from "concrete operation" to "formal operation." Preadolescents think concretely and manipulate the objects which they see and feel. In early adolescence, youngsters develop their ability "to manipulate ideas, isolate variables and deduce potential relationships which can be later verified by experiment."[9] Although youngsters from the ages of eleven or twelve to thirteen or fourteen can handle certain formal operations such as implication or exclusion successfully, they are not quite able to prove. But adolescents of fourteen or fifteen are likely to succeed in setting up proofs by using systematic methods of control. First they are able to think deductively and then inductively. This tends to affect the adolescent's thinking about God, and they shift from a concrete anthropomorphic concept of God to a more abstract concept of God. This

118

shift has moral implications.

British religious psychologist and educator
Ronald Goldman adopted the Piaget's overall interview methods, and developed a structural interview
based on three Bible stories and three religious
pictures. Among children (ages 6 to 17), he found
a developmental sequence including an intuitive stage,
a concrete operational stage, and a formal (abstract)
operational stage. The transition from the second
to the third stage took place usually between the
ages of 13 and $14\frac{1}{2}$. He also found that levels of
religious thinking correlated with the frequency of
church or Sunday School attendance and "total religious behavior" (Bible reading, devotion, parental
religious behavior, etc.). He tested for sex differences and found none.[10]

In the United States, religious social scientists Dean R. Hodge and Gregory H. Petrillo studied
a representative sample of suburban Roman Catholic,
Southern Baptist, and United Methodist Churches in
the spring of 1976. They sampled 241 Catholics, 225
Baptists, and 225 Methodists, and asked them to fill
out questionnaires in group under supervision. About
one-third did so, but the remainder were interviewed
at their homes. Hodge and Petrillo obtained complete
data from 152 Catholics, 151 Baptists, and 148 Methodists. They asked both parents to fill out short
questionnaires. The final sample was largely from
the upper-middle class (mean age, 16 years and 0
months, 97% white, 54% female). The result showed
that religious thinking levels tended to lag behind
overall thinking levels, that this gap tended to
produce faith rejection among adolescents, and that
more abstract religious thinking was associated with
greater rejection of doctrine and the church, except
for private school Catholics.[11] The intriguing di-
lemma for teachers in enhancing levels of abstract
thinking is that the more one succeeds, the more
likely adolescents will become negative toward the
doctrine of the church and the church itself.

With regard to adolescents' cognitive development and faith rejection, it may be well to refer
to a satirical poem by an eighteen-year-old high

school senior, entitled "Lord's Prayer."[12]   The poet
acknowledges the existence of God, but questions it
from his personal observation of the nation and the
world.   Thus he writes, "Our Father who art in Heaven,
where the hell have you been?   Our leaders are all
lunatics.   The world is full of sin."   This reflects
an adolescent idealism and rebellion.   Social and
political problems are powerful forces in undermin-
ing religious convictions.   "We have hostages being
held by Khomeini, who is a crazy man.   What should
we do about the Russians who invaded Afghanistan?"
the poem continues.   He wrestles with these problems
in relation to his faith in God and finds them un-
solvable rationally.   He is familiar with the religious symbols and languages he has been taught, but he
uses them to air his doubts and ambivalence toward
God and the world.   "I do not want to seem ungrateful
for all you have given us today.   That is why I'm
thanking you, God, for cancer, heart discease, and
even tooth decay.   Oh, give us this day our daily
deaths. . ." he writes.   The poem is a classical
questioning of God's love and power confronting the
evils of the world.   However, the poet seems to have
enough remnant faith to build up new religious convictions.   In the last part, he says "We pray to You
everyday of our lives.   We read the Bible--our Book
of Holy Lies.   We get on our knees and look up to
the stars and pray for You to tell us some more of
Your illogical idiocies.   So that we can justify this
nuclear wasteland world of ours.   Praise the Lord!
Halleluja! Help! Amen."   He may renew his religious
faith after struggling to reconcile illogical phenomena of the world with logic and reason.   In this regard
we may say that adolescent faith is transitional to
a new stage of "individuative-reflective faith."[13]

     Transition depends on capacities for logical
thinking, freedom to engage in questioning and doubt,
and successful synthesis of past experiences with
present thinking and planning for the future. Following rebellion, adolescents are likely to reflect on
their own beliefs and select those that have helped
them to cope with emergencies and major problems,
and thus have helped them to make sense of their
lives.   Although the majority of youth hold on to
conventional beliefs, there are adolescents who ac-

tively try to work out beliefs which express convictions born out of and related to their personal experience. Their ideas of God, expressed in daily living, are marked with their personalities.

In contrast to Goldman's findings just mentioned, Pierre Babin found distinct differences between girls' and boys' conceptions of God. He has pointed out that the notion of pure divine spirituality was never marked among girls, while it appeared frequently among boys; that the notion of a faithful and good God was typically feminine and that girls would say, "God is a Father who desires my happiness, who is my refuge, my protector, and my confidant, and who helps me." The girl desires God to be a solid, faithful, and present supporter, filling her needs for affection. Her need for God resembles her need for a father and an ideal man. She tends to imagine God the way she feels at a particular moment. "The boy sees in God a point to attain; the girl sees a relationship to realize."[14] However, whether this is socially conditioned needs to be examined, and any exaggeration of these differences may lead to falsehood.

In childhood one thinks of God in terms of a "big man," as one grows up, adjectives appropriate in describing God's attributes are related to personal qualities, such as "friend," "companion," "lifeline," "guide," "mind," "all-wise," "kingly," "forgiving," "absolute," etc. As pointed out by Goldman, "a child must spend a long apprenticeship in experiencing and understanding the data of life upon which religious thinking is based." The beginning of real religious insight is delayed until sometime in adolescence.[15] Then there will be a real struggle in working out one's beliefs. What will be its outcome? Nobody can say for sure, but we may well make nine hypotheses based on pastoral psychologist Charles W. Stewart's study of adolescent religion (1 to 6) and others' observations (7 to 9).[16] They are as follows:

1) If the adolescent has been "emotionally deprived" of parental love and acceptance in childhood, and has become overly dependent upon parents in early adolescence, he or she may "think of God as a controlling power," or may have difficulty believing in

God. God's love and forgiveness is relevant to his or her needs.

2) If the adolescent is afraid of the "burgeoning impulses of sex and aggression," and in need of external control, he or she may "think of God as ruler or lawgiver." The Ten Commandments may be relevant to such adolescents.

3) If the adolescent is anxious about personal power and relationships to authority figures, he or she may "think of God as a savior from evil powers" in nature or society. The Lord's prayer--"and lead us not into temptation, but deliver us from evil" may be significant to such adolescents.

4) If the adolescent intellectualizes the world in order to keep a distance from it emotionally, he or she may "think of God as an abstraction," and not respond to God as a "thou" with whom one can have personal communion. Such adolescents may find their concepts of God in philosophy. For them philosophy may be their religion.

5) If the adolescent is afraid of peer pressure, and desires the approval of peer groups above all else, he or she may "think of God as an approving or disapproving group authority." Such adolescents may find current emphasis on Christian community in several churches extremely appealing.

6) If the adolescent seeks identity and mastery of life situations, he or she may "think of God as the life-force sustaining" him or her in the nexus of personal relationships and events. Psalm 23 may have particular significance to such adolescents.

7) If the adolescent prefers the mother in parent-child relationships, he or she may think of God in terms of "Mother." Such adolescents may be greatly attracted to feminist theology.[17]

8) If the adolescent favors the father in parent-child relationships, he or she may be quite content with the traditional teachings of the church.

9) If the adolescent matures early, he or she may move away from the "religion of obedience" to the "religion of autonomy." Such adolescents may find the teachings of the New Testament more relevant to them.

The transition from the socialized conventional faith of middle and late childhood to the "individuative-reflective faith" of late adolescence and young adulthood seems correlate with Gordon W. Allport's typology of "extrinsic religion" and "intrinsic religion."[18] The former is practiced for the sake of social conformity, and other utilitarian motives, whereas the latter is a way of life, practiced for its own sake, and based on experience. On the other hand, the transition seems to be based on the shift from the punitive superego as its locus to the ego-ideal as its operational axis.

Furthermore, there are two modes in this transition, which William James called "gradual conversion" and "sudden conversion."[19] They reflect two types of personality--"once born" and "twice born." The "once born" Christians have a more or less smooth transition through life, with plenty of optimism and basic trust in the goodness of nature and the world. In contrast, the "twice born" Christians are subject to sudden conversion experiences in their transition; they are apt to have melancholy and neurotic temperaments and a basic dissatisfaction with themselves and with life. There are about 40 million people who call themselves twice born Christians, according to a recent report.[20] Some of them define "twice born" differently and do not necessarily have sudden conversion experiences. Early research by pioneering psychologist of religion Dr. Edwin D. Starbuck showed that a pattern of distress, relieved by a religious conversion experience, was common among adolescents between the ages of 14 and 17.[21] This led him to believe that conversion is often the normal means by which young people make the transition from a child's small universe to the larger and more complicated moral and intellectual frame of the adult world. However sudden conversion is not limited to adolescents.

In conversion, there is "self-surrender." Each

adolescent works out his or her crisis in a unique way, and religious beliefs and practices either help or hinder in coping with life's problems. For some adolescents, faith is liberating and freeing, while others find religious faith restrictive and enslaving. For the fortunate, religion is a creative force pushing him or her out, but for the unfortunate it is just an easy way to conform. Each adolescent may have a particular dominant orientation at a particular period of time, and shift to another type through growth and in response to challenges. If the adolescent accepts the challenge of becoming a mature person, he or she will often change egocentricity to concern for others, and isolation will be changed into participation in community. It is a challenge to "self-surrender" and to identify with a leader or savior in the process, without losing one's individuality.

The religious experience of Carmen Canestaro of Melrose, Massachusetts, is noteworthy.[22] He grew up in the college town of Ithaca, New York, in the late 1960s and early 1970s. Turned off by his father's negativism, he began using and dealing hashhish, marijuana, and LSD at the age of 15. He felt empty, and started going to seances, talking to the dead, and making friends with warlocks. At 18, Canestaro felt drawn to study his born-again Christian brother's faith, and went to his church in Boston. Praying with his brother and others, he "accepted the Lord," and said to an interviewer, "I felt happy and peaceful. All those feelings of searching for the right thing were over." He learned that drugs were counterfeit experience. His self-surrender to Jesus Christ made him integrated internally and feel happy and peaceful, and at the same time integrated externally with a Christian community for fellowship and support. In his self-surrender, he transcended and differentiated from his wretched state of egocentrism and emptiness, to a state of communion with God, who, for him, was above all and in all.

2. Young Adulthood and Existential Faith

Adulthood begins when one is engaged in society

124

as an independent responsible person. This takes
place after college or after a period of apprenticeship in society. Yound adulthood is a new stage,
which extends roughly from the ages of 22 to 35.
Physically, young adults are in their prime, energetic, and seemingly tireless. They have attained
a considerable degree of maturity. The two major
tasks in young adulthood are: 1) establishing a family,
2) establishing a career. Both of them are strongly
oriented to external integration. Childhood is centered on differentiation from the parents, adolescence
is centered on internal integration of self-images,
and young adulthood is centered on external integration with a marriage partner at home and career partners in society.

In adolescence, a person asks "Who am I?" but
now he or she askes, "Where am I going?" The process
of self-definition narrrows down from previous ex-
pansiveness and illusory speculation to a more realistic consolidation of self-image and life's goals,
after repeated testing of various ways of life, including meaningful relationships with persons of the
opposite sex and ways of support. Internally, a
young adult is now more definite in integrating various aspects of identity and is capable of attaining
intimate interdependence with other human beings.
He or she is now an independent person, participating
in an adult world so complex and full of entanglement
and danger that a young adult is bound to have a great
deal of anxiety and to put forward his or her best as
a kind of self-protecting armor. At the same time,
a person cannot help but conceal the Achilles heal
and life becomes extremely lonely, and sometimes it
becomes unbearable.

Young adulthood is a time to establish a home,
in which one can relax and take off the social masks,
because at home there is generally less need for self-
defense. So, young adults learn to select a mate,
and to live with a marriage partner. They learn how
to express and control feelings of anger, joy, disgust, and love. Some choose to live together without
the sanction of marriage. The current divorce rate
in the United States indicates that marriage is certainly not always sweet, nor is home always a rosy

garden. Conflicts mount and tension increases between newly weds, and both partners are often un-
speakably disillusioned. "Home is not sweet, nor is
it a castle for refuge," they say, "Home is another
battle ground." The task of establishing a happy
home is not easy. As indicated by the study of Roger
Gould of UCLA, adults from the ages of 25 to 50 cannot say, "For me, marriage has been a good thing."[23]
Some people get married for the wrong reasons; because
they were forced by parents; because marriage assures
financial security, political power, or solutions to
visa problems. Others get married without adequate
preparation; they have not been weaned psychologically from their parents; they have not quite defined
who they are and what they are going to do with their
lives; they do not really know their marriage partners.

Erikson defines the central theme of young
adulthood in terms of "intimacy vs. isolation."[24]
Having established identity, the young adult is generally not preoccupied with egocentricity, but reaches
out toward others, and learns to share in intimate
manner. In commenting on whether Erikson's view--
identity precedes intimacy, is more valid than H. S.
Sullivan's view--intimacy precedes identity, Dr. G.
W. Goethals says that possibly both are right.[25] It
seems to me that intimacy and identity reinforce
each other, because they constitute the paradox of
two polarities, integration (intimacy) and differentiation (identity).

Having formed an identity, the young adult is
ready to be ethically bound, and to abide by commitments in concrete terms, without fearing loss of self.
Intimacy may take the form of self-sacrifice, sexual
union, close friendship, or self-negating and mutually supportive colleague relationships. However, intimacy in young adulthood is prominently expressed
in the full reciprocity of two persons in the context of sexual relationships. The achievement of
such intimacy takes the edge off the hostilities
between the couple. Furthermore, it provides a context for the realization of equality between male
and female. On the other hand, we may conjecture
that such an intimacy signifies the basic reciprocity

and equality inherent in mother-child relationships
which created basic trust in the child. Genuine
mutuality and equality are deeply rooted in self-
giving maternal love, which recognizes the right of
the infant to be an independent human being in spite
of strong dependency on the mother. Now such reciprocity and equality have grown and blossomed in
adult psychosexuality, particularly in mutual love
and understanding. Mutuality and respect seem to be
the foundation for all happy interpersonal relationships.

Some young adults choose to devote their lives
to a career, to certain philanthropic causes, or to
the ministry, and may remain single for life. Others
prefer marriage, yet remain childless. Nonetheless,
the majority still expect to get married and have
children. A working mother may have a hard time
meeting the needs of her children, just as does a
father. Those who choose to be in such situations
need to take into account the long range impacts
their life-style would have on all persons involved.
It is evident that no one can serve two "masters"
very well at the same time.

Occasionally, parents may be tempted to send
a child to a grandmother or another close relative
without considering the effect on the child's growth
and mental health, or to have the child taken care
of by an inappropriate babysitter for a long time
without thinking about the consequences. It is unwise to sacrifice one's children for the sake of
material luxuries. Parenthood has its joys as well
as its anxieties, headaches as well as sacrifices.
Mounting literature on child psychology and rearing
may help parents to understand their children: what
to expect, what to take into account, how to deal
with behavior problems, eating habits, fatigue, self-
confidence, fear, social adjustment, discipline,
allowance, sex education, religious questions, etc.,
but parental maturity is most important.

For young working couples, raising children
can cause problems, but for unmarried singles, intimacy can be a problem. Young adults may be absorbed

in their professions, but their emotional needs as
human beings cannot be ignored. Singles bars may
offer opportunities for casual contacts, but uncertain noncommital relationships often make people
feel frustrated and lonely.

In a study of 40 men (ages 35 to 45), Prof.
Daniel J. Levinson of Yale University and his asso-
ciates found that during the period from ages 17 to
33, young men in this society face four major tasks--
1) "to define his dream of adult accomplishment,"
2) "to find a mentor to guide him," 3) "to develop
a vocation," and 4) "to open himself to a new intimate relationships."[26] The first three are interrelated, and largely oriented to career development.
This may also be true for most young women.

Independent from their parents, young adults
establish new homes. But that is not enough. The
other half of their developmental problem is to establish basic identifications in the adult world--
in their jobs, politics, religion, and other aspects
of social life. Identity formation is not completed
by the end of late adolescence. The process of defining one's dream goes on; dreaming is part of identity formation. Young adulthood dreams are different
from those of childhood. The former are reality-
oriented, whereas the latter are fantasy-oriented.
The adulthood dream is a vision, "an imagined possibility that generates excitement and vitality." It
sets goals and directions for future planning and
strategies, and taps hidden resources and motivations.

In order for a dream to be realized, it must
be set in concrete contexts and defined in concrete
terms. In adolescence, a person may dream of being
a scientist, a minister, an architect, a physician,
a lawyer, a politician. But in young adulthood, a
person dreams of a tangible success, and its steps
and details may be expressed in terms of projected
timetables and projects. These dreams are often
accompanied by a strong commitment and urgency as
well as great deal of idealism. More and more transcendence has its place in adulthood, and manifested
in these dreams, idealism, and value judgment.

128

Transforming a dream into reality depends partly on the accuracy of perception of potential, talents, resources available, and a prediction of the future. The dream needs to be connected in some ways with the developmental tasks of the past. It would be foolish for a young person to dream of becoming something for which he or she has no talent nor training. This signifies that transcendence must be accompanied by integration (dream with reality) and differentiation (fantasy from reality).

For a blind girl to dream of going from the United States to Japan to help people there requires careful planning and strenuous effort: learning the language, customs, geography of the land. Genevieve Caufield achieved her goals remarkably, and her youthful dream was not just a dream. Certainly it is not easy to keep a dream alive, and to strive toward its realization and fulfillment.[27] People forsake youthful dreams which are indeed true reflections of their talents, interests, and character, because of seemingly unsurmountable obstacles. This is wrong.

Whenever one sells out one's soul for a cheap bowl of porridge, he or she is going to regret sooner or later. A person's soul represents his or her basic commitment in life, their interests, and their dreams. Medicine is a respected and wellpaid profession. But not every physician is happy with it. Once a successful physician told me that he wanted to become an electrical engineer when he was young. But he went into medicine because it was his father's wish. He was very successful and wealthy, but somehow he found himself very unhappy in some respects. This is due to the disharmony of "three-in-one" "one-in-three" dynamics in human maturation: in this case, integration (following his father's wish) dominates differentiation (his individuality) and transcendence (his youthful dream).

Young adults may rejoice in winning independence from parental authority, but they are in no way totally liberated from authority. In order to grow in stature and ability in the field of his or her choice, the young adult needs to establish some kind

129

of mentor-protege relationship comparable to the
parent-child relationship of childhood. Functionally,
there are some similarities. The parent-child relationship is based primarily on human reproduction
and biological necessity, and secondarily on emotional
needs and satisfaction. No one can choose their father or mother. But the mentor-protege relationship
is built on personal choice and mutual attraction,
which may have the quality and intensity of husband-
wife relationships. There is a considerable degree
of mutual admiration and appreciation, love and care.
In this respect, the mentor often plays the roles of
parent, encouraging, guiding, caring, helping, and
creating opportunities. It has been observed by Dr.
Stanley H. King of Harvard Health Servide that M.D.s
have institutional mentorship once matriculated to
a degree program, whereas Ph.D.s need personal mentors. [28]

    The mentor-protege relationship may be termi-
nated by a transfer from one locality to another,
after the emergence of conflicts grown out of professional maturation on the part of the junior partner,
or purely out of ill will. Examples of such relationships include Emerson and Thoreau, Freud and Jung.
Some young adults choose mentors whom they have not
met personally, but psychologically find guidance,
stimulation, and modeling. Generally, they choose to
be artists, writers, and other self-employed professionals, whose professional growth is not bound by
institutions. The mentors can be male or female,
and some young adults may have mentors of the opposite sex. Just as the peer group is a crutch for
fuller differentiation from the parents, the mentor-
protege relationship is a crutch for fuller integration into society.

    In the process of weaning themselves from their
parents, adolescents seek refuge in and support from
peer groups whose approval and disapproval greatly
determine their decision-making and patterns of behavior. However, as they enter the adult world and
strive for acceptance, competence, and advancement
in their twenties or sometimes early thirties, the
peer group becomes increasingly less important and
is eventually abandoned. The more they become self-

130

reliant, the less they use friends as substitutes
for the family. Instead of peers young adults need
a special person, a marriage partner. This person
acts like another mentor, shares dreams, and echoes
aspirations; they generally agree on their achievements and support each other. Together they define
the boundaries within which to nurture dreams and
strive toward realization.

When two young adults are happily married, each
partner is intimate with the other at home and with
the mentor in the world. This is a successful integration. At home, sexual and romantic feelings add
fuel to the union. If each does not share the other's
dream, their marriage may end somewhere in the transitional periods possibly in their thirties, forties,
or fifties. Without realizing the deep-rooted cleavage within the marital relationship, a college professor was greatly shocked to hear one day that his wife
was leaving him in order to pursue her own career
for self-fulfillment. For him, their marriage had
been good, but for her it was not a fulfilling experience, although they had two daughters and grandchildren whom they both loved dearly.

Around the end of early young adulthood, a
qualitatively new life structure emerges, containing
some elements from the past which have new meanings
in the context of a new life situation. By the early
thirties, a person is almost certain to have married,
or divorced and remarried. He or she is now independent from parents, who may have passed away, or, if
still alive, have different relationships with the
person. A reversed role shifting is likely with the
young adult taking care of the aging parents. The
young adults' occupational life may also take new
shape and stability, or manifest drastic differences
from the original dream. In the early twenties, a
person feels great urgency to realize the dream. That
is the time to plan for the future; hopes are high,
expectations are great, and he or she is sure. The
young adult may appear cocky and arrogant, but when
he or she reaches the age of thirty, he or she is
likely to be uncertain and to waver, questioning
what he or she is doing, and why. As the young adult
becomes more reflective, he or she will discover the

deeper dimensions, neglected during the early twenties. Now the young adult needs to examine earlier commitments. A new crisis generally develops, and life begins to look more difficult and painful. Active life may decline, and marriage may also go down the drain.

Successfully selecting a mate depends partially on "the extent to which the chosen woman fulfills the man's conception of the kind of wife a person of his identity should have."[29] This is also true for a woman. Identifications and love objects of early childhood are the bases for selections later in life. However, accidental factors may play an important role in the final determination such as availability of the kind of person looked for.

After a period of turmoil and the "forty days and forty nights in the wilderness," young adults settle down till the turn of another decade. The period of settling down may last seven years (roughly 33 to 40). If they do not settle down by the age of 34, they are unlikely to have a satisfactory life structure, but nobody can predict for sure, because life is so dynamic, and human vitality is so potent.

Life is dynamic because integration is accompanied by differentiation and transcendence, and has three polarities, instead of one. Childhood differentiation from the family is accompanied by the internal integration of cognitive and perceptual development, and young adulthood integration in society is accompanied by the external differentiation of good and bad guided by transcendence (youthful dream, commitment, and value judgment).

What is the religious dimension of young adulthood? Any transitional period is a time for self-reflection and a time for reshaping relationships with the ultimate and the world. Jesus of Nazareth was believed to be tempted by the Satan at the age of thirty, then proclaimed the coming of the Kingdom of God, and ended his life on the cross during his young adulthood, because his teaching was unconventional. His faith was existentially vital and per-

132

sonally experienced.

Young adulthood is characterized with expansive vision, ambitious dreams, and the audacity to achieve them. The Christian experience at the Pentecost has similar characteristics: "I will pour out my Spirit upon all flesh, and your sons and your daughters shall prophesy, and your young men shall see visions, and your old men shall dream dreams." (Acts 2:17) The religious form of dream and reflection in young adulthood may be the Kingdom of God on earth. The young adult's dream is basically different from the child's fantasy which is magical, fairy-tale like, and other worldly: the young adult's dream is reality-oriented and this worldly. This is due to cognitive development and the need to be integrated with society. It is no surprise to hear that a young Chinese graduate student told a minister after a sermon how he appreciated the teaching of Jesus about the Kingdom of God on earth. A 27-year-old probation officer said, "I don't work for the state. I work for God."[36] God is no longer far away in heaven, but is close and near in this world. In childhood, God may be pictured literally as the Heavenly Father, but in young adulthood it is only symbolic. Furthermore, God is likely to be identified as the Holy Spirit dwelling in the hearts of men and women. Religion is not just something being taught; it is caught, experienced, and personal.

Because of their interests in the Kingdom of God on earth, some young adults are impatient about the church's lack of involvement in social issues. It is not unusual to see a young seminary graduate getting into trouble with leaders of the church and society on various issues. In politics, young adults may become revolutionaries fighting for social justice.

On the other hand, young adults emphasize the personal dimensions of religious faith, which helps consolidate identity and individuality of personality. Faith is not just a creed commonly read at the church services; it is a personal profession of convictions. The previous "We believe" confession of faith is conventional and objective, but now the confession of

133

faith is subjective and personal: "I believe." Faith becomes internalized with an increasing sense of responsibility.

Due to the tension created by an increasing ability to test reality, some young adults become disillusioned with the church and stay away from organized religions. They cannot tolerate discrepancies between church teachings and actual life experiences. They scrutinize the church's every aspect, and are discouraged by its ineffectiveness and slowness to change. Some join other churches, convert to Eastern religions, cult groups, or simply stay away from religion for a while. Zen Buddhism is attractive to some because it is the most down-to-earth type of Buddhism, and at the same time personal and highly subjective. Some change their denominational affiliations because of adolescent rebellion.

Existentialism is appealing to young adults, particularly college students, because it provides a philosophical framework for individuation and the reflective integration of personal faith and actual experience. In response to my casual inquiry about his religious faith, a young graduate student simply said, "Philosophy, not religion." His religious faith was his philosophy. When I probed further, it was clear that what he meant by "philosophy" was actually existentialism. He and his friends often engaged in animated discussions. They were disappointed by rationalists who stress the power of a priori reason to grasp substantial truth about the world and argue about the essence of things. Young adults are rational and idealistic, but they are aware of the destructive forces of irrationality in human existence. Reason cannot be praised in contrast to faith, tradition, and authority, although it is right to do so in contrast to childhood superstition. Rationalism is inadequate.

A young Japanese graduate student once said to me that he was greatly absorbed and enticed by Sartre's No-Exit, and he responded to its message so much that he felt like jumping into the Hudson River in New York. Some young adults experience inner

134

anxiety and dread which is beyond rational comprehension and control. They feel that existentialists rightly strike against rationalism, and rightly remind us that we are incarnate and must be concerned with our true existence, here and now, <u>Dasein</u>. From the rational idealistic point of view, maturity signifies the state of full growth, full development, and perfection. But from the existentialist point of view, maturity is not a state of being but a process of becoming, as pointed out by Dr. Bernard Boelen; and in young adulthood "the birth of primordial Being in man" is felt most acutely.[31] Young adults have learned the limit of human reason from personal experience and are more concerned about individuality, freedom, choice, and the authenticity of inner being.

The religious dimension of young adulthood has particular significance for the local church. A young professional said, "The best book I have ever read is Paul Tournier's <u>The Meaning of Person</u>." The book spoke to his existential needs of becoming an authentic person, when he had to protect himself by wearing facades that made him a hypocrite. Young adults wear social masks because they have just started in their careers and marriages. Social pressure creates a hunger for unconditional acceptance. Here again the fellowship of the church is of great significance. To be a person is to be loved and to love someone. This is essential to personality development, and its particular formula for young adulthood is intimacy versus isolation. Every person needs to be intimate with someone. If the church is not able to provide fellowship, young men and women are bound to seek intimacy elsewhere.

The first emotional impact some young adults receive in joining cultic groups is intensive love, acceptance, support, and intimacy all of which provide an effective atmosphere for indoctrination in subsequent meetings. During intimacy, people tend to lose their heads. When this occurs, they are likely to regress to the mother-child symbiosis of infancy. In distorted forms of religious mysticism, self is lost in ecstasy, totally submit their judgment and decision-making to the organization's leader, a father figure, or to the group itself, or union

135

with the deity is expressed in sex. Intimacy has
religious dimensions, but intimacy in young adulthood implies the completion of identity formation
in adolescence. If identity formation is oriented
to differentiation, intimacy is oriented to integration; and the two are intertwined and complementary.

Some young adults may not experience the transition from conventionally synthesized faith to
individuated and personalized faith. For them, the
transition may come in middle adulthood, or not at
all.

3. Middle Adulthood and Integrated Faith

Middle adulthood is the prime of life, the
peak of career development, and the climax of social
life for most people. It is often regarded as the
"creative years." Most positions of power are occupied by middle-aged adults. In the academic world
they may be full professors, deans, or college presidents; in the business world, they are likely to be
chief executives, department managers, or to chair
corporate boards. Self-employed professionals have
been well-established by now, and are enjoying the
fruits of their labors; they can now afford to take
care of younger members of their profession. Their
children are in college, or have married and left
home. In general, they are in their forties or fifties.

Middle adulthood is a period of further integration, differentiation, and transcendence. In
early childhood there is the Oedipus Complex; in
adolescence there is the identity crisis; in young
adulthood there is a transitional crisis; and in
middle adulthood there is another transitional crisis
around the age of forty. In some ways, the middle
adulthood crisis is as painful and perplexing as
that of adolescence. It is characterized by a heightened sensitivity to social position, and by a preoccupied reassessment of self, which implies a high

136

degree of introspection and insight into changes in career, family, status, and the ways in which things are dealt with internally and externally. It is a time for further exploration of one's goals and potential in order to make a final readjustment before time runs out.

By middle adulthood, accumulated experiences make a person conscious of the emotional, social, and cultural distance from younger generations. Middle aged adults are likely to feel the existence of a generation gap. In the middle of three generations, they ask "How should I relate to the young and the old, as a bridge of between the two generations?" Growing young people can hardly understand their middle aged parents, who are more sympathetic to older people. Middle aged adults wonder whether they will get old in the same way and feel that older people are in a better position to understand and appreciate middle aged responsibilities, opportunities, and problems; they project themselves in their contacts with older people.

The disparity between career expectations of the twenties and career achievements of the thirties, the death of friends or colleagues, and the decline of physical strength and bodily changes make middle aged adults sensitive to human frailties, limitations, and weakness. They suddenly become aware that time is running out. These and other things may make them more reflective and sometimes despondent. They may feel pressed to reorganize their self-concepts--a new identity crisis. In the mid-thirties, such awareness may just begin to work its way to consciousness; in the mid-forties, they find that it is time to rework the narrow identity by which they defined themselves, to reexamine their purposes, and to reevaluate spending their resources from now on. Untapped and undeveloped talents cry to be used so that life can be fulfilling. On the other hand, middle aged adults cry for self-acceptance, and, by accepting suppressed ugly self and the unwanted parts, they prepare themselves for reintegration of an identity which is uniquely their own, not something to please others or conformed to cultural standards and norms. Life needs to be restructured in terms of

137

what is left rather than in terms of what has been.
The key question is, "How can I best use the time
left?" By renewing their purposes and restructuring
their life patterns, they try to help a more authentic selfhood emerge and regain a sense of equilibrium.
This represents a further step of internal integration.

Middle adulthood transition involves changes
of value systems, motivations, philosophies of life,
and other related matters. The valuing of physical
power is replaced by valuing of wisdom.[32] Such changes are brought about by integrating what Sherrill
called "the acquired philosophy" and "the spontaneous
philosophy" of life; the former is "the meaning which
one has been taught to give to life and the universe,"
whereas the latter "the meaning we actually give to
life and the universe as it confronts us, and as we
deal with it day by day."[33] Naturally no one has to
wait until middle adulthood to begin formulating
his or her philosophy of life. In young adulthood,
in adolescence, in childhood, one is intuitively
searching for a formula of meaning with which he or
she can cope with life. The dynamic pattern which
we use in coping with life is largely in the realm
of feeling and emotion which is usually hidden from
our self-consciousness.

Aging makes people aware of decreasing physical
strength, stamina and youthful attractiveness, but
accumulated experience makes their decisions and
judgments wise, their choices more effective and
less affected by their emotions or extreme idealism
and generalizations. They no longer consider physical powers as the chief means for coping with life's
problems, nor do they accept material wealth as the
most important element in their value systems. In
middle adulthood, maturation is oriented to transcendence. Aging makes one transcend from the physical and material valuing.

In her middle adulthood, Eda J. LeShan wrote,
"I think one of the most important keys to a full
and happy middle age has to do with trusting oneself."
The more we trust ourselves, "the happier we will be,
and the happier we are, the nicer we will be to other

people." Another expression for her is: "I am present at my life." She compares this state of being
to that of "synergistic societies."[34] Self-trust
is not egoistical but an effort to integrate. In
social spheres, middle aged adults begin to give up
being a "social butterfly" and have fewer friends
but richer experiences. Self-trust has a dimension of
pleasing oneself, quite different from selfishness,
which involves self-honesty, inner-direction, and
responsibility for one's own life. Perhaps, the
process of reintegration in middle adulthood has
something in common with Carl Rogers' "client-centered
therapy."

In adolescence and young adulthood, people are
often driven by impulse. But in middle adulthood,
self-control is better and life becomes less impulsive. Sex becomes more an expression of interpersonal intimacy than a physical union, because
personal values have become more important than material or physical values. This is due to increasing transcendence in the process of internal integration, which should not be interpreted as isolation,
egotism, or alienation from others and the self.
Rather it should be regarded as the inevitable outcome of external integration, identification, and
contact. Egotism makes us isolated and lose touch
with ourselves; it creates a "false humanism" which
emphasizes isolation instead of interpersonal communion. In the effort to satisfy ourselves by isola-
ting from others, we frustrate ourselves. Attempting to control ourselves, we become uncontrollable.
Increased self-control is not egoistical manipulation;
it is an expression of internal integration in which
one has comprehensive contact with oneself and the
environment. These contacts lead to inner and outer
harmony with oneself and other people. Contact unifies the self, and lack of contact leads to its disintegration. Like gravity, contact brings the subjective and the objective polarities together and
integrates them. Loss of contact is precondition of
abnormality, isolation, and stagnation.

The first half of life is dominated by biological need, but somewhere around the age of forty
or forty-five, biological needs become less important,

and the search for objectives in life becomes more dominant. This does not mean that biological needs do not exist in middle age, nor does it mean that adolescents have no objective in life. Among middle-class Americans, career drives are likely to take precedence over other psychological needs, and dominate young adulthood; but formerly career-oriented young adults may turn to the family or the community for gratification in their forties or fifties. They have reached a new stage of maturity characterized by "generativity," as pointed out by Erikson. "Generativity" means primarily "the concern in establishing and guiding the next generation."[35] Successful middle aged adults are capable of handling internal and external problems; never before have they felt such a high degree of autonomy, competence, and self-confidence; they are ready to care for the next generation, and become mentors to young adults. Unsuccessful selfish middle aged adults stagnate.

"Generativity" also implies creativity and productivity. Studying 738 persons, each of whom lived to age 79 or beyond, Wayne Dennis concluded that a person's twenties were the least productive (except for artists who produced a large part of their lifetime output in this period) and that the highest rate of productivity of nearly all groups, including scientists and scholars, was reached in a person's forties or soon after. Unlike artists, the output of scholars suffered little decline from age forty onwards. After age sixty, scientists' productivity dropped considerably, and the output of artists, musicians, and writers dropped even more.[36] This might be due to the fact that artists' productivity depended primarily on individual creativity and, consequently, blossomed earlier; whereas scholars and scientists required a longer period of training and preparation for their careers and, as a result, their peak came later. Generally, middle adulthood is the most productive and creative period in life.

Age thirty is a critical time for those hoping to get married, whereas age forty is a critical time for those who have striven for success in their careers but have not achieved it. After middle age,

chievement needs decrease, but power needs increase.
Highly successful professionals may give up a well-
established practice for political office; a full
professor may want to become a college president;
or a highly respected minister may want to become
a bishop. During middle adulthood, most people have
attained the highest status and income of their careers.

Middle adulthood is also a time when parents
help their teenage children become responsible and
happy adults. The most important thing for them to
do is to set a viable model for their children to
follow, and to give them the freedom and guidance
they need. Throughout the critical years of adolescence, youngsters need continuing relationships with
their parents. Parents' supportive confrontation or
feedback may help children see clearly their own ways
of coping with life, both effective and ineffective,
to decide what to retain and what to discard. Furthermore, parents need to learn to listen, to be flexible,
and to trust their children. Parents too need feedback from their teenage children, demonstrating con-
vincingly that they are strong and yet open, democratic, and tolerant, that they are flexible and yet
principled, secure, and determined, and that they
are trustful and yet watchful and judicious. Parents
need to be detached and objective in understanding
both themselves and their grown-up children, and to
enjoy parenthood with a sense of humor, if possible.

One developmental task of middle adulthood is
relating to one's spouse as a person. With the satisfaction of motherhood, a married woman in her middle
years resumes the role of wife which was less significant to her and her husband during the childbear-
ing and childrearing years. Likewise, a middle aged
man resumes the role of husband, which he neglected
during the years of his greatest productivity and
vocational success. Often a husband desperately
needs the encouragement and appreciation of his wife
when they first marry. On the other hand, a husband
needs to understand his wife's special needs and problems as she goes through menopause, or feelings of
"empty nest." The couple in their fifties may suddenly find that their marriage has never been so good

141

as both try to meet each other's needs for affection, understanding, and privacy. Although personal comfort often decreases and marital happiness ebbs in the late thirties and early forties, there is a new turn later in the late forties and fifties in which both friends and loved ones become increasingly important as money has become less important.

Middle adulthood is the last chance to change careers. Sometimes it is too late to make major change, and a person has to reconcile "what is" with "what has been" as well as with "what is going to be." Life again settles down with acceptance of a new self-image and structure of things.

In middle adulthood physical power declines. Everyone must adjust to these changes and accept them, if possible, with grace. Body tissues show signs of aging; muscular strength diminishes, body functions slow down, elasticity of the lends (eye) decreases. Women undergo a profound physiological change, and menopause symptoms vary.[37]

Life is full of surprises. For many such surprises may come in the form of romance. Literature is filled with such stories, and the Germans have a term for it--"Torschlusspanik" meaning to panic at the shutting of the gates. Like teenagers, middle aged adults have to cope with disturbances in previously stable hormonal balances, and deal with an upsurge in sexual and aggressive energies. Nobody is exempt from this crisis. Levinson observes that some middle aged adults tend to have romantic fantasies as part of final attempt to solve "middlescence" problems of the "Young/Old polarity." They insist "on remaining youthful in the early adult sense, trying to have now the good times that" they "earlier missed."[38]

Blessed are those who have come to terms with their physical changes and lived with sufficient wisdom, dignity, and integrity to absorb physical decline and limitations, when envy for the youth and regret of the past may gnaw at their minds. The narcissistic adult whose life has been built on the admiration of others and pride in youthful attributes is likely to seek that which will never come back, and be tormented by resentment and bitterness.

Vocationally, people continue to change jobs throughout middle adulthood, but shifting from one job to another may create great difficulties in readjustment. Promotions may become blind alleys, and responsibilities are likely to increase as energy and malleability diminishes. Changes within a career may be more satisfactory than shifting careers. Some careers come to an end in middle adulthood; increasing automation forces some middle aged adults out of the job market, and they are not welcomed in fields in which they have had no training. Even when they are accepted, their resistence to retraining often creates problems. Middle adulthood is a time to get settled rather than to prove ourselves anew. Naturally, many new opportunities open for successful persons. Some learn to control feelings of resentment toward employers and find virtue in patience and other sources of self-realization. As age increases, future security becomes more important than opportunity.

For some people, the quality of "postparental life" can be good.[39] With grown children no longer at home, parents are free of financial responsibilities, free to move wherever they want, free from housework and other chores, and free to be themselves. They can let their hair down and take it easy without the restriction of being good models for their children. Previously they were devoted to their children and lived for their children's future, but after children are gone, they can work to comfort themselves, and get what they want. This newly-emerged freedom provides opportunities for middle aged parents to redefine their marital relationship and self-image. It may result in a better relationship with each other, and in greater satisfaction. But it may also lead to a weakening relationship with a general drop in marital satisfaction and loss of intimacy, confidence, reciprocal settlement of disagreements, sharing of activities, and eventually to disenchantment.[40]

Some middle aged couples realize they have

failed in raising their children. A coal miner expressed suicidal ruminations because he and his wife
had scrimped and taken extra jobs to send their two
sons to college. Now he is disabled and neither of
his boys wishes to study beyond high school.[41] Likewise, a successful physician and his wife became dis-
enchanted with their four children none of whom was
able to get into medical school. They felt a sense
of stagnation at this point in life.

Unmarried middle aged adults often find advantages and satisfaction with their life style diminished. What used to be meaningful turns out to be a
new burden. Sharing life with another person may
become completely impossible. Widowhood sometimes
means a decline in economic income and social status.
But generative people often find creative fulfilment
and meaningful participation in various enterprises
and causes.

What is the religious dimension of middle adulthood? The answer to this question is as complex and
multiple as that of adolescence. By middle adulthood,
there are innumerable differences in personal faiths.
Some people suddenly shorten the lagging process of
faith development in a single conversion experience
in middle life. A middle aged painter, in response
to my question, "How old are you?" said, "Forty-seven,
but I should say 'two and a half' because I had a
new birth two and a half years ago." Explaining his
conversion experience, he said, "My life has really
been changed for the last two and a half years. Before I had everything--drugs, alcohol, adultery, you
name it; and I wanted to die. But now I am converted
to Jesus Christ. I know I should seek something
higher." A father of nine children, with two in college, he was not satisfied with his painting job, and
wanted to go to a seminary. He had found a new direction in life, and was committed to a new cause. Middle adulthood can be a turning point in a person's
faith.

Middle adulthood is a time for integrated faith.[42]
In young adulthood, the process of individuating faith
begins, and in middle adulthood, the quest for and

the redefinition of one's meaning, values, and commitment in life becomes intensified to a breaking point. But for some people, their faith remains to be conventionally synthesized on the intellectual level as propositions or creeds or confessions, or even as systematic theology. However, for most middle aged adults, the quest for authentic integrated faith has to go a step further, asking, "What do I really believe?" "What is really the meaning of my life?" "What am I really working for for the rest of my life?" The adolescent threefold question--"Who am I? Why am I here? Where am I going?" is repeated with renewed urgency and seriousness. It is not enough merely to talk about the meaning of life and the world; a person must really possess it. Unfortunately, we cannot possess the meaning of life like a material possessions. It is experienced, and such experience cannot be made. It just happens, and in the strict sense, it is something given, independent of human activity or inactivity. The classical story of "The Burning Bush" is significant to our understanding of the religious dimension of middle adulthood in this respect. In his midlife, Moses saw a vision of "burning bush" and heard the divine calling, "Moses, Moses! . . ."[43]

In his Modern Man in Search of a Soul, Carl G. Jung discusses the very significant problem of middle adulthood with depth and profoundness. His patients were from "all the civilized countries of the earth," and many were well-educated. What is their problem? He says, "Among all my patients in the second half of life--that is to say, over 35--there has not been one whose problem in the last resort was not that of finding a religious outlook on life."[44] Moreover, "none of them had been really healed who did not regain his religious outlook." However, he also points out that this had nothing to do with "particular creed or membership of a church." He has found that "modern man has an ineradicable aversion for traditional opinions and inherited truths." Some exceptionally able, courageous, and upright persons "have repudiated our traditional truths for honest and decent reasons, and not from wickedness of heart." These people fear that traditional religion has grown empty. They cannot reconcile scientific and the re-

145

ligious outlooks. Their conscious life has lost
meaning and promise. It takes on the mood of meaninglessness that we often hear, "Let us eat, drink,
and be merry, for tomorrow we die," or "Why don't
you enjoy yourself?"

Meaninglessness is a problem for the middle
aged in transition than anybody else. It is a particular problem for those who have to struggle with
integrating a "spontaneous philosophy of life" based
on life experiences in the modern world, with an
"acquired philosophy of life" based on the dogmas
and teachings of the church in the ancient world.
For them, religious faith is valid only insofar as
it is in accordance with their own experiences in
the depth of their psychic life. Their inner conflicts are manifested in restlnessness and a quest
for a new vision of world order, a new purpose of
life, a "Burning Bush" which will rekindle their
hearts with a new sense of mission and direction.
They need the Spirit to touch their hearts so that
all the scattered and isolated pieces of their inner
life may be brought together again. Their hearts
are restless until they find rest in God like St.
Augustine centuries ago. But not every middle aged
adult experiences a religious reawakening. Some people fail to perceive the spiritual dimension of their
life until the moment of death.

Spiritual reawakening cannot be worked out
according to a schedule. It involves the participation of the Spirit, which is beyond human control.
It is a foretaste of entering into the Kingdom of
God. Psychologically, it is the reintegration of
inner selfhood. For Christians, it is "repentence."

Midlife crisis calls for further individuation
by integrating world views and an ultimate commitment
to reaching a state of authentic living, expressed
by Martin Luther's "Here I stand!" Its task is to
find the meaning of life by striving to relate not
only to parts but to the whole, not only to people
and things but to historical events; it is to make
sense of the past, present, and future. By touching
the "corner stone" of our inner beings, we make life
more abundant, we become eager to reach out and care

for the young, the needy, the oppressed, and to extend ourselves to almost all spheres of community life.

A recently retired church leader retrospectively said, "It was around the age of fifty-five that I preached from the gut level for the first time." Prior to that his faith seemed to be on an intellectual level. At fifty-five it became integrated with his innermost being. His power seemed to flow from his mouth when he preached.

Another minister in his middle adulthood divided his past seventeen years of pastoral experiences into four periods: the first five years were primarily from books and intellect, the second five years were partly from books and partly from pastoral experiences, the third five years were from personal reflections of life in general and experiences of some significance, and the last two years he had integrated them all in his preaching and other aspects of his ministry. For him, faith became subjectively authentic and objectively realistic.

In consolidating one's faith by integrating the contradictory aspects of one's outlook and personal experiences, one finds paradoxes, tensions, and discrepancies within oneself and others. More internally integrated, one can afford to be detached from oneself and accept others for who they are and for what they believe. Cognitively one is on the level of formal operation, but one's mental structure and construction becomes more pluralistic. So, the monistic synthesis of conventional faith in the previous time becomes the paradoxical faith of middle adulthood. The previously unexposed single perspective of the immature years is differentiated into the multiple perspectives of mature adulthood. The fact that faith has multiple dimensions becomes acceptable, because they can be coherently held together in one's mind without threatening internal well-being. One is able to live with ambiguous paradoxes in life, because one can transcend childish egocentricity and youthful absolutism, and accept the perspective of other persons and groups. Better integrated internally, self-awareness increases, and subjectivity become more

147

disciplined and principled. Increasingly, life becomes more inclusive and responsive.

4. Late Adulthood and Simplified Faith

"Old age" has different connotations for each
social class. The upper-middle class tends to believe it begins after the age of 65, whereas the
lower class believes it begins as early as 50. Living conditions of older people also differ according
social class. But there are some characteristics,
problems, and adjustments common to old age in all
classes. Gerontologists study physiological and
pathological phenomena associated with aging, but
that is beyond our scope here. A thorough sociological survey of the problems of old age is also beyond
our scope. Although the Unites States is strongly
youth-oriented, awareness of the problems of aging
and the impacts of demographic changes on the future
society is increasing.

Old age has both blessings and curses. For
many elderly adults, age brings more problems than
consolation. They are frustrated in finding satisfaction for their physical and emotional needs. Opportunities of meeting their social status needs are
reduced--retirement means reduced income, personal
worth, close friends, social contacts, valuable prestige, and institutional support. Retirement is a
critical time. A senior staff member of a petroleum refinery observed that several of his former
colleagues died shortly after their retirements. He
advised against retirement. Later he, too, retired,
and became seriously ill. He might have felt he was
no longer a worthy member of the society. His job
was the center of his life.

Retirement is particularly critical for an
academician who has not published a book of major
significance representing his or her life's work.
But this is not always so. Retirement for William
James was a blessing. Shortly before his sixty-fifth
birthday on January 11, 1907, James resigned and
Harvard President Eliot granted him twenty-six hun-

dred dollars a year. The next day he wrote in his diary: "Delicious feeling of leisure!" In the spring he wrote to his brother Henry saying, "You can't tell how happy I am at having thrown off the nightmare of my 'professorship.' As a 'professor' I always felt myself a sham, with its chief duties of being walking encyclopedia of erudition. I am now at liberty to be a reality, to be my own man, after 35 years of being owned by others. I can now live for truth, pure and simple, instead of for truth accommodated to the most unheard-of requirements set by others."[45] In middle and late adulthood, transcendence becomes increasingly prominent, and successful preparation for retirement requires an attitude of detachment as well as transcendence from the world.

With increasing age, older adults experience decreasing physical strength and health. The amount of energy invested in living also decreases. As the body ages, its cells accumulate some useless or poisonous materials, the nutritional processes slow down, and cells lose their self-repairing properties. The signs of aging may show up in the cardiovascular system, the kidneys, or the joints. Illness may make early retirement inevitable; or it may cause unsatisfactory occupational performance. For every person, death is an inescapable fact of life. The death of a spouse is hard for anyone whose marriage has been good. It is even harder for the aged. According to Chinese oral tradition, there are two kinds of miserable people: the motherless infant and the spouseless old man. They are the most helpless and loneliest people.

Older people are more cautious than young people, and feel more vulnerable to physical and socioeconomic loss. Based on his study of adulthood and aging, Dr. Douglas C. Kimmel identifies two characteristics in the thinking process of older people as: 1) "rigidity" and 2) "concreteness."[46] Their problem-soliving ability declines. Redundancy, difficulty in handling new concepts, and inability to make use of efficient strategies in problem-solving are common. Older people sacrifice speed for accuracy (rigidity) and sacrifice abstraction for functional conceptualizations (concreteness). But when

149

a decision cannot be avoided, older people are as likely to choose a high-risk solution as young people. Just as conceptualization ability declines in old age, creativity declines with few exceptions.

Forty-year-olds are different from sixty-year-olds in that the former see the world rewards risk-taking and courage, whereas the latter see the world as more complex and dangerous, no longer to be re-formed according to one's wishes and ideals.

Women tend to become more extreme and aggressive, when they get older; but it is just the opposite for men. Older women feel less guilty about aggressiveness and egocentricity. Consequently, they are more self-assertive and look stronger and live longer.

Both older men and women are preoccupied with themselves, and concerned with their own needs and satisfaction. The older they get, the more inwardly directed they become. Naturally, there are exceptions.

For the majority of old people, integrating a wide range of stimuli, and perceiving and dealing with very complicated situations grows increasingly difficult. But there are people whose ego-strength and enthusiasm shows no sign of decreasing even at the end of life's journey. For them age is not an important factor in determining their purposiveness, and late adulthood is not just a period of decline and idle waiting for death. In describing the last days of Jeannette Rankin, the first U. S. Congresswoman, Hannah Josephson said, "Although she grew feebler each day, she clung to her interest in the world outside enough to watch the hearings of the Senate Committee on Presidential Elections on television 'with glee.'" right up to the end.[47] Those people seem happiest when they find that there is still more to do in the world. It pleases them to know that their accumulated knowledge and wisdom can still be used to benefit others. They do not stand still or fail to utilize their resources to the utmost. Albert Einstein and Picasso are examples. Such unusual creative persons are fortunate in their adjustments to old age. Personality is an important dimension in viewing the relationship between social and psychological wellbeing. The productive lives of those creative geniuses confirm the observation that organism is purposive and its basic direction is forward. The ultimate force seems to be their relentless determination to grow and overcome whatever obstacles prevent growth. They are "self-actualized" persons, to use Abraham Maslow's term. They seem to have a strong desire to stay alive in order to maintain a sense of worth.

In an interview at his office after his retirement and shortly before his death, Harvard sociologist Talcott Parsons pointed out that, unlike some other professionals, he could continue to be active and write without being interrupted by official retirement, and each day he could tell how much he had done in a tangible way. This was one of the advantages of being an author. I could believe what he said, because I was made to wait outside his office till he finished his instruction to his secretary concerning the manuscript, and even after I was received into his office, he made another phone call to the copy editor talking about the necessity of putting exact pages in the footnotes, and then he made an apology for keeping me waiting, and casually commented that he was going to New York to speak at a meeting on his psychobiography the following week. As we talked, it became evident that the inspiration he received from the most influencial German sociologist Max Weber when he was young, continued to burn like an unquenchable fire in his old age.

Another type of active older people do not contribute, but control. They have been possessive mothers or fathers, unwilling to let their children grow up. They have been in the driver's seat for so long that they do not want to let younger people emerge as their successors. They can be properly called "controller" not just of money, but of all decision-making powers; they try to veto democratically processed decisions in the name of seniority. They can hardly be regarded as "self-actualized" persons. On the contrary, they may be "stagnated" persons.

In contrast to active older people, there are
passive older people, who withdraw from social commitment and pursue a more leisurely and contemplative
way of life. Passive people look forward to retirement with pleasure, joy, great anticipation. In a
casual conversation with a fifty-nine-year-old professional, I found that he looked forward to retirement. Without my asking about his future, he voluntarily and spontaneously disclosed that his inner-
most concern was his retirement in the near future.
He and his wife had bought a house in a resort area,
planning to live there among other retired professionals. Unlike those who wanted to continue writing
after retirement, it seemed hardly possible for him
to plan another project before retirement, as he subtly suggested. There is no clear distinction between
active and passive orientations. Every person is
somewhere in between the two polarities.

In traditional Chinese culture, passivity is
highly valued and patience and courtesy are considered
virtues. Passive personalities are dominated by a
sense of security. People of this orientation may
have high life satisfaction but low social activity;
they disengage from social activities with greater
comfort and remain content with life as a whole,
while others in similar situations show low levels
of satisfaction. They welcome freedom from responsibility and indulge in passive dependency. Their
disengagement from committed activity is voluntary
and not forced by declining physical strength or by
external pressure. Basically inner-directed and having a sense of self-esteem, these old people find
security in isolation, retirement, and freedom from
pressure and responsibility. For them, isolation
is not a sign of loneliness, nor is leisure demoral-
izing. They enjoy both, and are well-adjusted to
old age. Their life-style has continuity with the
past, and their needs are generally met. Both activity and passivity can be found among those well-
adjusted to aging.

One can find a detached pattern of aging among
the Chinese, who are content to hand over responsibilities to their sons instead of trying to dominate.
Their grown up children do not need to rebel against

them in the process of achieving independence and autonomy as adults. The detached pattern can also be found among people of different ages; it is not simply a phenomenon of late adulthood. But aging seems to sharpen personality patterns, and makes detached older people look more distinctly passive. In some cultures, there is little disengagement to be found among the elderly; but even so, older people are definitely not as active, virile, and physically strong as they were when they were younger. Aware of this, they readily accept the limitations imposed by their aging.

The third type of aging is that of the integrated personality. If the active type is symbolized by Yang, and the passive type is symbolized by Yin, then the integrated type is Yin-Yang. In actual living, Yin and Yang are always integrated in different proportions, and are never entirely pure. The integrated type of aging is characterized by flexibility, freedom, and spontaneity.

Culturally, every Chinese is in some ways influenced by its two major streams of thought--Confucianism and Taoism, and the recent cultural and political revolution seems powerless to uproot them. The political structure may have changed, but the basic polarities of Confucian-activism and Taoistic-passivism play their parts in individual as well as national life. The same phenomenon can be found in the West, as Carl G. Jung observes, there is femininity in man and masculinity in woman. The wholesome mature personality integrates the two polarities, the subjective and the objective.

The integrated type of aging reflects a basic style of life which has been developed from the past. This type is commonly seen among well-adjusted old people. Those who adopt this type of aging are neither strictly activist nor passivist, because they integrate the two, seeking proper balance and harmony with self and the external world. Sometimes they swing to the active achievement, but at another time to the passive satisfaction and contemplation. These people move easily into old age and are relatively free from neurotic conflicts, because they

are able to accept themselves realistically and find
genuine satisfaction in activities and social relationships as well as in passivity and isolation.
They feel that their lives have been rewarding and
satisfactory; they are able to grow old without regrets; they take old age for granted and make the
best of it.

In many ways, the integrated type manifests
maturity, health, and wholesomeness. Integrated
old people are not greatly affected by the past nor
are they going to be affected very much by the future. Their behavior is likely to harmonize with
their underlying needs and desires. They have complex inner problems but can competently integrate
and solve them; they maintain a comfortable degree
of self-control over impulses, remain flexible, and
are open to new stimuli; they are gentle but dignified, relaxed but firm; they have a high degree of
satisfaction; their wisdom, accumulated knowledge,
and competence enable them engage in a wide variety
of activity. They reorganize their activities after
retirement and give time to continuing professional
interests, personal reading, or church activities
and community activities. They may only have limited
activities, but they are highly selective, aware of
limited time, energy, and resources.

Dr. V. Clayton of the University of Southern
California raises a question as to whether most
elderly individuals resolve the last major crisis
of "ego integrity vs. despair," and emerge with a
concomitant virtue of wisdom. After examining the
basic tenets of Erikson's model, and relating it to
other organismic theories of development, she has
concluded that most individuals either seek foreclosure or enter a prolonged moratorium after adolescence, never reaching the last stage of the life
cycle.[48] Therefore, compromise rather than complete
resolution of forces at each major crisis of life
seems most common and realistic for the majority of
old people.

Unfortunately not everybody goes through aging
by a well-adjusted route. The maladjusted are un-
integrated, unhappy, and unproductive. Having failed

their goals earlier in life, they look back with disappointment and bitterness. They are often angry and blame others for their misfortunes and failures. Sometimes, their resentment and hostility turn inward and they become self-destructive. These angry individuals may become depressed and apathetic as they grow older. They are unable to reconcile themselves to the failures of the past, to increasing loss of social status in the present, to reduced income due to inflation, and to the loss of a spouse in the future. Their feelings of inadequacy and worthlessness may surmount any joy they may have in old age. They experience physical ailments, deteriorating thinking processes, or loss of emotional control sooner than the well-adjusted. They are low both in activity and life satisfaction.

Erikson describes negative old age adjustment in terms of "despair," which summarizes all the characteristics of maladjusted hopeless angry people all their lives. Despair does not come suddenly. It is accumulated, gradually reinforced by a long-standing maladjusted passivity and apathy. Personalities that change very little over the years follow the same pattern in their interactions with themselves and others in the world. They have been so frustrated from the beginning or at some critical point in their lives that neither the principle of differentiation nor the principle of integration has been able to function fully. Consequently, the principle of transcendence has not been fully operative. Their personality growth has been thwarted, and they have become self-haters, if not angry people. Angry people turn their maladjusted psychic energy outward, whereas the self-haters turn it inward. In contrast, well-adjusted persons make a circulatory flow of their energy with its hierarchical high and low tide as the stage of human growth may require in accordance with the principle of transcendence.

Despair in the elderly may take the form of mental illness. In a study of social isolation and mental illness in old age, Dr. M. F. Lowenthal found that lifelong loners tended to have better morale and less hospitalization than those who had tried and failed to establish social relationships with

others.[49]   In fact, the latter were more vulnerable
than the former. Isolation due to the death of a
close friend, a roommate, a relative, or a spouse is
unbearable. As a practical gesture for the improved
adjustment in old age, closeness with another human
being must be maintained. If the elderly have con-
fidants, they can decrease their social interactions
without too much risk of becoming depressed. On the
other hand, if an old person has no confidant, he
or she is more likely to become depressed. On the
other hand, if an old person has no confidant, he
or she is likely to become depressed, no matter how
active he or she is socially. Intimate relationships
are important to maintaining sanity, particularly
in late adulthood. Those who are well-adjusted often
live with another person whom they can trust and with
whom they establish an intimate relationship. Married people are most likely to have a confidant,
whether the person is the spouse or someone else.

     Many old people move to a new location after
or around retirement. But by and large they maintain close contacts with relatives and old friends.
As they get older, their capacity for making new
friends diminishes, and new friends are unlikely to
have the same meaning and intimacy as old ones. At
the same time, relatives become increasingly impor-
tant--not only children and grandchildren, but also
brothers, sisters, and others of the same generation.
For some old people, grandparenthood is a source of
pleasure and fulfillment. Through their grandchildren,
they feel young again, or see their personal lives
extending into the future. Previously, they might
have been too occupied to enjoy their children, but
now they are free from taxing responsibilities and
their grandchildren are sources of love and affection. Some old people are looked on as reservoirs
of family wisdom, or as surrogate parents.

     A cross-cultural study of adjustment in late
adulthood (based on a sample of men from ages 70 to
75 in 7 countries) showed that the primary task was
developing and expanding family roles especially
the role of grandparent and homemaker. The second
task was developing and expanding community roles
in churches, clubs, neighborhoods, friendship, and

and civic activities. The third task was cultivating new active hobbies or leisure activities. The fourth task was keeping a general, balanced slowdown of activity.[50]

What is the religious dimension of late adulthood? Any answer to this question involves the simplification and crystalization of religious beliefs in old age, and the meaning of life and death, and life beyond death. This is related to the fact that in late adulthood maturation is oriented to the principle of transcendence which implies the polarity of divinity in the metaphysical sense. The liberal activist Williard Uphause fought for international peace, and found himself becoming more conservative in his old age, while he was in jail because he refused to disclose names of those who participated in the conference he had organized. His beliefs crystalized and simplified, and his faith became more powerful and positive.[51] Simplified religious faith may come out as sermonettes instructing the young, or sayings which carry the weight and quality of proverbs transmitted orally and informally. "God is love" is an example. The phrase is simple, but powerful and profound. It comes out that integrity which embodies past and present experiences as well as hope and aspirations for the future. Perhaps, one can make it a credo. In late adulthood, the minute details of an elaborate belief system appear superflous. All sophistries and systems of rationalization become irrelevant. Simplicity is needed. Life incarnates belief.

Those who have had a simplistic faith and narrow conservative religious views may begin to widen their outlooks and become more tolerant and perceptive of religious complexities. At 62, Billy Graham said frankly, "I wish I'd read more and spoken less. I've come to understand there are no simplistic answers to the exceedingly complicated problems we face as a country--and as a planet." He who preached that God was on our side during the Cold War of the 1950s is now aware that "God does not choose countries. God chooses people." What he has not mellowed is his Biblical message: "Jesus Christ forgives sin, gives security and stability, purpose and meaning, in this life and in a life to come."[52]

A religiously-oriented older person may become a mystic, seeking direct and immediate experience with the divine, and become identified and unified with transcendent reality. Such experience is a total liberation, an unburdening of cargo from the self. Previously paradoxical and divided selfhood becomes unified and integrated into one whole by an ultimate commitment to and identification with God. Like the Incarnation, such direct experience with the divine brings together the sacred and the secular, the spiritual and the physical, and ego boundaries are transcended by love and universalizing compassion. The person is no longer preoccupied with survival, but ready to sacrifice self for love and justice, because he or she has become a part of the transcendent reality of God. Selfishness and ego-striving are consumed by unselfish love of God. For such an old person, death seems a mere transition from the visible to the invisible, a complete fulfillment of life. "Father, into thy hands I commit my spirit."

Secularlists may condemn the ill effects of both personal and organized religion on those who are approaching the end of life's journey. This seems to challenge the common assumption that people turn to religion as they grow older. [53] Elderly people are particularly interested in the idea of immortality. Religion provides solace, hope, self-esteem, and a way of life for the old. Even though life draws to a close, an old person needs self-esteem and purpose, beyond the days, weeks, or months to come. Religion is time-honored means of finding meaning and purpose of life, not only in the hope of life after death but also in the liberation from ego-striving and selfishness.

5. Meaning and Maturity

As we grow from infancy to old age, we are captured and motivated at each stage by whatever is meaningful. Meaning changes, yet always symbolizes and reflects our basic needs, interests, crises,

158

goals, values, and purposes. Maturity represents
not only what is normal in a particular socio-
cultural situation, but also what is ideal, best,
excellent, perfect, and ripened at each stage of
life as a whole. Maturity can be approached in two
ways: from the static perspective, and the dynamic
point of view. We can see maturity as a state of being, and we can also see it as a process of becoming.
In this age of relativism, maturity as a state of
full development and perfection is often unpopular
and the tendency is to equate maturity with maturation. But when maturity is seen as a state of being,
it represents the ideal, the transcendent, the perfect, the utopian; it is like truth, beauty, and
goodness to which we can aspire but seldom achieve.[54]
In this way, maturity symbolizes vision captured at
some point in our lives, and gives us a meaning for
living no matter how tough life is. This is where
religion has its place. Healthy, mature, and true
religion always gives us vision, inspiration, and
spiritual strength. Then, life becomes meaningful!

As we mature, our sense of values changes.
What is meaningful and important becomes meaningless
and unimportant. When we are young, we are judged
by what we do, by our position, or by our title. But
when we get older, we are judged by what we are, by
the breadth of our minds, by our inner lives, by the
quality of our love for others, by the intrinsic and
not the market value of what we bring into the world,
namely, by our personal maturity. As we grow, we
have new values, ideals, and purposes. When we are
young, every one of us is in a rush, everything is
urgent, and no one has time to think about the overall meaning of life. But as we get older, the day
comes when we suddenly stumble into a void like feverish toilers saying, "Vanity of vanities, all is
vanity." When we are young, we value activity, but
as we grow older, we value people. Modern culture
subordinates people to things. No wonder the search
for meaning becomes feverish and desperate. Life
becomes a desert and we ask, "What is the meaning of
life?"

This agonizing problem is argued fervently by
late adolescents, just as they are about to engage

in life. The key question for them is how to live, and they envision their future career, marriage, income, social status, and perhaps a new world order. They may agree wholeheartedly with General MacArthur: "You don't get old from living a particular number of years; you get old because you have deserted your ideals."[55] They may still live intensely as they advance in years. But one day, they find their physical strength has declined, productivity ceased, friends gone, spouse dead, and there is nothing left. There is no point in living, and life is coming to an end. Again, they are haunted by the question of meaning. When old people look for meaning, they are really asking the meaning of death and eternal life. Their underlying question is how to die. In response to my maturity survey among experts in related fields some years ago, a psychiatry professor wrote two very brief sentence fragments--"how one handles time and space" and "how one handles death." They are open ended, but behind the "how"s are the "why"s and "what"s of life and death, that is, the questions of meaning. Our capture of the meaning of life and death shapes our conception of maturity.

How is the meaning of life found and captured? --through personal touch of the deepest kind in non-directive interpersonal relationships and dialogue between intimate friends or between a psychotherapist and a client. This can be illustrated by an old woman's encounter with a surgeon.[56] She said to the doctor that she was infirm and wanted an operation. But the initial diagnosis did not confirm that she was ill. Clinical and laboratory tests were favorable, and there was no need for operation. The surgeon encouraged her to get up in vain. She just lay in the hospital, prostrate, indifferent, and apathetic. The surgeon asked her how long she had felt that way, and she answered, "Since my daughter died three years ago. My life has not been worth living since then." The surgeon had lost a son in the promising years of youth and had been broken hearted by it. Since this old woman happened to be occupying the room where his son had died, he talked about it as a personal testimony in a fellowship of common sufferers. The next day he found the woman paying more attention to life and determined

to get up and go out, and eventually restored her
normal life. She recovered because the meaning of
life reemerged in her. She had come to terms with
the loss of her daugther, and became reconciled with
herself. It was an internal integration through
self-acceptance. Meaning comes from integration,
internally and externally.

In order to find meaning in life, we need non-
directive dialogue and communion with others. This
intimacy is initially experienced in the mother-child
symbiosis which makes basic trust possible in future
experiences. Nobody can tell us what the meaning of
life is. Each one of us can recognize it only for
him or herself, because the meaning of life is subjective, and it is oriented to the principle of
transcendence. When we are poor, we get excited
about becoming rich. But when we become rich, we
may not be so happy about life itself, because whether
we are rich or poor, have social position or not,
our meaning of life alters very little. Outer circumstances do not make life meaningful.

The meaning of life is inconceivable without
reference to transcendence and God. When life is
charged with meaning, we do not just marking time.
When life is charged with meaning, time is not just
quantitative clock time (chronos); it is qualitatively
different time; it is the right "moment in time when
the eternal breaks into history" (kairos).[57] This divine participation in human life integrates the natural and the supernatural, the sacred and the profane,
the physical and the spiritual. It fulfills the
principle of transcendence.

Integration is essential to our perception of
meaning; when the things we perceive are not integrated in themselves and in our minds, they are meaningless, without form, character, and identity. No
one can recognize them. If the table on which I
put my typewriter and write this book disintegrates
into pieces, I cannot even recognize as a table.
When things are integrated in themselves, distinctions are clear and they are visible. In our perceptual fields, figures and ground are differentiated;
otherwise, the picture would be blurred and confused.

161

Similarly, for a society to have meaning, it must be integrated in itself, and for society to be integrated in itself, it must have order. Order makes distinctions clear according to law. So, when there is integration, there is differentiation, and vice versa.

Furthermore, when things are meaningful to us, it is because what we perceive is integrated into our existing mental structures primarily because there are corresponding features between outer and inner reality. As we mature, these experiences may lead us to a more accurate perception of the external world. Consequently, we are able to grasp the meanings of things, events, and persons more realistically. An accurate perception of meaning is a sign of maturity.

It is no accident that "integrated" is the adjective most commonly chosen by 23 experts in fields related to the concept of maturity, such as psychology, psychiatry, anthropology, sociology, education, and religion. They responded to my survey on maturity by choosing five words to describe their concept of maturity from an adjective check list.[58] The adjective check list was based mainly on cross-cultural personal interviews and an earlier study of the concept of maturity in psychology, Christian theology, and Chinese philosophy (Confucianism, Taoism, and Buddhism) in reference to the study of national characteristics by D. Katz and K. Brady and by G. M. Gilbert.[59]

A mature person is integrated and is integrating internally and externally. In a symbolic sense, there are two kinds of integration--1) "horizontal integration," and 2) "vertical integration." Secular cultures have the horizontal dimension and emphasize equality and relativism. Hierarchy is frowned upon, and there is hardly a sense of transcendence. Horizontal integration is socio-political and psychological, whereas vertical integration is self-transcending and sacred. The two are interrelated and inseparable in the dynamics of daily living. Sublimation is an important psychological mechanism for maturation and human growth, and it implies vertical

162

and transcendent dimensions through a better and
more sublime adaptation to socio-cultural norms and
standards. Sublimation makes unacceptable incestuous
urges into acceptable identifications with parents,
It turns aggressive energy into cognitive development
and rational behavior. In sublimation the two types
of integration are integrated best. The process of
sublimation is like a petroleum refinery which trans-
forms dirty crude oil into clean gasoline and jet
fuel.

Maturity is culturally conditioned and interpreted differently. But there are common themes inherent in the concept of maturity. We shall analyze
them in the next part.

NOTES

1. David Belgum, Religion and Personality in the
   Spiral of Life (Washington, D.C.: University
   Press of America, 1979), p. 3.

2. L. Joseph Stone and Joseph Church, Childhood and
   Adolescence (New York: Random House, 1967), pp.
   271-275.

3. Lewis J. Sherrill, The Struggle of the Soul (New
   York: The Macmillan Co., 1961), p. 48.

4. Theodore Lidz, The Person: Stages of Life Cycle
   (New York: Basic Books, 1976), p. 320.

5. Sherrill, The Strugle of the Soul, pp. 49-52.

6. Merton Strommen, Profiles of Church Youth (St.
   Louis: Concordia Publishing House, 1963).

7. Joseph Adelson, "The Mystique of Adoslecence,"
   Psychiatry, 27 (1964), pp. 1-5.

8. Charles W. Stewart, Adolescent Religion: A
   Developmental Study of the Religion of Youth
   (Nashville, Tenn.: Abingdon Press, 1967), pp.
   292-298.

9. B. Inhelder and J. Piaget, The Growth of Logical
    Thinking from Childhood to Adolescence (New York:
    Basic Books, 1958), pp. viii, 347.

10. Ronald Goldman, Religious Thinking from Child-
    hood to Adolescence (New York: Seabury Press,
    1964); Goldman, Readiness for Religion: A Basis
    for Developmental Religious Education (New York:
    Seabury Press, 1965).

11. Dean R. Hodge and Gregory H. Petrillo, "Develop-
    ment of Religious Thinking in Adolescence: A
    Test of Goldman's Theories," Journal of the
    Scientific Study of Religion, 17 (1978), pp.
    139-154.

12. "Let's Hope He Finds Faith," Boston Sunday Globe,
    July 27, 1980 , p. A2,

13. James W. Fowler, "Faith and the Structuring of
    Meaning," in Toward Moral and Religious Maturity,
    First International Conference on Moral and Re-
    ligious Development, Abbey of Senanque, France,
    1979 (Morristown, N.J.: Silver Burdett Co, 1980),
    pp. 71-72.

14. Pierre Babin, Faith and the Adolescent (New York:
    Herder and Herder, 1965), p. 36.

15. Goldman, Religious Thinking from Childhood to
    Adolescence, p. 277.

16. Stewart, Adolescent Religion, pp. 80-81.

17. Andre Godin, "Parental Images and Divine Pater-
    nity," In From Experience to a Religious Atti-
    tude (Chicago: Loyola University Press, 1965).

18. Gordon W. Allport, Religion in the Developing
    Personality (New York: University Press, 1960),
    p.33.

19. Wm. James, The Varieties of Religious Experience
    (New York: Longmans, Green and Co., 1928), pp.
    189-258.

20. "To Be Born Again," _Boston Sunday Globe_, August 17, 1980, p. C 14.

21. Edwin D. Starbuck, _The Psychology of Religion_ (New York: Charles Scribner's Sons, 1899).

22. "To Be Born Again," _Boston Sunday Globe_, p. C 1.

23. Roger Gould, "Adult Life Stages: Growth Toward Self Tolerance," _Psychology Today_, 12 (2) (1975), pp. 74-78.

24. Erik H. Erikson, _Childhood and Society_ (New York: W. W. Norton & Co., 1950), p. 265.

25. George W. Goethals and D. S. Klos, _Experiencing Youth: First Person Account_ (Boston: Little, Brown and Co., 1971), p. 16.

26. Daniel J. Levinson, "Growing up with the Dream," _Psychology Today_, 15 (1) (1978), pp. 20-31, 89.

27. Genevieve Caufield, _The Kingdom Within_ (New York: Harper & Row, 1960).

28. Based on personal interview on August 21, 1979.

29. Norman Cameron, _Personality Development and Psychopathology_ (Boston: Houghton Mifflin Co., 1964), p. 110.

30. "To Be Born Again," _Boston Sunday Globe_, p. C 14.

31. Bernard Boelen, _Personal Maturity_ (New York: Seabury Press, 1978), pp. 13-14.

32. Robert C. Peck, "Psychological Development in the Second Half of Life," in _Middle Age and Aging_, ed. by B. L. Neugarten (Chicago: University of Chicago Press, 1968), pp. 88-92.

33. Sherrill, _The Struggle of the Soul_, pp. 100-128.

34. Eda J. LeShan, _The Wonderful Crisis of Middle Age_ (New York: David McKay Co., Inc., 1973), pp. 326-329.

35. Erikson, Childhood and Society, pp. 266-268. Cp.
    Raymond C. Kuhlen and George G. Thompson, ed.,
    Psychological Studies of Human Development (New
    York: Appleton-Century-Crofts, 1963), pp. 161-
    171.

36. Wayne Dennis, "Creative Productivity between
    Ages of 20 and 80 Years," Journal of Gerontology,
    21 (1966), pp. 1-8;R.G. Kuhlen and G. H. Johnson,
    "Changes in Goals with Increasing Adult Ages,"
    Journal of Consulting Psychology, 16 (1952), pp.
    1-4; David C. McClelland, The Achievement Motive
    (New York: Appleton-Century-Crofts, 1953), p.
    119.

37. B. L. Neugarten, ed., Middle Age and Aging, pp.
    195-200. See also, B. Fried, The Middle-Age
    Crisis (New York: Harper & Row, 1967), p. 136.
    Cp. Nancy Mayer, The Male Mid-Life Crisis (New
    York: New American Library, 1978), pp. 85-252.

38. "The four polarities whose resolution is the
    principal task of mid-life individuation are:
    (1) Young/Old; (2) Destruction/Creation; (3)
    Masculine/Feminine; and (4) Attachment/Separate-
    ness." Daniel J. Levinson, et al. The Season of
    a Man's Life (New York: Alfred A. Knopf, Inc.,
    1978), pp. 207-221. It seems to me that these
    are four themes based on two dichotomous polari-
    ties.

39. Irwin Deutscher, "The Quality of Postparental
    Life: Definitions of the Situation," Journal of
    Marriage and Family, 26 (1) (1964), pp. 52-59.

40. Ernest W. Burgess and Paul Wallin, Engagement
    and Marriage (Philadelphia: J. B. Lippincott Co.,
    1953).

41. Lidz, The Person, p. 498.

42. Sherrill, The Struggle of the Soul, pp. 100-128.
    Also, John C. Cooper, Religion After Forty (Phil-
    adelphia: Pilgrim Press, 1972).

43. Ibid.

44. Carl G. Jung, <u>Modern Man in Search of a Soul</u>
(New York: Harcourt, Brace and World, 1935),
pp. 225-299.

45. Gay Wilson Allen, <u>William James: A Biography</u>
(New York: Simon and Schuster, 1969), pp. 456-
457.

46. M. A. Wallach and Nathan Kogan, "Aspects of
Judgment and Decision Making: Interrelationships and Changes with Age," <u>Behavioral Science</u>,
6 (1961), pp. 23-36. See also, Douglas C. Kimmel, <u>Adulthood and Aging</u> (New York: John Wiley
and Sons, 1973), p. 382.

47. Hannah Josephson, <u>Jeannette Rankin: First Lady
in Congress</u> (Indianapolis: Bobbs-Merrill Co.,
Inc., 1974), p. 210.

48. Erikson, <u>Childhood and Society</u>, pp. 268-269. Cp.
Vivian Clayton, "Erikson's Theory of Human Development As It Applies to the Aged: Wisdom As
Contradictive Cognition," <u>Human Development</u>,
18 (1975), pp. 119-128.

49. M. F. Lowenthal, "Social Isolation and Mental
Illness in Old Age," <u>American Sociological Re-
view</u>, 29 (1964), pp. 54-70; Lowenthal, "Interaction
and Adaptation: Intimacy as a Critical Variable,"
<u>American Sociological Review,</u> 33 (1968), pp. 20-30.

50. B. L. Neugarten and K. K. Weinstein, "The Changing American Grandparents," <u>Journal of Marriage
and the Family</u>, 26 (1964), pp. 199-204; Robert J.
Havighurst and Augusta de Varies, "Life Styles
and Free Time Activities of Retired Men," <u>Human
Development</u>, 12 (1969), pp. 34-54.

51. Williard Uphause, <u>Commitment</u> (New York: McGraw-
Hill Book Co., 1969).

52. M. Michaels, "Billy Graham: America Is Not God's
Only Kingdom," <u>Parade</u>, February 11, 1981, p. 6.

53. D. L. Scudder, ed., <u>Organized Religion and the
Older Person</u> (Gainsville, Fa.: Florida State

University Press, 1958). Cp. Howard Kauffman,
"Social Correlations of Spiritual Maturity among
North American Mennonites," Sociological Analysis,
40 (1979), pp. 27-42.

54. Carl A. L. Binger, "Emotional Maturity," in The
Encyclopedia of Mental Health, eds., Albert
Deutsch and Helen Fishman, Vol. 2 (New York:
Franklin Watts, Inc., 1963), p. 533.

55. Quoted by Paul Tournier, Learn to Grow Old (New
York: Harper & Row, 1971), p. 192.

56. Ibid. pp. 45-46.

57. Paul Tillich, Perspectives on 19th and 20th Century Protestant Theology, ed., Carl E. Braaten
(New York: Harper & Row, 1967), p. 238.

58. Charles Kao, "American and Oriental Identity
and Its Relations to Maturity," unpublished paper,
1974.

59. D. Katz and K. Brady, "Racial Stereotypes of
100 College Students," Journal of Abnormal and
Social Psychology, 28 (1933), pp. 280-290; G.
M. Gilbert, "Stereotype Persistence and Change
among College Students," Journal of Abnormal
and Social Psychology, 46 (1956), pp. 245-254.

PART THREE: MATURITY

CHAPTER

V

AUTONOMY AND INDEPENDENCE

Autonomy and independence are important, similar qualities which most of us want. They are also
the center of many political controversies and struggles. On the international scene, small and underdeveloped nations are often dominated by large and
strong nations. They fight for independence in order
to become sovereign states. Domination and inter-
ference by the super powers are not warmly welcomed,
if not rejected outright. Invasion by the neighbor-
ing countries triggers immediate action. As human
history shows, independence is one of the most powerful motivators of political revolution. No one really
wants slavery. Deep inside, everyone wants to be
free from control, politically or otherwise. We want
the right of self-determination and self-government.

In this chapter, we are primarily concerned
with autonomy and independence as signs of maturity
in human growth, their relation to automation in our
technological age, and their implications for religious experiences.

1. Autonomy and Maturity

What do we mean by "autonomy"? What do we
mean by "independence"? Are they the same? Are
they signs of maturity? What do we mean by "maturity"
and how are they related to it?

"Autonomy" and "independence" seem quite self-
explanatory, but they are often misunderstood. The
most common misunderstanding is the tenet that we
can do whatever we want, if we are autonomous and
independent, or that we can isolate ourselves, if
we grow up to be mature adults. Social problems

reflect this misunderstanding. One of them is the
topic of abortion. Does a pregnant woman have the
right to decide for the new life inside her to live
or to die without moral responsibility or impact on
others in the family and society? Should a teenage
girl be able to have an abortion without the approval
of her legal guardian? If so, would it mean true
autonomy and independence for her? Similar questions
are: Can a landlord do whatever he or she wants with
property? Can a talented man commit suicide as he
pleases? Can a terminally ill patient decide when
to die? These legal questions are not answered simply, because they are far from simple. "Autonomy"
and "independence" do not mean that we can do whatever we want. It would be immature to do whatever
we want, because self-indulgence is a sign of nar-
cissism, the opposite of maturity. A small child
wants to do whatever he or she wants, no matter
whether it is good or bad, harmful or pleasant. The
basic motivation is impulsive desire.

    "Autonomy" and "independence" are similar, but
not the same. "Independence" has strong political
overtones, and is affectively oriented; "independence"
signifies political autonomy, self-government, freedom from the influence, guidance, or control of
others and non-affiliation. But "autonomy" means
"self-principled" as its Greek form shows: "auto"
(self) and "nomos" (law). Therefore, "autonomy" is
cognitively oriented. Consequently, it is more a
philosophical term than a psychological term.

    "Independence" implies psychological weaning
from parents, characterized by adolescence. In
early childhood, we are very dependent on our parents.
In adolescence, we rebel in order to become independent. Cognitively, we have reached the formal operational stage, but we may not be fully principled in
our behavior. We begin to rapidly develop our principles with newly acquired reasoning abilities. Autonomy reflects integration which is central to perceptual and cognitive development, whereas independence is differentiation from the family.

    Because adolescent independence has rebellious
ingredients and flavor, it is in some ways "other-

directed" and reactive. Truly autonomous behavior
is inner-directed, and is done because it is good
and right. Adolescent rebellion is stimulated by
parental authority, which represents society. The
more authoritarian parents are, the stronger rebellion is likely to be. Parents become the testing
ground where the adolescent prepares to enter the
world, not as a rebellious radical, but as a mature
adult who accepts authority and finds a place in it.
Maturity brings an awareness of one's need for others
and an acknowledgement of mutuality, give-and-take,
communion, and dialogue in interpersonal relationships. The swing of the pendulum from infantile dependence to adolescent independence is part of the
struggle for identity, but adolescent independence
is not mature independence.[1] Mature independence
is, paradoxically, interdependence.

In politics, one cannot help but sense the
significance Mao Tse-tung's rebellion against his
father, and his identification with his mother and
the peasants in his early childhood had for his political leadership and the success of the communist
revolution in China.[2] His iron-willed adolescent
independence met the revolutionary needs of his people. But, as history shows, the political situation
has changed. Recent improvements in the Sino-American
relationship indicate a swing of the pendulum from
adolescent independence to mature independence. This
indicates how politically significant and powerful
the mentality of independence can become.

Although adolescent independence is not as mature as adulthood interdependence, it has a considerable degree of maturity in itself. Independence
possesses the basic mental structure for autonomy,
if not the full content. Affectively, adolescent
independence is a frame of mind for self-determination,
even if the mind has not formulated its principles
fully enough to make decisions and take actions.
Furthermore, independence possesses another important ingredient of maturity, "competence."[3] Incom-
petence leads to dependence. The mature person is
competent, and therefore, independent and self-reliant,
but neither isolated nor rebellious.

173

Psychologists are not quite unified in their definitions of maturity. Attempting to construct a commonly accepted version of anything in a highly individualistic and pluralistic society is often hopeless. Each attempt to define maturity will invariably carry a particular orientation which reflects an author's age, sex, cultural background and other aspects of life experiences.

In a recent novel The Women's Room, author Marilyn French describes changes in women's life styles during the past three decades. She describes her protagonist's emotional states: "Part of her knew that she was simply surviving in the only way she could. Dull day by dull day she paced through her responsibilities, moving toward some goals she could not discern. The word freedom had dropped from her vocabulary; the word maturity replaced it. And dimly[4] she sensed that maturity was knowing how to survive." For some people maturity is knowing how to survive. To survive, one must have a certain degree of competence in problem-solving.

"The fully functioning person" is described by Carl R. Rogers as the goal of psychotherapy.[5] The therapeutic process is characterized by "an increasing openness to experience," "increasingly existential living," and by "an increasing trust in his organism." This is his view of good life, which implies maturity. To be mature is to be open to new experiences, new ideas, and new challenges. To grow up is to increase decision-making abilities as well as to take responsibilty. Maturity as "knowing how to survive" may be a cynical way of expressing the fact that the search for autonomy and independence is constitutional. It is cynical because somehow the purposiveness of the organism becomes aborted and its forwardness of direction thwarted. Preservation of life is instinctive, but maturity is more than just instinct. Mere survival is not what autonomy and independence mean; to be autonomous, one must survive, but this is not enough. Survival merely prolongs life. We must proact, not just react. We must develop basic principles, moral and religious values, and goals in order to become autonomous. A person who proacts is motivated internally, whereas a person who reacts is

174

motivated externally. One is inner-directed, whereas the other other-directed.

Tom Wicker's concluding remarks in his book
about his personal experiences with the six past U.
S. Presidents and their dealing with the press illustrates this vocationally.[6] Retrospectively he commented, "Not so incidentally, it seems to me, the
most respected reporters, and usually the best professionally, are those who most strongly assert their
own independence and are willing to rely heavily on
their own qualities of intellect and experience."
This is also true in other professions.

Apparently, independence was one of Albert
Einstein's characteristics.[7] "He was, as he often
said, the kind of man who did not work well in team.
Furthermore, his mental stature was such that he
needed little stimulation from other workers in his
field." This was not due to his dislike of other people, but to his unique mind. In writing to his parents in October 28, 1910, a visitor said, "the more
I speak with Einstein and this happens often, the
more convinced do I become that I was right in my
opinion of him. Among contemporary physicists he
is not only the clearest but the one who has the most
independent of brains, and it is true that the majority of physicists don't even understand his approach." His independence was related to his creativity and professional maturation.

Mentors are very important to aspiring new
comers, but there are times when each mature professional must leave the mentor and stand on his or her
own feet, making independent contributions. Professional maturation may bring about strains or conflicts
between mentor and protege, but not always. One does
not always have to experience bloodshed in the course
of achieving professional autonomy and independence.
Smooth weaning may result in enjoyable friendships
characterized by mutuality and equality. Smooth weaning depends on the mentor's willingness to let go and
the protege's willingness to pay respect continually.
According to the Grant Study at Harvard, mentors are
less important after the age of forty, as pointed out
by Dr. George E. Vaillant. [8] Mentors often are like

parental figures, but they are different from parents.
Those who have successfully weaned themselves from
their parents in adolescence are likely to experience
smooth weaning from their mentors.

A study on vocational maturity was made of 207
vocational rehabilitation clients and 59 graduate
students, rating the importance of 21 reinforcers
and 11 values.[9] Those who were high in vocational
maturity considered the following important: 1) a
feeling of accomplishment, 2) work that is not felt
to be morally wrong, 3) steady employment, 4) independence, 5) opportunities for using special talents,
6) challenge, and 7) self-satisfaction. On the other
hand, those who were vocationally immature considered
different items important: 1) telling other workers
what to do, 2) position in the community, and 3) prestige. Autonomy and independence are important in
this study. Competence and principles are high priorities among the vocationally mature.

A person's vocational maturity depends largely
on his or her emotional maturity because the two are
interrelated. Autonomy and independence are expressed
in both, but there are other elements in emotional
maturity which are summarized by Boris Blai in simple
terms: 1) setting priorities, 2) going easy with
criticism, 3) maintaining perspective, 4) being sensible, 5) talking it out, 6) controlling anger, 7)
responding to others, 8) taking charge, 9) being
generous, 10) temporarily escaping, 11) occasionally
giving in.[10] Emotional maturity is the basis for
inner security and is related to the degree to which
an individual is encouraged to exercise choices.

We can see significant levels of integration
and transcendence manifested in the component characteristics of emotional maturity. "Setting priorities" implies both integration in forming a hierarchical structure of values and principles into a whole
as well as differentiating one from the other and
making one transcend the other. "Going easy with
criticism" focuses on harmonious integration with
the external world and self-transcendence. "Maintaining perspectives" and "controlling anger" again
emphasize transcendence--the former cognitively, the

176

latter affectively. "Being sensible," "talking it out," "responding to others," "being generous," and "occasional giving in" are related to external integration with others. "Taking charge" and "temporarily escaping" have significant levels of differentiation, but they are accompanied by a certain degree of integration internally and externally. None is exclusively oriented to the principle of differentiation.

In discussing the basic styles of adaptation based on the Grant Study at Harvard, Vaillant composed a hierarchy of adaptive ego mechanisms and divided it into four levels:[11]

Level I--Psychotic Mechanisms (denial of external reality, distortion, and delusional projection).

Level II--Immature mechanisms (fantasy, projection, hypochondriasis, and passive-aggressive behavior, or acting out).

Level III--Neurotic mechanisms (intellectualization, repression, reaction formation, displacement, and dissociation).

Level IV--Mature mechanisms (sublimation, altruism, suppression, anticipation, humor).

Interestingly, none of the four mechanisms classified as "mature" is oriented to differentiation in the egoistical sense. They are oriented mainly to integration and transcendence. "Sublimation" is both integration and transcendence based on a hierarchical moral value system for the process; suppression is focused on internal integration and inner-directed self-transcendence; anticipation is perceptually oriented to external integration with reality; and humor is an expression of self-objectification and transcendence. Mature autonomy and independence are not egoistically differentiated, but internally and externally integrated and transcended manifestations of human personality. Understandably, all of the three mechanisms classified as "psychotic" are oriented to egoistical differentiation; no integration with external reality, no self-transcendence.

177

2. Autonomy and Human Development

In his discussion of biomodal consciousness,
Dr. Arthur Deikman points out two types of consciousness: 1) "action mode," and 2) "receptive mode."[12]
In human development, it seems that the receptive
mode originates and functions maximally in infancy,
and is gradually dominated by the action mode as
one grows. What characterizes the receptive mode of
consciousness is its organization around intake rather
than manipulation of the environment; its dominant
agency is the sensory-perceptual system rather than
the muscle system; its prominent functions tend to
be parasympathetic rather than sympathetic; its
attention is diffused rather than focused; its thought
process is paralogical rather than logical; its baseline of muscle tension is decreased with its electroencephanograph moving toward the alpha waves.

As the human organism interacts with the environment, the action mode of consciousness develops.
The human mind is increasingly organized to manipulate the environment by the increasing function of
its sympathetic nervous system and the striate muscle
system; its attention becomes increasingly focused;
its perceptual boundary heightened; its thinking
object-based and logical; and above all, it becomes
increasingly goal-oriented and strives to achieve
personal goals, social rewards, sensual pleasure, or
avoidance of pain. The more one becomes action-moded,
the sharper one's perception becomes.

Perceptual maturity depends greatly on perceptual sharpness: the sharper it is, the better its
manipulation of the environment. This sharpness was
expressed by a senior member of the National Security
Council in a comment on the CIA operation: "The agency
is best when there's something very specific that
you want to know, preferably a question that can be
answered with numbers, or, if not with numbers, then
at least with nouns. The fewer adverbs and adjectives the better it tends to be."[13] Specificity is
a sign of perceptual development. Sharp perceptual
boundaries are matched by the sharp conceptual boundaries which we need to succeed in the world.

178

In the course of human development, the action mode improves biological survival. The baseline of muscle tension in the action mode increases with its electroencephanograph showing beta waves. The progressive development of striving brings about the notion that the action mode is proper for adult life. In fact, the receptive mode also develops, and is also necessary, but it is overshadowed by the action mode.

Autonomy has a psycho-physiological dimension. Erikson regards the second stage of human development as one which is centered on "autonomy vs. shame and doubt."[14] At this stage, a child's muscular maturation enables him or her experiment holding on and letting go in toilet training. It is a time when a child experiences a budding sense of autonomy and control. Children in this period are encouraged by their parents to stand on their own feet. If not well-guided, this may lead to the formation of precocious conscience, obsessive repetition, or stubborn and minute control in dealing with the self and the environment. Shame is essentially rage against the self, a negative self-destructive and inwardly-directed sense of autonomy.

The toddler's upright posture is an important sign of autonomy, and is rooted in the action mode of consciousness. The infant's reclining posture indicates dependency, rooted in the receptive mode. However, even in receptive infancy, there are signs that the child is in a state of "alert inactivity"; the infant begins to assimilate what is in the outside world. This state of "alert inactivity" occurs most frequently when the child is relatively free from tensions such as hunger. At such times, the child's eyes are open and there seems little motor activity other than eye movement, which may indicate the beginning of cognitive development. It is clear that the infant is already interested in stimuli that can serve as nourishment for cognitive development. Thus we may say that the receptive mode is the mother of the action mode, if not the twin.

By receiving sensori-motor stimuli and emotional nourishment from parents and other significant individuals, the child accumulates raw materials for cognitive development, and moves away from pure reflexes to the pursuit of ends-in-view, exploring the objects, and feeling the ways for adaptation to and mastery of the world. The child, then, becomes capable of inventing new ways of problem-solving through combinations of available resources. This inner-directed discovery of new problem-solving is an initial sign of automous act; it requires the use of symbols through internalization and insight. Autonomy is essential to creativity.

Basic trust is important to autonomy, because without trust healthy identifications are impossible: Consequently, are also internalizations. Thus basic trust is the cradle of autonomy. Furthermore, we can trace basic trust to feelings of pleasure and well-being experienced in the mother's warm love, during eating, sleeping or after bowel movements. The feeling of well-being is nurtured to constitute one's volition, the will to act and to make free choices, a sense of autonomy and pride, which may eventually be formed as a political claim for human dignity and basic human rights. The cornerstone of autonomy is a firm sense of inner goodness and trust in oneself and the world. It is through faith from within and the corresponding affirmation from without that autonomy is nurtured.

Autonomy is often misunderstood as achieving total independence from others through absolute negation of receptivity. In fact, the action mode cannot be cut off from the receptive mode. Without identification and internalization of others, there can be no autonomous selfhood. Empty ego-striving is a sickness and not autonomy, isolation and not independence. Worst of all, it is mere impulsive self-will, which manifests deep inner anxiety.

In my personal interviews, parents were often remembered for their trust in giving their children freedom to choose whether to go to church or not. The adolescent needs freedom and not isolation from parents. In the process of becoming autonomous and independent, the adolescent must not cut off from parents. Adolescents need, not self-destructive de-

180

fiance, but changing the nature of their relationships with their parents; building a new type of relationship, rather than destroying the relationship altogether. Adolescents do not need to fight their parents, but to grow toward "adulthood maturity." They do not need to bring their parents down to an adolescent level of thinking and acting, but to improve themselves and reach the adult level. The principle of differentiation itself is not enough, it must be accompanied by the principles of integration and transcendence. This applies to any form of struggle for autonomy and independence. Autonomy is not egocentric, nor is independence narcissistic. Differentiation by itself makes us isolated and rebellious. Integration must be present, either in tension or harmony.

Autonomy implies moral development, theories of which have been given by psychologists. The best known of these is Harvard psychologist Lawrence Kohlberg's "Six Moral Stages."[15] But, fundamentally, there seem to be only three levels: 1) "Preconventional," 2) "Conventional," and 3) "Post-Conventional" or "Principled." Autonomous morality is principled; it is rooted in internal authority and self-authenticated laws and principles. Conventional morality is social conformity; it is anchored in external authority and subject to externally imposed laws and principles. On the other hand, preconventional morality is anomous and egocentric, individualistic and instrumental. The three levels of moral development may be considered three ways of life, or three philosophical positions, if one does not take into consideration the principle of transcendence in formulating a hierarchical system of moral values. When we discuss maturity, the principle of transcendence is indispensible, and the level of autonomy is the most mature and the highest in a hierarchy of moral value system.

Autonomy is an important part of Kant's moral philosophy.[16] Autonomy implies that a person as a moral agent is both subject to and author of law. Authoring law does not mean creating law according to personal interest and desire: It signifies a genuine moral imperative and "obedience to a law that is universally binding on all rational beings." The autonomous person is self-authenticatedly principled, but self-authenticated principles are universal and objective. Thus, autonomous self-legislation integrates the subjective and the objective.

One cannot become autonomous by self-assertion alone. As observed by Piaget, peer groups cradle autonomous morality. It is through interactions with peers that the child becomes less egocentric and able to understand and sympathize with others. Through identification, the child becomes aware that other people have their own points of view. This awareness of others indicates development of perceptual abilities and clearer self-other boundaries. It results from both differentiation and integration--cognitively differentiated from others but affectively integrated with them. The sharper the boundary, the greater the differentiation from the environment; the stronger the self is differentiated from its environment, the more autonomous it becomes. But for a person to be differentiated, he or she must be integrated and identified with others. In nurturing autonomy, it is important to interact with the environment. Without interaction, nothing will be internalized for the formation of principles or ideas. This is why the mutuality and equality of peers is so important for nurturing autonomy, because autonomy is born out of heteronomy. An example of this was reported by a journalist. On Tuesday, January 10, 1978, shortly before noon , a teenage girl went to a church and took a .38-caliber pistol, pressed it against the center of her forehead, and pulled the trigger. She died instantly. Many of the mourners at her funeral were children, her classmates. None, however, had been close to her. She was a child without friends. In deep despair, she had withdrawn into a fantasy world, leaving a pathetic message, "I don't want to live."[17] She was a "high average student" but a friendless girl. Many of the children were sad and could not understand the death of this unknown classmate. It took her death to break the barriers which had kept her apart from others. They were deeply touched, but too late. Isolation is not independence, nor is it a sign of autonomy. It is a tragic state. Running away from home is not an act of independence;

it is the first step on the road toward death.

The nurture of autonomy depends greatly on the parents' behavior toward the child. Affectively, parents-child interaction cultivates basic trust through loving care; cognitively, it develops symbols and language. By mastering language, one symbolically increases manipulative powers over the environment. Language is the symbolic means by which one plans strategies for interacting with the world; it is the instrument by which one accumulates knowledge, facilitating effective interaction with life. Significantly, public education is restoring the three basic disciplines: reading, writing, and arithmetic, which are cognitively oriented. As early as 1934, Vygotsky pointed out that the dialogue of speech and gesture between parents and children was indispensible to the development of the thought process.[18] In this dialogue, the child is both a subject and an object. A child's right to be independent is respected by parents, and this respect is the seed for autonomy and independence.

Volitionally, the parents' challenge to children to stand on their own is significant to the nurturing of autonomy. It is often remembered and appreciated later in life. A counselor recalled the excitement of crossing a street by herself. Later she was challenged to make up her mind in her choice of food, clothes, toys, and going to Sunday School. Each challenge was a significant preparation for autonomous life and responsible living. A similar challenge can be seen in the biography of Nelson Rockefeller.[19] The Rockefeller children were challenged to accept duties such as tending luggage, polishing boots, or buying tickets while they were on a journey. At home, they were challenged to keep accounts on how they spent money. Each was expected to choose which college to enter and what career to pursue.

The parents' challenge must positively encourage, rather than negatively prohibit. Training in decision-making begins with the simple items related to actual living. A sense of competence enhances a child's autonomy and self-mastery. With confidence, they often welcome hard, and positive choices rather than

try to escape them.[20] This is a sign of inner strength.
It is an essential ingredient in autonomy. The child
may gain confidence instead of frustration. The parents' challenge becomes a source of strength, rather
than defeat. The following considerations are important to the development of a child's self-confidence:[21]

1) Parents should guard against overprotection,
which may deprive children of the most satisfying
experience in childhood. Protection is important,
but overprotection is harmful.

2) Parents should let children experience success and the joy of discovery. Inner satisfaction
enhances their sense of autonomy and independence.
Each child should not be neglected; he or she should
be questioned and praised. Each should strive for
success, and success must be arranged that each can
get it.

3) Parents should evaluate each child in the
light of his or her own ability. Harmful comparisons
may make a child feel complacent or inferior.

4) Parents should take their children's fears
seriously. Fear may make a child speak out bois-
terously or act aggressively. Talking about fear
or avoiding fear-producing objects can help the child
overcome fear.

5) Parents should administer their powers carefully. Learning by trial-and-error is superior to
learning by rote, and learning by insight is superior
to learning by trial-and-error.

Moral development implies autonomy, and we can
differentiate the heteronomous child from the autonomous child by the way he or she appreciates humor.
A recent study on moral development and children's
appreciation of humor by developmental psychologist
Paul E. McGhee shows that the heteronomous child is
able to respond freely to humor regardless of its
moral unacceptability, but the autonomous child's
sense of humor becomes diminished if the event is
perceived as the result of morally unacceptable behavior.[22] The autonomous child is inner-directed

184

and possesses a sense of moral value and principles. The process of internalization has taken roots in him or her.

There are socio-cultural factors to the development and nurturance of autonomy and independence. About two decades ago, developmental psychologist Leonore Boehm compared the development of independence in two cultures by interviewing 181 American children and 80 European children ranging in age from kindergarten to high school.[23] In thought and action, the American children became independent of their parents at earlier age than did the European children. American mothers unwittingly shifted some of their children's dependency to peers as early as the preschool age. They were eager to bring up their children to become independent. In our rapidly changing society, parents may no longer be sure of their own moral values and standards, and may suffer from a lack of self-confidence and direction. Parents believe that peers know better what moral standards are important and what ideals and goals a youngster must have. Naturally, children lose confidence in their parents and become critical of them. There is no easy way or short cut in the development of independence and autonomy.

Developmentally, heteronomy precedes autonomy. Without going through a stage of heteronomy, a person cannot reach autonomy; without learning and internalizing moral values and standards from parents, teachers, heroes, and other significant individuals, a person cannot build a mental warehouse. An autonomous person shares common points with others. Autonomy should not be misunderstood as egocentrism, because autonomy implies an objectivity in which inner laws and principles are constituted, from which consistent references are made, from which everyone can find a common perspective, and without which there can be no social order.[24] The true meaning of freedom can only be found in autonomy which is based on a common law. In order to become strongly autonomous, a person has to undergo rigorous heteronomous discipline and training, which may appear contradictory. Life begins with the receptive mode, and in terms of modern cybernetics, we begin with input.

Often modern education emphasizes freedom so much that it neglects proper discipline. Increasingly, people want their children to receive a traditional education, which is characterized by heteronomous discipline. Through teacher's discipline, children become aware of responsibility. But external authority is not enough; there must be internal authority. A mature person is not at the mercy of external contingencies. The control is mutual. As pointed out by Francis Bacon, nature must be obeyed as well as controlled. Herein lies true autonomy.

At the heteronomous stage, "if you changed the environments of thirty little Hottentots and thirty aristocratic English children, the aristocrats would become Hottentots, for all practical purposes, and the Hottentots little conservatives," quotes B. F. Skinner.[25] But at the autonomous stage, this is not true. The environment which shapes human character is also under human control.

Anomy is centered on external differentiation; each child is egocentric and impulsive. But heteronomy is focused on internal differentiation and external integration; each child is taught to behave well and become socialized. Autonomy focuses on internal integration and transcendence of egocentrism manifested in the birth of self-authenticated and yet objectively valid principles. True autonomy is auto-heteronomous; and true transcendence is an integration of the subjective and the objective. Without transcendence, there is little communication; and true autonomy comes when one is mature.

3. Autonomy and Automation

We live in an age of increasing automation. We often hear how automation threatens human autonomy. Perhaps the time will come when all living beings are slaves. The future is hard to predict. Does automation really threaten our autonomy as human beings? Is there any way by which individual freedom and autonomy can be preserved? Is there any means by which we save ourselves from becoming robot-

controlled or computer-controlled slaves? Could
such a pessimistic prediction come true?

Automation has speeded up our conquest of nature. But are we more autonomous and independent
than our ancestors a century ago? Our democratic
system requires the decision-making of well-rounded
citizens, their active participation, and informed
consent. Does automation help us become more democratic? Automation certainly increases our leisure
time. But unlimited leisure is disguised curse.
Wouldn't automation lead us to hell rather than to
heaven? Questions about automation are many, and
they are beyond our scope. Our main concern is to
see its impacts on autonomy and human maturity.

Modern science and technology have made the
West dominant in the world. They have freed us from
a preoccupation with mere physical survival, improved
living conditions, and created labor-saving devices.
The West has dominated the world with its scientific
and technological know-hows, which have enabled us
to explore farthest and deepest in the physical world,
and opened up a whole range of possibilities for
speedier communication, calculation, management, and
self-destruction. Indeed, we are physically independent from nature and freer from geographical limitations; modern science and technology have eliminated
our physical limitations and enabled us to fly like
birds and swim like fish; we are free to do almost
anything we want to in this world. This seems to
indicate that we have become more autonomous and independent than, say, people in the middle ages. But
are we?

Increasingly, modern science and technology
eliminates physical labor and manual work. Automation has relieved pain and sweat of our bodies; man-
made machines have taken the place of our hands, feet,
and even our heads. Strong utopianism and dynamism
in modern technology carries us through to a "good
life"; life is enhanced in undreamed of ways, and
we are made "wiser," "happier," and "healthier."
What was impossible yesterday is possible today and
will become inevitable tomorrow, as modern science
and technology advance. But are we more mature?

In this world, every pleasure has its counter-
part in pain, and every valuable thing has its price.
Automation has brought us pleasure, but it has also
created problems. Automation may increase leisure,
but it displaces workers. For the unemployed, work
was not only a way to earn a living, but also a means
of sustaining self-respect, identity, and human decency. Psychically, they are crippled and wounded.
Displacement by machines has been with us since the
invention of the automatic knitting machine by the
Rev. William Lee in 1589. Two workers now do the
job of two hundred, making radio sets: Ten people
do the work for four hundred, producing auto motor
blocks. This was made possible by automation.[26] Do
unemployed workers feel autonomous and independent,
even with unemployment compensation?

In spite of optimistic predictions, automation
has displaced many people and forced them out of work
to live through anxiety and financial loss. They
live in a state of uncertainty and loss of self-
respect; they have fewer alternatives to choose from,
and less freedom to make decisions. Some technolo-
gists say that automation provides more jobs than it
eliminates. But this was one of the five fallacies
John I. Snyder, President of U. S. Industries, re-
portedly acknowledged.[27] The rate of displaced workers was from twenty to forty thousand per week according to one of reports by Walter Davis of the AFL-CIO.[28]
It is often assumed that displaced workers can be
rapidly retrained, but many of them are simply not
retrainable. It is not true that anyone who wants
to work can find a work. Machines can do more jobs
more efficiently than human beings. We may someday
see a workless society in which the work ethic is
irrelevant. If human dignity depends on work, then
human dignity will be lost. If autonomy and independence depend on inner dignity, then there will be
no autonomy and independence in the future.

Another price we pay for automation is dehumanization. We are deprived of human qualities unknow-
ingly and massively. Our chances of making decision
are subtly taken away. We find this dehumanization
in the way customers are treated; they are tamed by
rope barricades like domestic animals, in banks, post

188

offices, or bus terminals.

Furthermore, as automation is widely applied,
emphasis on personalized service decreases, according to the prediction of a peace researcher in Washington, D.C.[29] This prediction has already come
true. A woman went to the hospital to see a doctor,
but instead was asked to tell a computer about her
problems. The computer gave her a prescription. She
complained that seeing a physician would have taken
a few minutes, whereas replying to the CRT took her
almost half an hour. This was just an experiment,
but the day may not be far away when computers replace doctors. What she missed most was the personal
and quick response one can get from a physician. In
dealing with machines, we are becoming dehumanized;
and in dealing with us, machines are becoming human-
ized.

Automation is believed to be useful especially
in dealing with massive social planning, such as
traffic control, financial transactions, political
voting research, mass demands of consumers, etc.
Consequently social planners are likely to ignore
individuals. Somewhere down the line, individuality
may disappear, leaving groups of manipulators or a
single commander-in-chief who pushes key buttons.
Under these circumstances, the majority of people
may not have autonomy and independence. Many managers of large institutions now respect the individuality of their employees although the influence of
each individual is too insignificant to deserve attention. The individuality is too precious to be sacrificed at the altar of institutions.

Are we going to blame technology for all the
problems we have today? Are we going to destroy
technology to solve our problems, like the Luddites
who, between 1811 and 1816, rioted and destroyed
textile machinery? It took two hundred thousand
years for human beings to move out of the Stone Age;
metal tools appeared only about ten thousand years
ago; and the Industrial Revolution is only about two
centuries old. Now there is a new technological revolution. How are we going to deal with it? How are
we going to preserve human autonomy and independence?

Technology is amoral. It is created by people, developed by people, and used by people. People are responsible for what technology does to human beings, not technology itself. As pointed out by Luther H. Evans of Columbia University, the people who control technology are largely entrepreneurs, and their use of technology depends on profit-making possibilities. The overriding factors which dictate automation are: 1) production costs, 2) labor requirements, 3) inventiveness, 4) process expediting, 5) productivity, and 6) fuller and faster information for decision-making.[30] Technology can be used to enhance human living conditions and physical freedom. But it should not be used to gain profits at the expense of other human beings' self-respect, personal feelings, human dignity and possibilities of becoming autonomous and independent.

When automation replaces workers and manufactures products without human labor, unemployed workers will not receive wages to buy the products of industry. As a result, stock in warehouses may pile up, and markets may stagnate. Profiteers may no longer be independent and autonmous, like unemployed workers. It is a vicious circle. One person's autonomy is another's heteronomy because of the reciprocity between them. Well-regulated dynamism in industry and society as a whole is needed, so that serious stagnation can be avoided. Basically, this dynamism is rooted in human development toward autonomy and independence. Whenever the system stagnates, it either dies or changes through revolution or reformation. Therefore, responsible management should not be dominated by the egocentrism of profit-making. Avaricious, power-addicted manipulators need to regulate themselves so that there will be social harmony, which is indispensible for human autonomy and independence. On the other hand, the egocentrism of the workers needs to be guarded against by society, if social harmony is to be reached. In this dynamism, we can see the full play of three principles of human development: differentiation, integration, and transcendence.

Samuel Butler predicted that the machine might take control of humanity. Will his prediction come

190

true? We hope not. But we cannot be sure. Are we still the masters of technology, or have we been conquered by it? Dr. J. Kemeny, a pioneer and proponent of computer education, predicted that the ultimate relation between human beings and computer would be a "symbiotic union of two living species, each completely dependent on the other for survival."[31] This reminds us of the mother-child symbiosis, dominated by the principle of integration. There must be differentiation and transcendence so that we may be differentiated from computer dependency and become transcended to be its master as well as part of it. Otherwise, human autonomy and independence wil be destroyed. We follow the rule of the machine in order to use it and not in order to be its slaves. By following the rule of the machine, we become autonomous and independent to harness its power for our purposes. What is important is our vision for the future. Seeing a vision is an attribute of the autonomous and independent person. This leads us to the religious dimension of autonomy in human growth.

4. Autonomy and Religious Experience

In this age of increasing automation, we need to emphasize spiritual and human values to protect our autonomy and independence, and, more importantly, our human nature. Materialistic values are advocated by avaricious manipulators to justify their ruthless exploitation of other fellow human-beings. Material values are an important part of human life, but not everything: We do not live by bread alone. When our basic needs for food and shelter are met, we look for safety and security, love and belonging, self-esteem and self-actualization (Maslow). We have not only bodies, but also minds and souls. There is a religious dimension to human development at each stage. In addition to physical growth, there is gradual formation of symbols, meanings, and moral values in human psychic structure. They do not just continue sensorimotor development, but are a qualitatively different level of development. They belong to the spiritual and religious sphere of human existence. Religious faith can contribute to our security, self-esteem,

191

meaning of life, and human dignity, although it can
also destroy them. They are important to the development of autonomous and independent personality.

Many Christians affirm the value of human personhood, and believe in the love of God who "sent the
Son into the world, not to condemn the world, but
that the world might be saved." We are created in
the image of God in the Judeo-Christian tradition.
This religious faith is significant to self-esteem
when accepted wholeheartedly and, conseqeuntly, to
autonomy and independence. It provides a vision of
God, human identity, and the world. Seeing a vision
is an attribute of an autonomous person who is goal-
oriented, makes choices, and acts. As theologian
Karl Rahner points out, full autonomy is the pre-
supposition and consequence of an immediate vision
of God.[32]

Avaricious manipulators use fellow human beings
like machines for their profit-making. Their view
of people is negative and low. Cocksure materialists
think that men and women are objects, "it" not "thou."
Often this materialistic value is applied only to
others, and not to themselves. Other people are machines to be used, but not "me." "I am god, not just
a being created in the image of God." The decline of
human autonomy and independence may be attributed to
the lack of vision of God, being human, and the world
among secularists. With Copernicus and Galileo, we
human beings ceased to be the center of the universe,
attended by sun and stars; with Darwin, we human beings ceased to be the creation of God with soul and
reason; with Freud, we human beings ceased to be
governed by a rational mind. Now, with the developing capacity of computers to control as well as to
serve us, what importance can we claim for ourselves
to justify our self-esteem, dignity, and to define
our destiny, if our faith in God and ourselves is
wrong? Answers to this question affect our autonomy
and independence.

As pointed out by Dean Turner in his The Autonomous Man, "the more real importance a person finds
in himself, the more he will act to fulfill his needs
and to expand his value and meaning for himself and

192

others. The more importance he sees in his neighbors as ends in themselves, the more sensitive he will care for their wellbeing and happiness. In the act of caring, the more he will fulfill himself."[33] Such caring and loving reciprocity is rooted in a positive view of ourselves, and is essential to true autonomy and independence. This is a sign of maturity, and this is what Christian faith affirms.

The typology of autonomy vs. heteronomy does not only appear in education and philosophy, but also in psychotherapy and religion. The controversy over free will and determinism is a cliche, but has never become irrelevant to human life. It appears in various forms. In his luncheon speech to almost 2,500 persons at the Hotel Astor celebrating his seventieth birthday on October 20, 1929, John Dewey pointed out one of the basic problems in America; "the changing character of individuality and the need to safeguard its integrity." American life is characterized by "externalism," namely, "the attempt to find happiness in external things."[34] This is a secular statement of a spiritual problem. It is also a statement of autonomy vs. heteronomy, the internal vs. the external The ancient Socrates's midwifery approach to education and the modern client-centered therapy are designed to develop human autonomy and independence. The person who gives birth to a new pattern of behavior takes full credit for it as an autonomous agent. The patient is not told by the therapist how to solve problems, but is helped to work out his or her own solutions.

In Christianity, autonomy vs. heteronomy may be interpreted to have developed into two streams of thought, liberalism vs. conservatism. Liberals will advocate the subjective authority of the believer, whereas conservatives will advocate objective authority of the Bible or church tradition in dealing with controversial issues. However, such typology should not be pushed too far. Stating unequivocally that the liberals are autonomous, whereas the conservatives are heteronomous would be misleading and oversimplified. Nonetheless, the dichotomy cannot be ignored. The truth is not "either or" but "both and." True autonomy comes from heteronomy. In human growth,

193

differentiation and integration are intertwined with transcendence.

Subjectivity is the source of dynamism in life and the springboard of initiative and autonomy. The Reformation in the sixteenth century was rooted in the subjectivity of faith. Later, objectivity was found necessary, and a new kind of orthodoxy developed. The Roman Catholic Church and the Protestant Orthodox are heteronomous in different ways: the former advocates the authority of the Church, whereas the latter, the authority of the Bible.

Enlightenment thinkers advocated human autonomy as one of their fundamental principles. Kant defined enlightenment (Aufklärung) as the human conquest of immaturity, which is the "inability to use one's own reason without the guidance of somebody else," as Paul Tillich interprets him.[35] The courage and freedom to use reason is the essence of enlightenment. The guidance of other people would be more comfortable and secure, in religion, politics, education, and other fields, but this is against human nature, which aspires to autonomy. The law of reason is implicit in our rational structure; it is inside our true being. However, autonomy is not lawless subjectivity. Some people equate autonomy with individual willfulness and arbitrary egocentricity. Instead, autonomy is living according to the law of reason in all activity; it is having the courage to think and use reason.

For Enlightenment thinkers, not autonomy but ultimately heteronomy is willful and arbitrary. The word "heteronomy" comes from two Greek words--"heteros" and "nomos." The former means "other," "foreign," or "strange," and the latter "law." Heteronomy means being subject to a strange authority; it is an attempt to escape fear, not by courage but by subjection to an authority that gives comfort and security. Religious heteronomy subjects the individual to the church or Bible. "Reason" does not mean business calculation, rather it means awareness of truth and goodness, fighting the oppression and distortion of humanity by arbitrary authorities. Today, many people seek the security of heteronomy. This is dangerous.

However, in the Christian experience autonomy
and heteronomy are not irreconcilable. Paul Tillich
uses the word, "theonomy" to describe the integration
of the two. "Theonomy" comes from two Greek words,
"theos" (God) and "nomos" (law). Belief in the Holy
Spirit is significant in this regard. The divine
Spirit is believed to be transcendent, and yet is
immanent in human hearts and the world, giving power,
meaning, and direction to men and women who believe.
Inner potentialities are fulfilled through the presence of the Spirit. So, "theonomy implies our own
personal experience of the presence of the divine
Spirit within us, witnessing to the Bible or to the
Church," says Tillich. "Autonomy, which is aware of
its divine ground, is theonomy; but autonomy without
the theonomous dimension degenerates into mere humanism."[36] Heteronomously authoritarian John Calvin
strongly proclaimed the indwelling witness of the
divine Spirit if the authority of the Bible is to
be accepted. When there is no inner witness, the
Bible is meaningless. Theonomy is autonomy derived
from the presence of the Spirit. If the Spirit works
in us, truth is self-authenticating.

In the state of theonomy, autonomy and heteronomy are united. In divine transcendence and imma-
nence, differentiation is integration, and integration is differentiation. Through the presence of the
Spirit, subjectivity and objectivity are integrated,
and yet differentiated. One characteristic of theonomy is "its permanent struggle against both an independent heteronomy and an independent autonomy.
Theonomy is prior to both--at the same time, (it) is
posterior to both," says Tillich.[37] The freedom of
the human spirit, as well as the divine, is not repressed, and valid demands of justice are not rejected in the name of God. Likewise, valid acts of
personal determination are not perverted in the name
of the Holy Spirit. True theonomy is not distorted
into heteronomy. In this state of theonomy there is
true communion and communication. Religion and culture are not divorced; culture provides the forms of
religion, and religion the substance of culture. The
secular and the sacred are united, and at the same

time, differentiated. Faith and reason are not in-
compatible; the immediate presence of the Spirit is
felt in the act of knowing. Divine "inner light"
is also autonomous reason, which is the structure
of universal reality, within and without. Theonomy
is a state of religious maturity.

Unfortunately, autonomy is often misunderstood
as a human revolt against God. This is due to an
equation of autonomy with arbitrary pleasure oriented
lawlessness. If autonomy is based on the rule of the
divine spirit within, it cannot be a revolt against
God. Human goodness and its fulfillment become a
reality through the presence of the Spirit, but at
the same time is under the judgment of the Spirit.
Without the presence of the divine Spirit, we cannot
have true autonomy. If the Spirit works within us,
it is self-authenticating, and our autonomy is no
longer an empty autonomy, which is often attacked as
"humanism." The Spirit provides the content of autonomy and witnesses truth, goodness, and beauty.

Theonomy is beyond human logic. It unfolds
as one grows more mature spiritually, just as true
lovers take off their protective defenses layer after
layer. Theonomy is a mysterious paradox: In autonomy
we are not simply subject to the law of reason, truth,
and goodness; we are so subject to it that we become
self-legislating, and only within the heteronomy of
submitting to the divine Spirit can autonomy be realized. Obedience to a law of which our wills are the
source is self-destructive and nonesensical. This
idea makes sense only when the will which we obey is
indeed another Will residing in us, and is "a Will
in obedience to which we can alone find our own true
selfhood and our wills their real freedom," as pointed
out by theologian John Baillie.[38] This mysterious
paradox is what we first experienced as infants in
the mother-child symbiosis, and subsequent develop-
ments through the interplay of differentiation, integration, and transcendence.

In dealing with patients, Dr. Paul Tournier
finds that "the aim of psychology is the moral autonomy which men strive so hard to achieve," and that
"it is when one abandons oneself to Jesus Christ that

196

one attains inner freedom."[39] Through symbiosis
with Jesus Christ, Christians experience true autonomy and inner freedom. This is what Paul the Apostle meant when he described his inner struggle and
subsequent liberation. He could will what was right,
but he could not do it; he found, in his inner-most
self, another law at war with the law of his mind,
a law that made him captive; he exclaimed in great
despair and said, "Wretched man that I am! Who will
deliver me from this body of death? Thanks be to
God through Jesus Christ our Lord!"[40] In self-
surrender, we find true autonomy. Autonomy is not
strictly independence, it is interdependence.

Between early childhood and the thirties, a
person normally experiences increased mastery of the
environment and competence. As a result, the feeling
of autonomy increases. But after a physical peak
in young adulthood, physical strength decreases, and
there may be a parallel decrease of autonomy, mastery,
and competence. However, this is not always so. Autonomy is related to socio-economic class, education,
self-confidence, and social involvement.[41] Autonomy
is manifested in the degree of an elderly person's
inner freedom, strength and integrity, and it determines how well the elderly person adjusts to the
aging process. Autonomy is a manifestation of spiritual strength. Without this spirituality, life is
not the best it can be. An eighty-year-old man suffered from the incurable cancer that was spreading
slowly through his body. He had undergone surgery,
chemotherapy, and other treatment, but all seemed
futile. He had been strong and virile, but now he
was so thin and weakened. His friends and relatives
visited him and showed sympathy. But he was strong
within. In spite of the unbearable pain and anguish,
his eyes shone brightly and he looked very dignified.
His spirit inspired all who visited him. His inner
freedom did not waste away like his body, which dete-
riorated slowly everyday. He showed dignity and composure, a gift from the presence of the Spirit. His
spiritual autonomy was not affected by physical decay. He looked to the transcendent and eternal with
great hope and certainty. Religious faith is the
source of spiritual autonomy.

NOTES

1. David Belgum, Religion and Personality in the
   Spiral of Life (Washington, D.C.: University
   Press of America, 1979), pp. 68-69.

2. Roy MacGregor-Hastie, The Barbarians: The Life
   and Time of Mao Tse-tung (London: Boardman,
   1961); George Paloczi-Horrath, Mao Tse-tung,
   Emperor of the Blue Ants (London: Secker and
   Warburg, 1962); Robert Payne, Mao Tse-tung,
   Ruler of Red China (New York: Henry Schuman,
   Inc., 1950); Emi Siao, Mao Tse-tung, His Child-
   hood and Youth (Bombay: People's Publishing
   House, 1953); Siao Yu, Mao Tse-tung and I Were
   Beggars (Syracuse, N.Y.: Syracuse University
   Press, 1959).

3. Douglas Heath, Maturity and Competence: A Trans-
   cultural View (New York: Halsted Press, 1977).

4. Marilyn French, The Women's Room (New York:
   Summit Books, 1977), in Book Digest, March 1978,
   p. 180.

5. Carl R. Rogers, On Becoming a Person (Boston:
   Houghton Mifflin Co., 1961), pp. 187-192.

6. Tom Wicker, On Press (New York: The Viking
   Press, 1977), in Book Digest, March 1978, pp.
   35-65.

7. Ronald W. Clark, Einstein: The Life and Time
   (New York: The World Publishing Co., 1971), p.
   131.

8. George E. Vaillant, "How the Best and the Bright-
   est Came of Age," Psychology Today, 14 (9) (1977),
   p. 41.

9. Richard Walls and Steven P. Gulkus, "Reinforcers,
   Values, and Vocational Maturity in Adults," Journal of Vocational Behavior, 4 (1974), pp. 325-
   332.

10. Boris Blai, "Who Is Emotionally Mature?" _Psychology_, 12 (1975), pp. 35-38.

11. George E. Vaillant, _Adaptation to Life_ (Boston: Little, Brown and Co., 1977), p. 80.

12. Arthur Deikman, "Biomodal Consciousness," _Archives of General Psychiatry_, 25 (1971), pp. 481-489.

13. "Shaping Tomorrow's ᎶIA," _Time_, February 6, 1978, p. 17.

14. Erik H. Erikson, _Childhood and Society_ (New York: W. W. Norton & Co., 1963), pp. 251-255.

15. Thomas Lickona, ed., _Moral Development and Behavior: Theory, Research, and Social Issues_ (New York: Holt, Rinehart and Winston, 1976), pp. 34-35.

16. Robert Paul Wolff, _The Autonomy of Reason_ (New York: Harper & Row, 1973), p. 177. See also, Alasdair MacIntyre, _A Short History of Ethics_ (New York: The Macmillan Co., 1973), pp. 190-198.

17. Charles E. Claffey, "Suicide Ends the Despair of a Child's Life," _Boston Sunday Globe_, February 12, 1978.

18. L. Vygotsky, "Thought and Speech," _Psychiatry_, 2 (1939), pp. 29-52.

19. Alex Morris, _Nelson Rockefeller: A Biography_ (New York: Harper and Brothers, 1960), pp. 27-50.

20. Jerald M. Jellison and John H. Harvey, "Why We Like Hard, Positive Choices," _Psychology Today_, 13 (3) (1976), pp, 47-49.

21. Donald M. Maynard, _Your Home Can Be Christian_ (Nashville; Abingdon Press, 1952), pp. 56-69.

22. Paul E. McGhee, "Moral Development and Children's

Appreciation of Humor," *Developmental Psychology*, 10 (4) (1978), pp. 514-525.

23. Leonore Boehm, "The Development of Independence: A Comparative Study," *Child Development,* 28 (1957), pp. 85-92.

24. John A. Rawls, *Theory of Justice* (Cambridge, MA: Harvard University Press, 1971), pp. 516-517.

25. B. F. Skinner, *Beyond Freedom and Dignity* (New York: Bantham Book, 1971), p. 175.

26. Arnold B. Barach, "Changing Technology and Changing Culture," in *Automation, Education and Human Values* ed. William W. Brickman and Stanley Lehrer (New York: School and Society Books, 1966), p. 58.

27. Walter Davis, "A Labor View of the Social and Educational Implications of Technological Change," in *Automation, Education and Human Values,* p. 230.

28. *Ibid.*

29. Donald N. Michael, "Cybernation: The Silent Conquest," in *Automation: Implications for the Future* ed. Morris H. Philipson (New York: The Vintage Books, 1962), p. 92.

30. Luther H. Evans, "Automation and Some Neglected Aspects of Society and Education," in *Automation, Education, and Human Values,* p. 235.

31. "The Computer Society," *Time*, February 20, 1978, pp. 44-59.

32. Karl Rahner, *Foundations of Christian Faith* (New York: Seabury Press, 1978), pp. 83-84.

33. Dean Turner, *The Autonomous Man* (St. Louis: Bethany Press, 1970), p. 179.

34. George Dykhuizen, *The Life and Mind of John*

Dewey (Carbondale, Ill: Southern Illinois University Press, 1973), p. 243.

35. Paul Tillich, _Perspectives on 19th and 20th Century Protestant Theology_ (New York: Harper & Row, 1967), p. 24.

36. _Ibid._, pp. 26-27.

37. Paul Tillich, _Systematic Theology_, Vol. III (Chicago: University of Chicago Press, 1963), pp. 248-268.

38. John Baillie, _Our Knowledge of God_ (New York: Charles Scribner's Sons, 1959), pp. 246-247.

39. Paul Tournier, _A Place for You: Psychology and Religion_ (New York: Harper & Row, 1968), p. 209.

40. Rom. 7:7-21.

41. Rosina C. Lao, "Is Internal-External Control an Age-Related Variable?" _The Journal of Psychology_, 92 (1976), pp. 3-7.

CHAPTER

VI

IDENTITY AND EGO-IDEAL

Another theme in maturity is identity and ego-
ideal. Human growth is a process of individuation.
To be mature is to be an individual person. To become an individual person is to find one's identity
and ego-ideal. It is knowing who we are, why we are
here, and where we are going. To be mature is to
find our ego-ideals. Identity and ego-ideals are
complementary. Identity forcuses on who we are,
but ego-ideal focuses on what we are going to become.
Identity is a product of individuation, but ego-ideal
provides a norm for future self-actualization. We
become what we contemplate. Identity refers to the
continuity with the past, but ego-ideal refers to the
continuity with the future. A mature person has a
distinct and yet adaptable identity and ego-ideal.

Today many people are attracted to the problem
of identity. The world is changing and the old stability is no longer there. The child becomes an
adolescent, the young grows old. But change in human
growth is not the only reason for us to be concerned
with identity. Socio-cultural and political changes
make us wonder about our identity in new situations.
Identity is a problem for refugees from Cambodia,
Vietnam, Cuba, and other parts of the world. It is
a problem for immigrants from Mexico, Russia, and
other places. They have moved from their homelands
to a new socio-cultural environment, and have found
they are unable to live the way they used to live,
or are treated in ways they are unaccustomed to.
"Who am I?" "Am I somebody?" We may think that identity is a problem only for unfortunate "boat-people"
and aliens. But this is not so. People move from
one place to another for various reasons, and are
not free from the quest for identity. The quest
for identity is the destiny of being human. An em-
ployed person may suddenly find him or herself laid

off, and the problem of identity hits hard.

1. Quest for Identity

In ordinary conversation, we ask: "Who are you?" "What is your name?" "Where are you from?" "What do you do for a living?" and the like. By asking these questions, we attempt to define the identity of another person. If a person on the telephone does not introduce him or herself, we ask "Who is calling please?" If we want to know about an author, we look him or her up in Contemporary Authors, The International Authors and Writers Who's Who, or Who's Who in America. On the other hand, we want to know who we are and introduce ourselves to others. The quest for identity is as ancient as human history. It is an expression of self-awareness.

As indicated in the previous chapter, a person cannot obtain autonomy and independence unless he or she has formed a positive identity. In the growing process, every child wants to reach maturity, exhibit autonomy and independence, and have a clear sense of identity and ego-ideal. The struggle for autonomy and independence is partly a struggle to achieve identity and the image of future becoming.

A young professor, like many young people, was inspired by the youngest President in U.S. John F. Kennedy, and considered him a hero. Kennedy's portrait hung in the professor's office, as if he were still in the White House. Young people identified with Kennedy as they grew from adolescence to young adulthood. But this seemed not to be the case for the youngest boy in the Kennedy family, who was striving to become a man on his own right and by his own merit. In an interesting and psychologically conceivable report, Lester David, who wrote Senator Ted Kennedy's biography a few years ago, gave us a glimpse of the youthful Kennedy's fight for identity under the shadow of his older brothers. One day Ted Kennedy, then a young man, went to court to change his name. He said to the judge, "Kennedy is well known politically. One Kennedy is President, the

204

other a high-ranking Cabinet member; Your Honor, I want to become a success on my own." The sympathetic judge asked him what he had in mind. He replied, "Well, I think Teddy is all right as a first name, but I'd like to change the last name." "To what?" "What about Roosevelt?"[1]

Similarly, but apparently for different reasons, Michael Herbert Dengler wanted to change his name to a number, "1069," but a Minneapolis judge refused his request. In the judge's opinion, allowing him to do so "would only provide additional nourishment" to what the judge considered an increasingly dehumanized society.[2] Problems of identity are not only personal but also socio-cultural and communal. The battle to win an acceptable identity is fought not only in one's mind, but also in the politico-cultural arena in which one is born and raised.

Our quest for identity is twofold: 1) personal, and 2) collective. Each person searches for his or her "soul" as an individual and as a species: 1) "Who am I?" and 2) "What is to be human?" "What is man?" "What is woman?" etc. The mature person comes to terms with these questions. In this age of increasing automation and socio-cultural change, the quest for identity is an uphill battle. This struggle is part of the mental construction of oneself and the world at large: This battle is being fought by many people in the world today. The recent revival of ethnic consciousness is an expression of the quest for identity.

In our quest for personal identity, we often come into conflict with the expectations of others, notably our parents and other significant individuals, because to find our identity is to be differentiated from them. Thomas Woodrow Wilson is an example. His father was a minister and wanted him to become a minister. In 1873, he experienced a religious awakening, felt that God had chosen him for a great work, and that he was "guided by an intelligent power outside himself."[3] On the other hand, he wanted to become a politician. He tacked a portrait of the British Prime Minister, Gladstone, on the wall behind his desk. When Jessie Woodrow Bones asked him whose portrait it was, Wilson replied "That is Gladstone, the greatest statesman that ever lived. I intend to be a statesman too." During his second year at Princeton, he had a decisive experience which determined his quest for identity: he found an article entitled "The Orator" which electrified his mind and he felt he was like Gladstone. After reading the article, he no longer doubted his vocation and never again considered entering the ministry. He was sure he could and would conquer the world with his moral earnestness, his choice of words and gestures, like Gladstone.

The quest for identity is a struggle to become an individual. It is a task of self-definition, seeking to answer the questions "Who am I? What is the core of my life? What is my ultimate commitment in life? What kind of person am I going to become?" The quest for identity is acute in the United Sates, where individuality and freedom are strongly upheld. To survive in this society, one must become a strong individual. "Change is king," mobility is constant, and the principle of differentiation dominates all sphere of life.[4] On the other hand, destructive forces make achieving the goal of becoming a strong individual in this scientific and technological society difficult. There is a great demand for identity, but identity is hard to find and keep. The quest for identity is so acute in America that renowned psychoanalyst Erik H. Erikson has capitalized on it and made an academic fortune by analyzing the critical nature of the identity crisis in adolescence. He defines ego-identity as "the confidence that one's ability to maintain inner sameness and continuity is matched by the sameness and continuity of one's meaning for others."[5] In this constantly changing society, "sameness and continuity" are hard to come by. Identity diffusion may be the order.

2. Identity Formation

Identity formation is a process of differentiation, but in order to be differentiated a person must be identified and integrated first. In order

to become an independent individual at the end of
childhood, a person needs to have had a symbiotic
relationship with his or her mother at the beginning
of life's journey. If there is no intimate identification with mother, a child may die or become psychologically crippled. The child is then like a
seed unable to put roots into the soil, and eventually the child withers. The child first develops
selfhood at about the age of two through introjection and projection of the appraisals by the mother
and other significant adults in the process of identification. The child then has a sense of "me" or
"I," differentiating from "mother" without breaking
with her. "I am a good child; I love Mom." The
child identifies with the "mother" as a "loved one."

Later, the child further identifies with significant adults of the same sex by imitation and role-
playing. As selfhood becomes stronger, the child
needs to become an independent individual. With the
onset of puberty, child introjection and projection
become useless. A new selfhood is emerging, and ego-
identity is being formed. When identification with
parents predominates, the child is still in the stage
of heteronomy. But when a new selfhood and identity
emerges, he or she moves to the stage of autonomy.
Just as autonomy is born out of heteronomy, identity
is born out of identifications.

This is also true professionally. A person
becomes identified with a field, and deeply rooted
in it through the help of an experienced and established mentor. Even in a small business, a person
learns the various aspects of it as an assistant or
a helper to an established boss before opening a
store. Very rarely does a person go directly into
a new field without assistance and succeed in forming a professional identity.

Sooner or later, every successful apprentice
emerges with a separate professional identity, and
makes a unique contribution to the field. Those
who succeed in differentiating themselves from their
mentors are more likely to reach the top, whereas
those who remain under the influence of their mentors cannot, and are likely to be discarded by the

mentor in the end. When a person's professional
identity is formed, the subordinate relationship
with the mentor is transformed into that of equals.
But initially, identification is needed for identity
formation.

This is also true in a group setting. In a
study of identity formation, Dr. Arnold R. Beisser
of California has found three phases.[7] Phase one
is called "dedifferentiation," and is synonymous
with "identification" because "dedifferentiation"
means the opposite of differentiation. It is an
inclusive phase. When a person first joins a group,
he or she looks for people with similar qualities
and characteristics for identification, in addition
to presenting his or her best social dexterity and
most attractive qualities to others. By achieving
a high degree of identification with others, he or
she begins to have "we" feelings, "my people" sentiments, or an "our group" consciousness. During
this phase, social distance is minimized, and the
person tries to be as close to other people as possible.

Phase two, called "differentiation," occurs
when a person begins to differentiate from the rest
of the group. Previously, the person responded with
a constant "yes," but now he or she is likely to
give an affirmative "No, I disagree." Each person
seeks uniqueness and individuality within the context of group interaction. This phase is often
accompanied by self-assertion and aggressiveness.
However, each member of the group still strongly
identifies with the group. The task of seeking
authentic self in relation to the group and one's
place in it is completed in this phase. The authentic self appears, without threatening to disrupt the
cohesiveness of the group.

Phase three, "true identity," is a completion
of phase two, and is characterized by a person's
readiness to affirm truly who he or she is without
fear of embarrassment to, or rejection by, others.
Self-understanding corresponds to the appraisals of
others. When this happens, the person experiences
a sense of liberation and awareness. In this phase,

208

self-image and the image of others sharpens. This
is a stage of mature perception, which is accurate
and realistic. A sense of oneness and congruency
occurs between being and feeling; a sense of getting
oneself together. In this last phase, previously
dedifferentiated and the differentiated states are
integrated. The dedifferentiated state is largely
heteronomous, the differentiated state is partially
autonomous, and the "true identity" state is truly
autonomous. "True identity" symbolizes maturity.

As pointed out by Erikson, "identity formation
emerges as an evolving configuration, which is gradually established by successive ego syntheses and
resyntheses throughout childhood."[8] Each significant identification of the past contributes to the
multiplicity of dimensions and components of identity, which are integrated, coherent, and wholesome.
Social changes and mobility increase the number of
diversified interactions with the environment. Too
much diversification of identification increases
the difficulty of integration. When parents and
leaders do not provide direct guidance and role models, children are likely to be lost, not knowing
what to do in the situation in which they live.[9]
Identity diffusion is the inability to integrate all
dimensions of experiences in the past into a meaningful and hierarchical whole.

There are people who have never traveled. They
may think themselves provincial and narrow-minded.
But too much traveling may make a person equally unhappy. Unlike his brother Henry, William James moved
a great deal physically and professionally. His
trips to Europe made him restless, and his emotional
wellbeing was threatened. This can be seen in his
letter to Carl Stunpf dated January 24, 1894. He
wrote that he regretted bringing his children abroad.
He should have waited "until they are old enough to
have the Grand Emotion. One should not be cosmo-
politan, one's soul becomes 'disintegrated'; as
Janet (his wife) would way. Parts of it remain in
different places, and the whole of it is nowhere.
One's native land seems foreign. It is not wholly
good thing, and I suffer from it."[10] Crucial to
identity diffusion is the disturbance in interper-

sonal relationships and misunderstanding of social reality and self.

However, not all changes contribute to identity diffusion. A study on social change and identity formation was made at Helsinki based on two places--one characterized by rapid social change and high standard of living, the other by slow social change and low standard of living. It was found that improvements in the standard of living brought better possibilities for identity formation, consequently conditions favorable to mental health.[11] Therefore, if social change enhances the possibilities of achieving goals and realizing ego-ideals, it is not bad. Identity diffusion may not happen because of social change, but it would be unwise to condemn all social change in the name of identity diffusion. It is crucial that social changes better our chances for realizing our ego-ideal, social recognition, and acceptance.

Cognitively, identity has multiple dimensions, each representing certain values. Identity formation is an integrative process of major values which a person has acquired in life's journey. Each dimension is expressed in concrete interactions with the envirnment. Sometimes, an action implies several dimensions of identity and basic values. The healthy mature person has a well-organized and integrated hierarchy of values and various dimensions of identity. When a person has an integrated identity, he or she can make decisions easily.

Identity is the core of the total self, integrating basic value and all aspects of the self, and not just physical self or social status and political affiliation. A gifted young woman said that if someone rejected her as an actress, she would feel partial rejection, but this would not destroy her. However, if one of her friends came and told her that she was a "lousy human being without decent values," it would destroy her.[12] There seem to be different layers in the formation of identity. Attacking the central layer may lead to identity diffusion. But if the peripheral layer is made central by some unfortunate circumstance, the result may be identity

foreclosure. Identity foreclosure is caused by inadequate search and exploration of self and the environment, and is often prompted by a lack of opportunities to test oneself in career development. Sometimes, identity foreclosure is simply due to social
injustice which chronically limits chances for education and job training.

There are unfortunate people whose self identity is totally negative and who have created negative self-images. They may have been ill-treated
in early childhood. An inner voice repeatedly says,
"Yes, I am a bad child. I am useless." When they
grow older, they become delinquents or bandits. They
use their talents and gifts to destroy human lives
and create misery. Some people consider them devil-
ish and satanic. In fact these unfortunate people
have negative identity.

Thus, identity formation is a key problem in
psychotherapy. As pointed out by Carl R. Rogers,
"profound changes occur in the perceived self of
the client during and after therapy."[13] The perceived self becomes similar to the valued self. The
client's negative identity must be positively transformed, and his or her self-perception must become
more comfortable and adjusted to others. The principle of transcendence plays an important role in
this process.

Identity formation is uniquely human. The
loss or breakdown of identity is a constant threat
to us, because we are human. This danger is unknown
to animals under natural conditions. By nature, we
are required to define our identity in encounters
with the environment.

3. Identity, Culture, and Community

Identity formation is often understood to be
egocentric introspection and isolation, cutting ties
with others, standing in front of a mirror and looking at oneself intensely in order to find the true
selfhood. This misunderstanding excludes the social

211

aspects of identity formation. Figuratively speaking, identity is "an anchorage of the self in the social matrix," as pointed out by Dr. Kenneth Soddy in his discussion on mental health and value system.[14] Individuality and identity cannot exist in a vacuum. Identification can take place only in a community; in the family, church, club, or neighborhood.

It is a mistake to conceive of identity only in the individualistic sense. Identity can also be used in a collective sense, as in "American identity" which signifies the characteristics of the American people collectively.[15] Erikson proposed that "a national identity is derived from the ways in which history has, as it were, counterpointed certain opposite potentialities; the ways in which it lifts this counterpoint to a unique style of civilization, or lets it disintegrate into mere contradiction."[16] Collective identity is often manifested in various forms, fashions, fads, rituals, cultic movement, recreation, heroes, celebrities, or crusaders. Collective identity is the soul of culture. It constitutes the norm for socialization into the community.

In Chinese culture, identity is largely understood in terms of a collective identity centered on family in traditional society, and on the State in communist society. A Chinese aphorism says that the "small self" must be sacrificed for the sake of the "larger self"--the individual must make sacrifices for the welfare of the community, nation, and world. In traditional society, the family is the basic context for individual identity. The basic unit in that society is not the individual person, but the family. The individual person is identified as a member of a family, clan, or local community rather than as an individual with a separate identity. Consequently, a particular sense of closeness is felt for those from the same family, clan, or locality in a foreign land and different culture.

Due to Western influence in recent years--urbanization and the breaking up of the extended family--the individual in Eastern culture has more to say and greater power to decide. But the traditional practice of calling one's family name first and then personal name remains. In the West, personal names precede family names except in business or bibliographical references. This shows that in the East, collective identity is more important than personal identity, but in the West, personal identity is more important than collective identity.

In traditional Chinese society, there are two characters in a child's name with few exceptions. One is common to all the brothers or sisters of the same generation, whereas the other is personal. Thus a person can be identified by his or her place in the family or community very easily. In spite of Western influence, the Eastern emphasis on collective identity has not changed much, because in the quest for identity people need community and family. This can be seen in the experiences of immigrants in this country.[17] The "melting pot" image is a threat to those who are afraid of losing their identities in a new land. They form ethnic communities, where their identity is formed, affirmed, and reinforced again and again. Through interpersonal interactions and mutual identification a person can synthesize his or her self-image. In order to avoid the loss of identity, some people prefer the image of "salad bowl" in describing social unity. No matter whether it is "pot" or "bowl," we need a community in which to find ourselves.

"Salad bowl" implies unity, diversity, and mutual tolerance, whereas "melting pot" is strongly integrative. "Salad bowl" symbolizes a more mature stage than "melting pot." Unity keeps a community whole; diversity safeguards the identities of its members; and mutual tolerance makes interactions and mutual identification possible. The image of "melting pot" may be compared to the mother-child symbiosis which is yet to be differentiated, whereas "salad bowl" may be compared to the stage of paradox between two polarities of subjectivity and objectivity.

We need a community whose solidarity is organic. By being organic, a community assumes inevitable social changes and is capable of absorbing changes

without losing its unity or members' identities. We
need a community whose collective and individual
identities are preserved, affirmed, and reinforced.
"Melting pot" may mean the loss of individual identity for the sake of collective identity.

Identification is needed for identity formation,
but it is not the whole process. Identity formation
is also a process of differentiation. The melting
pot symbol menaces identity formation, not because
of its emphasis on unity but because of its lack of
articulate differentiation. People accept its dreams,
and strive to melt into this common pot of immigrants
and their decendents. But in American history, many
have rejected it strongly and unequivocally. This
is also true for those who have had cross-cultural
experiences.

In his study of American immigrants, Harvard
historian Dr. Oscar Handlin pointed out that in the
early days of European immigration, the Church of
Sweden advised its members coming to the United
States to join the Episcopal Church. But once here,
Swedish immigrants neither accepted the advice, nor
joined other European groups. They created their
own churches and found their own synod. Handlin remarks, "Almost at half century after the great immigration of Irish and Germans, these people had not
become indistinguishable from other Americans; they
were still recognized as Irish and German."[18] The
same phenomenon can be found today among immigrants
in the United States.

Moreover, identity problems can also be found
among the people of Asia. They have been influenced
by Western science and technology, goods from America, movies from Hollywood. Above all, they are hard
hit by world politics, and struggle to find who they
are and where they are going culturally. Those who
suffer most are the urban elite. Identity anchors
the self in the social matrix. So, when the social
matrix changes, the anchor is affected. Identity
helps us see ourselves in relation to the environment, and examine changes brought about by our interactions with the environment. The following
study is an example.

Some years ago, anthropologist E. M. Bruner made a study of identity problems in Sumatra, Indoneisia.[19] The people there had particular ways of living and traditional moral codes. The villagers were still living in the traditional culture, but the urban elite were no longer under its tutelage. Their life styles were not very different from those in the West. As the social order was changed by Western culture and politics, their ego-identity shattered. Previously they had designated various degrees of importance to different dimensions of living. Now, the order of reference has been broken, as the pattern of interpersonal relationships changed. Conservative villagers kept their personal and cultural identity intact. But the urban elite, who rejected traditional moral codes were on the threshold of an identity diffusion. They had forsaken sociocultural orthodoxy, and as a result males were no longer dominant. Previously, there was a hierarchical order among the siblings, but now all brothers were equal regardless of birth order. It was a great threat to their self-image and created a social and cultural crisis. The old self-image had been destroyed, but a new one has not been found. They feel alienated and restless.

We are living in an age of cultural crisis. What is happening in Asia, Africa, and Latin America makes us wonder whether we are in fact in the same boat with people in the Third World assaulted by the winds of cultural and political revolutions and counterrevolutions. Decades ago, Pitirim A. Sorokin wrote about the crisis of his age.[20] But what is happening today was beyond human prediction a few generations ago. The traditional social matrix has been shaken to its foundations by the Women's Movement, the Civil Rights Movement, and recently by a hightened ethnic consciousness. What is happening elsewhere may be just what occurs at the heart of the free world, namely, the United States; what we see elsewhere may be ripples from the center. Where are we heading in the future culturally? Our old culture has been torn down by whirlwinds from modern science and technology, and what we see is just the widely scattered pieces of it. Where are we going to live spiritually? Can we build a new resting

place for our minds and souls? As a college professor said after a conference at Big Bear Lake some
years ago, "Things are upside down nowadays." Can
we put them back? Today we find new conservatism
emerging in religion, politics, and education. Can
it put the Humpty Dumpty together again?

The "melting pot" symbol has been tested and
recently forsaken. It was a phase of "dedifferentiation." The current quest for identity, ethnic
or personal, is a phase of "differentiation." Will
there be a phase of "true identity"? Let's hope
we may reach a new mature phase. This nation is in
danger of being dominated by differentiation to the
extent that it has become the arena of struggle
among different factions. Each ethnic group curves
out a small colony of its own and exercises considerable influence on foreign policy and internal affairs. This is the stage of differentiation in which
identity is emerging. But reaching a stage of true
identity may take some time. In a more mature stage
one's identity is always affirmed in the matrix of
the nation and the world. In a mature stage, we
find not only differentiation, but also integration
and transcendence.

When we have integrated identity, decision-
making will be efficient. Even though there are
things for us to brag about, we do not do so. We
are in harmony with ourselves and the environment,
and there is no need for bragging. If we need to
boast, we still have identity problems. In a mature
stage, there is no need to do so. Affirmation of
ourselves should not be taken for bragging. However,
affirmation is easily misunderstood by those who have
identity problems.

In an interview with a sociology professor, I
found that he was not concerned with his identity.
His family had been in the United States for many
generations, and his identity seemed so well-established that he was not bothered by it. He was a
member of the majority, and he said that he had made
a survey about identity among the students in his
class after World War II, and that mostly Jewish and
other minority members were identity-conscious. Will

216

there be a time in the future, when every member of
any ethnic group in the United States feels at ease
with him or herself and the environment and affirms
positively?

   Traditional culture's main problem in human
development is socialization, whereas the key problem for modern culture is identity formation. Traditional culture is authoritarian and heteronomous;
the locus of authority is external, in the hands of
rulers and the traditions by which they rule; rulers
demand social conformity and obedience without question; truth is absolute. German philosopher Oswald
Spengler called it "Appolonian culture."[21] In contrast, modern culture is called a "Faustian culture,"
built on the assumption of conflicts. In modern culture, the locus of authority is internal and in the
hands of the people. Individuality is central, and
truth is relative. Nothing is absolute, and change
is a virtue. Personal identity is of paramount importance. This can be seen in a study of "the relationship between the life style and identity synthesis and resynthesis in traditional, neotraditional,
and nontraditional women."[22] Nontraditional women
conceived of their identity as strong and personal
throughout life; but this was not so for traditional
and neotraditional women--they conceived of their
identity as significantly stronger when they had
school-age children. Traditional culture is based on
integration, whereas modern culture is dominated by
differentiation. Will there be a time when our culture emphasizes transcendence, one that is intertwined with integration and differentiation. If so,
we will have reached a more mature stage.

   Being human, we are destined to forever define
our selfhood and ego-boundaries in our minds. By doing so, we create identity, individually, and culture
collectively. Culture manifests the identity principle. Thus, the cultural maturity of a society depends greatly on the maturity of its people. There
are two things a healthy person can do well according to Freud: work and love (lieben und arbeiten).[23]
Maturation is a never-ending process of work and love
which guarantees identity reinforcement, identity
maintenance, and identity re-creation. Culture is

the guide as well as the object of our work and love.

4. Identity and Religious Experience

What is the religious significance of identity and ego-ideal in human development? We can answer this question experientially and cognitively. Religious experience has been an important element in the formation of identity in the life of individual believer as well as in the religious community.

Identity is formed through identifications with persons or the community in which the individual lives. Models in the church or in the teachings of the Bible can form our image of our future self. This can be seen in the life of a teenage girl who said, "I am set apart, chosen, so to speak, to be the good girl of the family." How did she form such an ego-ideal? She pointed out that this was largely the outcome of her identification with the loving charitable Sunday School teacher she met at church.[24] Through her heroine, she identified herself with the teachings of the church, and saw herself as the "good girl of the family." The expressions "set apart," and "chosen" apparently indicate the religious impact on her thinking and cognitive articulation of her self-image, her personal identity.

As a Christian, Dr. Paul Tournier said that for him, the meaning of life is the Kingdom of God.[25] Like many other Christians, he identified himself with the goal which Jesus of Nazareth taught his disciples to have in prayer: "Our Father who art in Heaven, . . . Thy kingdom come, Thy will be done on earth as it is in heaven." This religious symbol became a central element in his mental as well as actual living. Unlike other physicians and psychiatrists, he found this religious symbol very meaningful. This is also true for Alan Paton of South Africa, who has devoted himself to social justice.

Since World War II, the quest for identity among peoples of the Third World has been capitalized on by their leaders, rediscovering their unique

cultures and ethnic consciousness. The quest for
identity has also been a great force in the theological reflections of Christian leaders in Asia,
Africa, and Latin America, in their construction of
a liberation theology, Asian theology, African theology, and a black theology in the United States. Previously they mingled within the denominations of
Western Christendom. They echoes Western theology
after reading Karl Barth, Emil Brunner, Rudolf Bultman, Paul Tillich, H. Richard Niebuhr, and Reinhold
Niebuhr. They reacted against Western theology as
they had tried "to assume the role of a prophet in the
midst of a search for national identity."[26] They
were no longer able to live as "a spiritual colony
of Western Christendom."[27] As a politically oppressed
minority, they identified with the historic experience of Israelites and focused on the Exodus story.
Furthermore, as pointed out by Stanley J. Smartha,
Director of the World Council of Churches' Programme
on Dialogue with People of Other Faiths and Ideologies, "Christian minorities can easily identify themselves to be on the side of the suffering Messiah,
claiming at the same time a share in the power and
privileges of the conquering Messiah."[28]

In the United States, black theology is also
based on the significance of the Exodus, and finds
meaning in the return of God's people from Babylon
and the teaching that God is the Liberator of the
oppressed.[29] As they struggled for emancipation,
their quest for identity and political independence
became virtually one. In fact, these quests are
often manifested in religious movements, such as
today's Islamic Revolution. Without the formation
of identity, the spiritual strength necessary to
fight for freedom and justice is missing. In this
way, religion may become the handmaiden of politics.
If so, such religion symbolizes the mentality of
"God is on our side," and lacks self-transcendence.
Thus, theology may become a rationalization of egocentricity.

Interestingly, the word "moratorium" which
Erikson used in discussing the problem of identity
formation in adolescence, was officially adopted as
a new policy recommended to member churches of the

All Africa Conference of Churches in May 1974.[30] One of the major aims of the moratorium was to achieve self-reliance and selfhood. The moratorium debate divided people into two camps: those who were strongly opposed to it and those who supported it. This indicates that younger churches in Africa and elsewhere have been facing identity problems in recent decades. The word "identity" has become a popular term among the leaders of these churches, although they are not psychologists, because they are facing an identity crisis as they struggle to become independent and autonomous in their own cultures in Asia, Africa, and Latin America.

Every identity crisis has religious significance. It is an opportunity to reorganize the self, a time to make new commitments, and faith is a form of ultimate commitment. Every identity crisis is a time for discovering new faith. Religious conversion is a process of new identity formation. It is a rebirth of selfhood. After the rebirth of selfhood, a new name is needed, just as Saul of Tarsus became Paul the Apostle after his conversion.[31]

The identity crisis is a time of inner struggle. The story of Jacob in the Bible is symbolically significant. In response to his request for blessings at the end of his struggle before dawn, Jacob heard, "Your name shall no more be called Jacob, but Israel, for you have striven with God and with men, and have prevailed."[32] The process of identity formation is a striving not only with others but also with God. The outcome of each identity formation is a new name. Naming is a solemn act. A new name, "Christian," was given to the early church, when the community of believers had become unmistakably differentiated from the rest of Jewish community.

In order to preserve its identity, the early church defined its orthodoxy by formulating the Apostles' Creed. In the history of the church, there were efforts of defining Christian orthodoxy in later times, such as the Nicene Creed and the Westminster Confession. Even today, there are various reinterpretations in this country. They all try to define what the church believes, just as a person tries to

define ego-boundaries in the formation of identity.
The Bible and other sacred literature have the similar function of defining the identity of a religious
community and its beliefs.

Heresy trials, excommunications, the Inquisi-
tion, and witch hunting were attempts to redefine
the identity of the religious community. Redefinition is needed when there is an identity crisis in
the church. Such an identity crisis may appear in
heated disputes and controversies among ecclesiastic
dignitaries. The sense of insecurity which characterizes an identity crisis may be a motivating factor in creating religious intolerance and persecu-
tion on the one hand, and self-righteousness, hypoc-
risy, and conservatism on the other.

Identity formation is a dynamic, continuing
process, just as the process of individuation goes
on till the end of life's journey. Identity crisis
is like a tidal wave; when the upheaval is over,
everything becomes crystal clear, and all unpure
elements are washed away. The motto "ecclesia semper
reformanda" of Reformers during the sixteenth century is highly significant to the identity formation
of the church at all times: It calls for the church
to continue its reformation and spiritual renewal.
Likewise, every Christian believer must always renew
him or herself spiritually in reaching the maturity
of divine perfection in the process of being sancti-
fied.

The danger of secularization is an identity
diffusion or loss of identity in the religious sense.
There is a similar danger in syncretism. For the
same reason, idolatry is condemned in the Bible:
"You shall have no other gods before me."[33] The
danger of the ecumenical movement is the loss of denominational identity which implies a particular
tradition and heritage. The similar danger can be
found in the current emphasis on the ministry of the
laity and the priesthood of all believers, if these
lead to identity diffusion or loss of identity for
both clergy and laity. A mature encounter with secular, other ideologies, or other cultures does not
lead to identity diffusion or loss of identity; on

221

the contrary, it enriches the believer's faith. Likewise, mature partnership and co-operation do not mean
the loss of boundaries. If ecumenism is designed to
promote a religious "melting pot," it is bound to
meet resistence in the principle of differentiation
in human growth.

A brief comment on sexual identity in relation
to the Christian faith is needed. Sexual identity
is believed to be a part of God's creation. In recent discussions on sexual identity, there is a trend
for some theologians and feminists to attack traditional patriarchal overtones in the Bible and the
church, as previously mentioned. There are various
reasons for these attacks but they should be kept in
a proper perspective. It is questionable to propose
a re-writing of the Bible by replacing the masculine
"He" with the feminine "She" in identifying God.
Although the reality of God has been expressed in
human terms and sexually identified as masculine,
God transcends human language and sexuality. It is
out of historical necessity that the Bible has been
in the language and culture of the ancient Middle
East.

Patriarchal expressions are offensive to those
who pay attention to the letter rather than the spirit
of the Scriptures. It is wrong to use the Bible as
a political weapon in justifying egocentricity, just
as it is wrong to use religion as a means of political oppression and exploitation. The root of the
controversy over the language of the Bible is not
the Bible itself; rather it is human egocentricity
and immature perception of divine reality.

Historical facts cannot be changed arbitrarily.
or abolished according to our own desires, although
our interpretations of them may differ from age to
age. When a person has solved identity problems,
the question of patriarchal overtones in the Bible
are transcended. When we solve identity problems,
"there is neither Jew nor Greek, there is neither
slave nor free, there is neither male nor female,
for you are all one in Christ Jesus."[34] When a
person has solved his or her identity problem, he
or she will not brag about sexual identity; When we

222

solve the problem of identity, we are wholeheartedly
committed to significant causes, as pointed out by
Prof. Jerome S. Bruner of Oxford University in his
discussion on identity crisis.[35]

NOTES

1. Lester David, Ted Kennedy: Triumphs and Trage-
    dies (New York: Grossett and Dunlap, 1972), p.
    122. Cp. "Ted Kennedy was undergoing no identity
    crisis in his late twenties." See, James MacGre-
    gor, Edward Kennedy and the Camelot Legacy (New
    York: W. W. Norton & Co., Inc., 1976), p. 71.

2. " A Number Just As Fair," Boston Sunday Globe,
    February 19, 1978, p. A4.

3. Sigmund Freud and William C. Bullitt, Thomas
    Woodrow Wilson: A Psychological Study (Boston:
    Houghton Mifflin Co., 1967), pp. 16-18.

4. "Year Out," Boston Globe, January 1, 1971, p. 1.

5. Erik H. Erikson, Childhood and Society (New York:
    W. W. Norton & Co., Inc., 1963), pp. 261-263.
    See also, Erikson, Identity and the Life Cycle
    (New York: International Universities Press,
    1956).

6. Gail Sheehy, Passages: Predictable Crises of
    Adult Life (New York: E. P. Dutton, 1976), p.
    132.

7. Arnold R. Beisser, "Identity Formation within
    Groups," The Journal of Humanistic Psychology,
    9 (2) (1971), pp. 133-146.

8. Erikson, Identity and the Life Cycle, p. 116.

9. Talcott Parsons, "Youth in the Context of Ameri-
    can Society," Youth: Change and Challenge ed.
    Erik H. Erikson (New York: Basic Books, 1963),
    pp. 115 f. See also, Kenneth Keniston, The Un-
    committed (New York: Harcourt, Brace and World,

1965), pp. 239-240.

10. Wilson Allen, William James: A Biography (New York: Simon and Schuster, 1969), pp. 322-364.

11. Juhani Hirvas, Identity and Mental Illness (Helsinki: Westermarck Society, 1966), pp. 72-74.

12. Ralph N. Harris, "The Meaning of Personal Identity," The American Journal of Psychoanalysis, 31 (1971), pp. 39-47.

13. Carl R. Rogers, On Becoming a Person (Boston: Houghton Mifflin Co., 1961), pp. 231-236.

14. Kenneth Soddy, ed., Identity: Mental Health and Value System (London: Tavistock Publications, 1961), p. 3.

15. Erikson, Childhood and Society, pp. 285-325.

16. Ibid.

17. Oscar Handlin, The Uprooted (Boston: Little, Brown & Co., 1951); T. C. Wheeler, The Immigrant Experiences (New York: The Dial Press, 1971).

18. Handlin, The Uprooted, p. 241.

19. E. M. Bruner, "Urbanization and Ethnic Identity in North Sumatra," American Anthropologists, 63 (1961), pp. 508-521.

20. Pitirim A. Sorokin, The Crisis of Our Time: The Social and Cultural Outlook (New York: E. P. Dutton, 1941, 1957),

21. Oswald Spengler, The Decline of the West tr.by C. F. Atkinson (New York: Alfred A. Knopf, Inc., 1926).

22. Agnes N. O'Connell, "The Relationship between Life Style and Identity Synthesis and Resynthesis in Traditional, Neotraditional, and Non-

224

traditional Women," Journal of Personality, 44
(1976), pp. 675-688.

23. Erikson, Childhood and Society, p. 229.

24. Cp. Helen's religious identity. See, Charles
   W. Stewart, Adolescent Religion: A Developmental
   Study of the Religion of Youth (Nashville: Ab-
   ingdon Press, 1967), pp. 32-57.

25. Paul Tournier, Learn to Grow Old (New York:
   Harper & Row, 1971), p. 209.

26. Choan-seng Song and Gayraud Wilmore, Asians and
   Blacks: Theological Challenges (Bangkok, Thai-
   land: East Asia Christian Conference, 1972),
   pp. 1-16, 34-48.

27. Ibid.

28. Stanley J. Smartha, "Areas of Concern in Asian
   Theology," in African and Asian Contributions to
   Contemporary Theology ed. by John Mbiti (Bossey,
   Switzerland: W. C. C. Ecumencal Institute, 1977),
   p. 20.

29. Lk. 4:18-19, Gal. 5:1. Song and Wilmore, Asians
   and Blacks, pp. 50-63. Also, James H. Cone,
   Black Theology and Black Power (New York: Seabury Press, 1969); Cone, A Black Theology of
   Liberation (Philadelphia: J. B. Lippincott Co.,
   1970).

30. John Mbiti, "Some Current Concern of African
   Theology," African and Asian Contributions to
   Contemporary Theology, p. 12.

31. Acts 9:1-23, 13:1-12.

32. Gen. 32:28.

33. Ex. 20:3.

34. Gal. 3:28.

35. Jerome S. Bruner, On Knowing (Cambridge, MA:
   Harvard University Press, 1962), p. 164.

CHAPTER

VII

CREATIVITY AND CARE

Just as autonomy and identity are interrelated, identity and creativity are also interrelated. They are like closely linked chains or tightly twisted strands that form the mature personality. If we have one, we are likely to have the other, depending on our degree of maturity.

Behind our quest for personal identity is our quest for identity as a species. Our scientific name is Homo sapiens, Latin words meaning "man as a thinking creature as distinguished from other organisms."[1] People used to have a narcissistic self-image: We thought of ourselves as the crown of all creation and the center of the universe. But that idea has been dethroned by scientific discoveries, and rapidly advancing brain research has forcefully challenged the traditional concept of free will. Modern computers are said to be so advanced that they surpass human brains in memory, speed of calculation, and efficiency. We can no longer be proud of being the only thinking animal. Then, "what is the unique element in us that makes us superior to the computer we make?" "What makes us uniquely human?" The key word is "creativity," as pointed out by George J. Seidel in his discussion on the crisis of creativity.[2]

We are not merely mammals, like other mammals distinguished by self-regulating body temperature, hair, and milk-producing mammae. Furthermore, we are not merely primates, like monkeys and apes, which breathe, eat, digest, grow old and die. We have the intelligence to create: the ability to learn from experience and solve new problems. Our brain is not just larger than the gorilla. Through a combination of intelligence and social interaction, we can develop speech to share knowledge, feelings, and insight from

227

one generation to the next. Even the most primitive
men and women had the creativity to make tools to
dig, cut, and protect themselves. By using creativity, they advanced from Stone Age by staying in one
place and growing plants and animals for food and
clothing. They created jars, bowls, and other pot-
tery. By using creativity, they learned to use first
the softer metals, such as copper, and then, in the
iron age the harder metals. They made, not only
tools and weapons, but also ornaments and vases that
are still admired for their beauty. By using creativity, modern men and women have invented machines
for spinning thread (James Hargreaves and Richard
Arkwright, England, about 1765), the power loom (Edmund Cartwright, England, about 1785), the steam
boat (Robert Fulton, U.S.A., about 1807), the cotton
gin (Eli Whitney, U.S.A., 1793), the reaper (Cyrus
Hall McCormick, U.S.A., 1831), the electric telegraph
(Alexander Graham Bell, U.S.A., 1876), the incandes-
cent lamp (Thomas A. Edison, U.S.A., 1879), etc., etc.

Is human creativity expressed only in scientific and technological inventions? What is creativity? What are the conditions which make a person
creative? What are the dynamics of the creative process? How is human creativity related to religious
experience? These are the major questions in our
reflection on the nature of creativity. In relation
to maturity, we also ask "Is a mature person creative? Is a creative person mature? Is creativity
in conflict with maturity? Does creativity imply
care as well? Can we just create without care?"

1. Creativity and Maturity

Human creativity is manifested in every aspect
of life. Whenever human creativity is manifested,
there is change, improvement, and progress. About
a decade ago, a news reporter depicted the American
ethos in three words--"Change is king."[3] During the
past ten years, things have indeed changed. A middle age professional witnessed numberous changes in
his immediate environment saying, "The building remains the same, but it has been remodeled and turned

228

into condominiums. Those living in it have been changed; the lights, walls, and the mailbox have been changed. The landscape of nearby Washington Square remains the same, but its stores have been greatly changed; a pharmacy was changed into an ice-cream parlor, an A & P was changed into a Chinese restaurant, and a Chinese restaurant was changed into a Jewish restaurant. A new bank and a new traveling agency have been opened, and they are flourishing. . . . A bunch of old stores remain the same, but their interior decorations and details have been changed." In every change, there is a manifestation of human creativity to improve conditions. Improvement can be economic, esthetic, social, or spiritual.

Life is creative. A few years ago, I received a hand-made birthday card from my niece. It was made of an ordinary piece of paper with a flower on it. The flower stem and leaves were drawn with a green pen, but the flower itself was a folded piece of blue paper, which had wrapped a piece of chocolate. Apparently she ate the chocolate, and instead of throwing the cup-shaped, bud-like paper away, she pasted it at the end of the flower stem she drew, and wrote "Congratulations. Happy Birthday." This manifested her creativity as a small girl. Other children may express their creativity in making a snow Santa Claus in the garden in the winter and a sand castle by the seashore in the summer. In each stage of life, creativity is manifested differently.

In school, children learn English, biology, social science, mathematics, etc., acquiring knowledge for their future lives as citizens. They are encouraged to use their intelligence and imagination creatively to solve problems, co-operatively and by themselves. Furthermore, they are encouraged to express their creativity by writing stories, essays, plays, or in the making of artifacts such as chair, stool, and others. As they grow older, their creativity will be expressed in developing friends or creating more sophisticated projects inspired by science fiction, pep talks, or pure fantasy. In young adulthood, each person imaginatively seeks a career by successive experiments with creative potentialities, and by checking the opportunities available. Another area of creative expression is the establishment of a home. New born babies are wonderful creations that express the parents' creativity not only in the creation of another human beings, but also in the care of the coming new generation.

After young adulthood comes mature adulthood. Interestingly, middle age is often called the "creative years." According to a study done by Harvey Lehman, the peak of outstanding creative work comes in the half-decade between the ages of 30 and 35, followed by another half-decade between 35 and 40, and thereafter, a decline in almost all fields except leadership in politics, diplomacy, finance, and the church, where the peak often occurs much later.[4] So, human creativity is manifested in the process of maturation and corresponds to it. This can also be seen in Wayne Dennis' study, mentioned in our discussion on middle adulthood.[5]

Creativity is present to some degree in every person, and is manifested in a variety of creations and products. The normal person has it, and the handicapped person has it. One of my former students was impressed by exquisite embroidery made by a physically handicapped and slightly retarded teenage girl, who, after a long period of despondence, was inspired by encouragement from the right person at the right time. Each person's identity is largely shaped by the creative works he or she has done. Each creative act enhances self-understanding. Each creative work adds an "element of self-discovery"; and, through creative work, we find our identity. American composer Aron Copland said "I must create in order to know myself, and since self-knowledge is a never-ending search, each new work is only a part-answer to the question 'Who am I' and brings with it the need to go on to other and different" creative works.[6] People find personal identity through creative work, which gives shape to selfhood through the meanings their products convey to them. The tree is known by its fruits, and people are known by their creative works. Creativity is very much related to identity, because it is tied to the ego-ideal. Find-

ing herself able to create something beautiful and
exquisite, this physically handicapped and slightly
retarded teenage girl was able to smile and live a
happier life because her self-image had been changed.

Although creativity is present in every person
as a potential, it is not equally distributed among
all people, nor is every creative expression equally
significant and of equal value. Manifestation of
creativity is part of the growing process, and there
are different levels of maturity in different creative acts. A creative act may not always be mature.
Some years ago, a youngman in California attracted
the attention of the mass media by building a nest
on a tree and living there for as long as he could.
This could be regarded as an expression of his creativity, but could hardly be called "mature," because
he did not contribute something highly significant
and valuable to the common good. What he did was
not profound in terms of truth, goodness, and beauty:
it was only unconventional. Consequently, some people might call him a crazy man, who should be institutionalized. The principle of transcendence is also
operative in creativity, and in this case, it is
negative in terms of value.

Mature creativity is a response not only to
internal but also to external reality. Any artist
can create, but the mature artist brings the relevant messages to the people, and thus, has a great
impact on society, shaping the culture and future
direction of the world. What the mature artist
creates will not pass away like a quickly rising
mushroom in the rainy season. The messages power-
fully conveyed to us through music, pictures, or
writing are not swept away by tidal waves of human
faddishness. They capture our minds, hearts, and
souls forever and we honor them as timeless classics,
because they speak to all people at all times. The
creation of an immature artist can only satisfy our
needs momentarily and passes into oblivion without
notice. The difference between mature and immature
creativity lies in the artist's perception of reality. The mature artist perceives more accurately
and profoundly what truly is within and without the
self, and is less dominated by narcissistic fantasy.

In this way, mature creativity is tied to a mature perception of reality.

The creation of another human being by a loving couple is the most beautiful thing in the world, and the most precious expression of human creativity. At the same time, it is the most awesome and responsible act any human being can undertake. Unfortunately, children are often neglected, beaten, tortured, and even killed by their parents. Recently a couple tried to exchange their baby for a car. Babies have been found in trash bags, and thrown away like a garbage. Not every creation of another human being is a mature act. Mature creativity is characterized by the care of the creation. Care and creativity are inseparable, just as identity and ego-ideal are inseparable.

Furthermore, the relationship between the creator and the creation is not independent, but interdependent. As soon as we create something, we are affected by it in one way or another. We may create something, and throw it away immediately afterward. We are not as independent as we think we are. In discussing "generativity vs. stagnation" of the mature stage in middle age, Erikson says "Mature man needs to be needed, and maturity needs guidance as well as encouragement from what has been produced and must be taken care of."[7] Maturity is interdependence.

2. The Creative Person

Creativity can be understood in two ways: generally, and specifically among creative geniuses. In a broad sense, everybody is endowed with a certain amount of creativity, expressed by solving problems in daily life. In the interpersonal relationships of day-to-day life, the creative person puts him or herself in others' shoes: creativity leads to empathy. And empathy can help avoid divorce, broken relationships, or perhaps even riots and wars. But, normally, creativity refers to a very special act. It refers to an exceptional group of very talented,

imaginative, and inventive people. Who are they?
How are they unique? What characteristics do they
manifest?

The creative person often demonstrates an adventurous "divine discontent," and is always trying
to reach out for something new, unexplored, and untrodden. There are two diametrically opposed trends
in human life: centrifugal and centripetal; the former is a reaching out, the latter a shrinking back.
The two symbolize life and death, depending on the
situation. The creative person is full of vitality,
resiliency, and versatility. Although the desire
to create something new, unconventional, and unique
is inherent in every person, the creative genius is
particularly so inclined. Each creative person is
an adventurous Columbus, well-equipped for adventure
in thinking, doing, and acting. Specialized fields
become so confining and stagnated that new pastures
are needed to satisfy the adventurous spirit. The
creative person has the courage, determination, and
guts to move out of a familiar discipline and field
and into an unfamiliar, challenging one. This is
one of the characteristics of creative persons.[8]

Interdisciplinary interests are "a prerequisite
for path-breaking intellectual activity." This is
confirmed in a study done by Robert E. Maizell of
the American Institute of Physics.[9] Highly creative
scientists are different from others in "information-
gathering behavior." In general, creative scientists
come from homes where the habit of reading and owing
books is highly valued. Their interests and academic
pursuits are not confined to their fields, but extend
to other sciences. Such adventurous spirits have
made them more resourceful and versatile. They spend
more time than others reading published materials
such as journals and monographs. Creativity is a
dynamic source of power which drives talented people
to explore new and deeper knowledge and move on with
a creative vision. Thus, "a creative scholar provides a flow of new ideas, drawing upon deep resources
of accumulated knowledge."[10]

The creative person has an inquiring mind which
hungers for new knowledge and explores new frontiers

in other fields for a cross-fertilization of ideas,
For instance, the existentialist philosopher Karl
Jasper was a physician; likewise, the Harvard philosopher and psychologist William James was a physician; statesman-scientist Benjamin Franklin was
a printer; Mendel, who founded the science of genet-
ics, was an Austrian monk; Joseph Priestly, who
discovered oxygen, was a British clergyman; Sir
Winston Churchill, the British Prime Minister, won
the Nobel prize in literature. Some journalists
become bankers via public relations. Others become
politicians or publishers. Instead of remaining
journalists, they explore related fields and allow
their adventurous spirit its full play. Each new
adventure into other fields brings about a cross-
fertilization of ideas and new insight.

In a study of creative people, Prof. D. W. Mac-
Kinnon of the University of California at Berkeley
found that highly creative architects felt freer
to describe themselves frankly, critically, and in
unusual ways than those considered to be relatively
uncreative.[11] Highly creative people have the courage to be themselves in the fullest sense, and feel
less threatened by social pressures. Highly creative architects stressed their inventiveness, independence, individuality, determination, enthusiasm,
and industry. Ninety eight per cent of them said
that they were imaginative, and 92% said that they
were active. On the other hand, less creative architects tended to stress their good character, virtue,
and sympathetic concern for others. This indicates
that highly creative people are not so socially and
conventionally minded. Originality means more to
them; it symbolizes inner freedom.

Dr. Frank Barron of Berkeley studied a group
of most creative writers, and a group of successful
and productive writers, who were not the most creative, and compared the two groups. The most creative group scored lower on measures of socialization,
self-control, desire to make a good impression, and
achievement via conformity. The less creative group
was more concerned with popularity, "doing the right
thing," dependability, responsibility, and other
moral and conservative values.[13] The creative per-

son is not as concerned with the standards, expectations, and opinions of others. Similarly, a study of United States Merit Scholars showed that creative students scored lower on measures of socialization and superego strength. More creative students expressed preferences for unconventional occupations and less rigid adherences to convention.[14] However, such creative unconventionality should not be regarded as anti-social. It comes from a better grasp of reality and truth, which captures the whole being of the creative person. But not every unconventional person is creative and devoted.

Sometimes, the creative person appears to be egocentric and arrogant, but deep down one can trace these traits to total devotion and concentration of energy on creative work. For these reasons, the creative person may be looked upon as a rebel, like Socrates who was sentenced to drink hemlock, or Jesus of Nazareth who was crucified, and other countless reformers or inventors who met similar fates. In fact, they were not socially irresponsible, as they were condemned to be. They were guided by values and standards they set for themselves, according to their better grasp of reality and truth; they were independent and original thinkers; they were self-confident and self-sufficient in many ways.

The creative person has less of a need for external stimulation or encouragement from others, like Edison or Einstein. But no one can live in a total isolation, and the creative genius is no exception. Creative scientists in the past have had to master the knowledge and methods available to them in order to break into new and original fields. One can assume that the creative scientist must be reasonably learned, and that his or her creative originality is likely to be manifested predominantly within the framework of the discipline.[15] Although the creative person has less of a need for external stimulation, he or she is not cut off from external reality, or independent from the framework of their discipline. The highly creative person may join fewer organizations and social groups than less creative contemporaries, but he or she is not isolated or friendless.

We meet creative but unconventional people now and then. They wear shabby clothes or unmatched socks: They are distinguished by their propensity for breaking rules. Their unconventionality may be interpreted as a sign of weak superego control. But, as psychologists R. B. Cattell and J. E. Drevdahl have shown, the scientists selected for their eminence in biology, physics, and psychology whom they studied, scored significantly higher on a measure of compulsive superego or will-control, although they indicated less identification with the standards of the group.[16] Such independence may be attributable to the precocity of ego development noted by Freud and others.

By the same token we hear the story of the so-called "absent-minded professor" whose mind is too devoted to the creative work at hand to remember other things. Albert Einstein was "casual of dress, unconventional of habit, with the happy-go-lucky absentmindedness of a man concentrating on other things which he was to retain all his life." He used to forget his key, and had to wake up his landlady in the middle of the night shouting, "It's Einstein-- I've forgotten my key again."[17] But on the whole, there is little evidence among scholars in the exact sciences showing the great lack of socialization and unconventional Bohemianism, or the impulsiveness and emotionality which are frequently seen among artistically creative persons.

A creative person is characterized by an unusual sensitivity in the area of specialization and concentration. A mentally ill person is also sensitive, but there is a qualitative difference between the two. Creative sensitivity is reality-oriented and derives from strength, whereas neurotic sensitivity is fantasy-oriented and derives from weakness. One is other-directed curiosity, the other inner-directed anxiety.

However, creative sensitivity may lead to anxiety, and is often accompanied by creative anxiety. Creative persons are more open to inner experience and external reality than less creative persons, and

236

are more perceptive than judgmental. Such openness
inevitably makes them feel overwhelmed by their extraordinary amount of sensory-perceptual or imagi-
nary inputs, confused and anxious. Generally, the
creative person scores higher on anxiety measures
than less creative peers. However, he or she often
has mechanisms for controlling anxieties.

The "radar" of creative people is larger and
more efficient in receiving messages from the environment. They are capable of responding to multiple
and incidental cues which are unnoticed by ordinary
people. They often have sensitive temperaments
which may make others uncomfortable. To have such
temperaments is energy consuming. Perhaps it was
due to such a sensitive temperament that Darwin
avoided social evenings spent in animated conversation, lest he should be exhausted the next day.

Why is the creative person more sensitive and
perceptive? Why is the creative person more insightful? Why is the creative person more intuitive to
hidden realities? It is difficult to give an exact
answer to these questions, but we can hypothesize
that it has something to do with the structure and
content of the creative mind. It seems to me that
the creative mind is open (absence of fixed pre-
conception), integrated (presence of well organized
ideas and information), and differentiated (accumulation of substantial ideas and information). Openness is a liberal attitude. It implies the availability of better ideas in the future, and is tied
to the principle of transcendence in human development. The creative person does not just memorize
facts and ideas, but sorts out interrelationships,
similarities, and differences, organizing them for
future reference. Such efforts develop the fluency
of ideas and association of facts, and, consequently,
increase sensitivity to messages from the environment. The creative person always sees something new
in the world.

Creative sensitivity may be inborn, because
it has a childlike quality to it, and is sometimes
called "second naivete" or "innocence of perception."

237

Yet it has wisdom: it has the "spark of life." It
can also be developed. "The broader the scientist's
experience, and the more extensive his stock of
knowledge, the greater the possibility of a real
break through," said Dr. A. Roe.[18] The "storage" of
knowledge and experience may contribute to creative
sensitivity.

This "storage" is diversified, extensive, and
integrated. The creative person is not only sensitive but also imaginative, intuitive, and intelligent. He or she has multiple perspectives as well
as an acute sense of form and pattern-making ability.
In describing the creative person, some writers
stress "divergent-thinking abilities," while others
emphasize "convergent-thinking abilities." But, in
fact, the creative person often has both. "Among
the mechanisms that aid creative thinkers in the
sciences and the arts is a developed sense of gestalt
perception," said Dr. Howard Gardner.[19] Human perception is a process which involves divergence as
well as convergence; the first half of expectation,
attention, and selection of the sensory input in
perception is divergent, while the second half of
"trial-and-check" and formation of perceptual set
is convergent. Human perception is differentiated
as well as integrated. A further discussion of perception appears in the next chapter.

Many people are afraid of problems, complexity,
and incompleteness. But creative people are not.
Generally, the uncreative individuals prefer easy answers and clear-cut simplicity. In psychological
tests they select orderly cards most of the time,
whereas creative individuals express a clear preference for chaotic cards and show an ability to tolerate the tension and anxiety of creating a new order
out of chaos. Existential psychologist Rollo May
observed that his mentor, Paul Tillich, one of the
most creative theologians of this century, loved uncertainty and that there was a significant correlation between his creativity and his doubts.[20] This
can also be found in Tillich's autobiography On the
Boundary, which symbolically indicates characteristics of his life. Ambiguity is not a difficult
problem for creative individuals. They can tolerate

238

it because they have the ego-strength to cope with it, knowing that it is a part of creative life. "To state the matter more positively, ego-strength requires a flexible repression-mechanism, so that the person may be said to be optimally open to experience, though capable of excluding phenomena that cannot be assimilated to the structure of the self," remarked Dr. Frank Barron.[21]

The limits of human creativity are unfathomable and unknown. As soon as one goal is achieved, another dawns, and new and vaster horizons appear in the creative mind, prompting it move toward further creative endeavors.

The creative person is also characterized by intensive motivation, manifested in a dedication, passionate participation and involvement, and unusual concentration. If there is any detachment from the world, it is a withdrawal before further involvement and active participation. Even in the later years of life, the creative person manifests a quality of "deathless childhood vitality." Creative individuals lose themselves in what they do. This passionate desire to lose oneself in a larger whole can be traced to the symbiotic stage in which the child begins life unable to differentiate self from mother.[22] Such a regression is at the service of the ego. It is often characteristic in the creation of arts. It is paradoxical that one loses oneself in the creation, but at the same time in losing oneself one's identity is found.

Perhaps the story of Chief Carpenter Chuang can help us grasp this aspect of creativity. He was wellknown for carving wood in making a stand for musical instruments which was miraculously exquisite. The Prince of Lu, astonished at Chuang's artistic skill, summoned him to court and asked him, "What magic have you used in completing your artistic masterpiece?" Chuang answered, "No magic, your Majesty, and yet there was something. When I was about to make a stand, I guarded myself against dimunition of energy. First, I reduced all distractions in such a way that I was able to make my mind absolutely quiescent. Being in this condition for three days,

I became oblivious of any reward to be gained. For five years, I became oblivious of my four limbs and my physical frame. Then, with no thought of the court in my mind, my thought became concentrated, and my skill superb, and all distractive elements from the external environment gone. Then I entered some mountain forests and searched for a suitable tree which contained the form required. I saw the stand in my mind's eyes, and then set to work on it. Beyond that there was nothing. I brought my innate capacity into working relations with that piece of wood. What was suspected to be miraculous or super-natural in my work was due solely to this devotion." Passionate interest and devotion tap the reservoir of human creativity.

Sometimes we are amazed by the questions children ask, because they have new ways of looking at the things around them. They show originality in their questioning and ingenuity in their play, but they do not manifest the dedication of mature crea-tive adults. Children give up very quickly and easily; they show little persistence and forget their questions soon. Children may be curious, but they do not have the passionate love for truth which Goethe considered the first and last task required of genius. They are forgetful, but not "self-forget-ful" in the way creative artists and scientists im-merse themselves in what they do. The creative per-son passionately loves truth and is dedicated to it. Deep interests and steady concentration on the task at hand uplift mental powers to the level of crea-tive imagination, and prolonged absorption in a theme eventually stimulates the imagination and brings it to a creative point. Edison had a habit of devoting himself to his inventive projects for hours and days at a time with little food or sleep.

Such absorption gives the genius the power to create. But it alienates the genius from others so much that he or she appears extremely eccentric. The genius has little energy left for others. The crea-tive genius prefers solitude in order to prevent dis-traction by others. And they have other odd habits, because their creativity demands total immersion in their subject matter.[23] The creative person allows

the distinction between the subject and the object
to disappear during the act of total "immersion,"
which we find in mystical experiences or in the experience of falling in love with someone. Creativity
works best when reason and passion are integrated.
The title of Silvano Arieti's recent book <u>Creativity</u>:
<u>The Magic Synthesis</u> is indicative of this point.[24] The
creative person is able to reconcile the rational
with the irrational, and to integrate passion with
reason.

3. The Creative Condition

So far, we have focused our attention on the
characteristics of the creative person. Now, we
turn to the creative condition and ask, "What social
conditions enhance our creativity, and what inhibits
our creativity? Under what conditions can we expect
to be more creative? What makes a person stagnated?"
In our attempt to asnwer these questions, we will
no doubt come back to the creative person because
external social reality has a great impact on the
person who lives in it. Likewise, we will refer to
the creative process.

Creativity is actualized in a social context
and in the interactions between the individual and
the environment. The creative process has a social
dimension, and creative individuals are influenced
by social forces in the environment. What forces
are more favorable to creativity?

There is likely to be much disagreement concerning the types of situations and social forces
that facilitate creativity and those that inhibit,
because each situation will not be equally conducive
to creativity for each person. However, some common factors deserve our attention:

1. Freedom. There is no future for the creative person in a totalitarian society. The police
state restricts creative thoughts, words, and deeds.
Alfred Bernard Nobel was a creative Swedish inven-

tor who was given a total of 129 patents; the Nobel Prize winners are the most creative in the fields of medicine, physiology, physics, chemistry, literature, and peace. There are more Nobel winners in the free world than in the totalitarian countries. Freedom facilitates creativity.

Freedom for creativity implies a social climate which encourages diversity rather uniformity. It is one which acknowledges the importance of individuality and pluralism in socio-political life. Ideologically, it is oriented to the future, rather than the past. Truth is seen as something to be found and not something which has already been found. Such freedom makes it possible for the creative person to envision a new heaven and a new earth to come, and to safeguard the independence of thought and autonomy of action.

2. Challenge. Creativity can only be realized when there is a need for it. If there are no problems to be solved, the creative mind will be passively dormant. During his long life, Edison received 1,009 patents and worked on at least a thousand other inventions. Why did he do it? Edison once said, "I find what the world needs, then I go ahead and try to invent it." On another occasion he was asked the secret of his success, and replied, "Hard work, based on hard thinking." He continued to work and think hard, because there were problems to solve.

Challenge for creativity may be found in our deprivation. Newton, showered with honors, terminated his creative career in his early forties; but in contrast, Galileo, under house arrest for his challenge of the established thinking of his time, continued his remarkable career into his seventies. Indian Prime Minister J. Nehru wrote his best books in prison. So also did John Bunyan, the 17th century English preacher who wrote Pilgrim's Progress.

Creative challenge may take the form of positive encouragement from parents, teachers, or other significant individuals. This can be found in the personal experiences of those I interviewed. Their

creativity seemed to be awakened by the appropriate
words they heard from teachers, parents, or friends
at the right time. Some illustrative samples have
been given in the second chapter according to various contexts. Many creative scientists have come
from families in which one or both parents engaged
in professional activities and highly valued knowledge and excellence as a way of life according to a
study by Philip H. Abelson.[25]

Something less than complete satisfaction in
childhood may play an important role in the development of a rich inner life and higher motivation toward creative excellence. A proper amount of negative experience or positive encouragement may create
an empty space within, which may appear in terms of
an "inner gap" in need of fulfillment. Such inner
tension may propel creative individuals to concentrate on accomplishing their tasks. For some people, such tension may be brought about by deprivation in childhood, but for others it may be caused
by perfectionistic expectations of parents. Any
creative achievement is a reflection of inner tension in one way or another, and its resolution.
Freudian psychoanalysts like to trace it to various
stages of psychosexual development.[26]

3. Security. The creative person often takes
risks. Behind what seems like a hazardous venture,
we often find supportive parents, teachers, church
groups, friends, or unknown Good Samaritans. These
altruistic people love and support unconditionally.
This kind of love and support provides the creative
person with security and dispels fears of failure.
Edison was an unusual little boy, always observing
and investigating. When he was six years old, his
father found him sitting on a nest of goose eggs,
trying to hatch them. At the age of nine he started
experimenting in a laboratory in his celler. He was
punished for the disasters his experiments caused,
but his mother supported him wholeheartedly.

The parents of creative people often show
their children great respect, allowing them to become independent, free to explore the universe, and
make their own decisions. These children are ex-

pected to act responsibly, and they know that their parents love them deeply. Somehow they are able to develop what Erikson calls a "basic trust" in life, which becomes a source of inner security, allowing them to venture into new creative work. Due to this basic sense of trust fostered in and through the supportive care of parents, creative people go on in spite of rejection later in life. Some creative individuals are regarded as "deviants." In a study of 975 British men of genius, 160 of them were imprisoned one or more times.[27] Highly creative children are often disliked by their teachers.[28] Without a firm sense of security, the creative genius will not be able to stand up under social rejection.

Later in life, such security can be experienced in the acceptance of significant others. In an interview, a Harvard undergraduate said that whenever he felt assured of personal esteem, whenever he felt someone was willing to take a chance on him, his productivity sprang into high gear.[29] Whenever he experienced forced cockiness, he felt his creativity was impaired. Creativity requires that a person be oneself and let down defense mechanisms. Forced cockiness implies a strong ego-defense. Authenticity is important to creativity, and we are most creative when we are true to ourselves. So, creativity needs conditions which foster a sense of security and inner strength.

4. Relaxation. A detailed discussion of physiological characteristics of the creative person is beyond the scope of this book, but we should note that creativity is tied to the production of alpha brain waves which indicate a relaxed state. The creative condition is a physically and mentally relaxed state. This is one of the reasons why so many people today are attracted to TM and other methods of relaxation. Tension shuts the gate to creative energy.

French mathematician and physicist Jules Henri Poincare's experience has been quoted by many writers on creativity. For days, he struggled with a mathematical problem in vain, until one night he drank

244

a cup of black coffee in a relaxed mood. Then the solution came to him quite unexpectedly.[30] Suddenly ideas crowded his mind, colliding, sometimes interlocking, and finally making meaningful combinations. Shortly afterward, a profound insight flashed into his mind as he put his foot on the step of an omnibus on a geological excursion. This may induce us to take public transportation for relaxed moments of creative thinking instead of fighting traffic on our own.

Gestalt psychologist Wolfang Köhler disclosed his own creative experience: "For my own, far less important, new insights always occur when I am particularly inactive, either when taking a warm bath in the morning or, a bit later, when I am shaving-- in both situations my eagerness to do mental work is exceedingly small."[31] A well-known physicist in Scotland once told Köhler that this kind of thing was generally recognized by the physicist's colleagues in Britain. "We often talk about three B's" he said, "the Bus, the Bath, and the Bed. That's where the great discoveries are made in our science."

But relaxation does not mean laziness. After a period of active problem solving, sudden insights may occur when the mind is relaxed.

5. Heterogeneity. The experience of moving from one culture to another enriches personal living and creative expression. Even the experience of moving from one subculture to another in the same country greatly benefits creativity as so often mentioned in the personal interviews cited earlier. Although too much mobility may also cause mental anguish, anxiety, and disintegration, the right amount of heterogenous experience in different cultures can be of great value to creativity. It will replace boredom and monotony with a certain amount of cultural shock and excitement.

Creativity is highly personal and individual. But it needs stimulation from others. Creative individuals need personal encounters and dialogue with creative peers for mutual enrichment. The peers can be professionals from other fields, or people from different backgrounds. Interdisciplinary dialogue in the academic community is important.

When we look at creative problem solving, we note that centralized networks produce faster solutions to simple problems, but complex problems need decentralized networks. Heterogenous groups may produce solutions of higher quality than homogenous groups. Mixed sex groups are more creative than single sex groups.[32] Groups may lose creativity if they last longer than five years because members become familiar with each other, and get little new stimulation and mutual enrichment. Tenured faculty who stick together for life may be secure, but not creative, unless they are highly creative and need no stimulation from other scholars.

4. The Creative Process

Curiosity is the first stage of the creative process, and the inquisitive mind is its base. In order to be creative, we must learn to ask questions. By asking questions, we develop our minds. Questions stimulate creativity, and are themselves creative acts of intelligence. They open our minds and ignite ideas. The first level of asking questions is asking random and frequent questions. The basic principle behind asking as many questions as possible is differentiation. Ideas grow like cells.

The second level of questioning is integration. Questions to be asked are deeper, more detailed, and highly relational. The task is to analyze each question, see how one question is related to the other, and determine whether there are common factors involved in the questions being raised. This level is a step of further differentiation, but is aimed at the integration of all questions. The first half of this level is dissecting questions into more questions, and the second half is integrating them as much as possible. By integrating them, we may find the dynamic relationships among questions.

246

The third level of questioning is transcendence. Questions are existential, valuational, and specific. Our task at this level is to reflect on the basic goal of life; "What is the most important thing in my life at this time in history, here and now?" In the process of asking such questions, we refer to identity and to concrete living situations, e.g., our needs and social problems. This is an essential part of the creative process, although it may look remote and unrelated. Without asking these questions, we are unlikely to make commitments to what is to be done. By reflecting on the most important thing in life, questions are formulated hierarchically, and the top priority becomes clear. The most creative question transcends other questions in value, urgency, and significance. The success of creative people depends on their asking the right questions at the right time and place.

The second and major stage in the creative process is hard work. It includes preparation, planning, and visualization. This again follows the pattern of differentiation, integration, and transcendence. At this stage, we need not only the left half of our brains, but also the right half. At every level, the creative process involves hard work. The creative process differs from the non-creative process in the exceptional degree of hard work and concentration involved. This may explain why "high anxiety and excitability appear common, but full-blown neurosis is quite rare," among creative individuals.[33] Creative individuals invest unusual energy into what they do and are more anxious than others. Naturally, they are more excited when they succeed, and more worried about failure, in addition to being constitutionally different in their personality structure. They are likely to be less social and talkative, because they invest so much emotion in their work.

The creative process is not limited to the creation of something new and useful. It is also a process of becoming and self-actualization. The creator is a part of the outcome of the process: not only the subject of the process, but also its object.

247

In this process, the subject and object are differentiated and yet integrated. After creating a masterpiece, a creator is a different person. From this point of view, every piece of information one has acquired in childhood, adolescence, and young adulthood is part and parcel of the creative process in mid-life. The creative process is extensive and intensive; the creator is deeply involved. This is why one has to ask existential questions in the beginning.

In psychological literature, "the extension of the self" and "environmental mastery" are used to describe the characteristics of the healthy mature personality.[34] The creative process has the same characteristics; it invovles extensive accumulation of knowledge and mastery of the environment. In the creative process, the mind has to work hard to reach a point of creative imagination. In order to reach the point, we must have the mastery of skills, languages, techniques, and necessary experiences in the field. Creativity is often hampered by too little preparation, too little knowledge, too little information, and too little motivation.

Einstein took notes while sailing on a lake. It was supposed to be a time of relaxation, but it was also a time for his mind to work creatively. He accumulated ideas all the time and kept them for later usage, and his ideas grew constantly. He took notes under street lights while walking on a snowy evening.

Similarly, Whitt N. Schultz of the Creative Education Foundation suggests the term "Idea Banks" in the form of $8\frac{1}{2}$ x 10 inch envelops.[35] Each one is labeled with the subject matter of interest. Make deposit whenever you capture an idea you can draw later whenever you need it. We need to develop a strong curiosity about people, places, and things. We need to be perceptive and think sharply. "Widen your friendships. Read widely, wisely and occasionally pick up books at random on subjects outside your main fields of interest."[36] This extensive search for ideas, knowledge, and information is a differentiative act. It is a conscious effort and labor of the mind.

The third stage in the creative process is concentration, consolidation, and integration. After the general and extensive accumulation of knowledge and brain storming, comes a time to select relevant ideas and focus them on the central problem, stimulating solutions. Checklists can extend our supply of intuitive ideas for problem solution. But check list must have imagination-prodding quality. However, there is no substitute for an active imagination and visualization of solutions. When we come to an impasse, and tension mounts, we must consider the next step.

After a period of persistent and hard work, we need to detach ourselves from the problem for a while, and let our unconscious and subconscious find an appropriate solution. The hard work remains, but can now be done on a subconscious or unconscious level. Human creativity is rooted in the unconscious and subconscious, which remain largely a mystery. We have glimpsed them through hypnosis or dreams. The hard work goes underground, but is still under the control of the ego: a period of incubation. Unlike regression, which leads to serious neurosis or even psychosis, this incubation period is at the service of the ego, just as undercover agents work under the direction and supervision of the Police Department.

Next comes a moment of discovery and intense exhilaration, when we are overjoyed by our new insight. Hard work is now rewarded with a tangible and workable solution to the problem. There is nothing in the world more exciting than discovering the answer to a problem a creative person has worked hard on. We see new meanings, new forms, and a reality not known before. It is a moment of penetration into the problem's secret by the formation of new ideas through interaction and cross-fertilization of old ideas. Creative originality is fully expressed at this moment.

The moment of discovery cannot be planned ac-

cording to a timetable. Funding agencies often do
not receive results at the time proposed. True creativity depends on free association, the flow of ideas
at the unconscious or subconscious level after the
hard work of the conscious. Without freedom, it is
hardly possible to cultivate originality and creative thinking. In this respect, there is an element
of trascendence in the discovery of new insight. As
pointed out by Dr. Gardner Murphy of Karl Menninger
Foundation, "illuminations come when they are ready
to come."[37] They transcend our conscious efforts.
Readiness comes when the inner logic of the mind
matches the outer logic of the environment. The
conscious ego is somewhere between the inner and the
outer. Some people deny that unconscious conflicts
play any role in creative functioning, but others
emphasize the role of the preconscious during the
period of elaboration from which sudden solution or
insight emerges into consciousness.[38]

English philosopher and mathematician Bertrand
Russell wrote that, when he was young, every fresh
piece of serious work seemed beyond his powers. He
was afraid that his work would not come right. Later
he discovered that he needed a period of "subconscious incubation," which could not be hurried. "Having, by a time of very intense concentration, planted
the problem in my subconscious, it would germinate
with blinding clarity, . . . as if in a revelation."[39]

Discovery favors the well-prepared mind. Repeated experiences eventually consolidate into a
structured patterns. A well-practiced musician becomes sensitive to melodies and harmonized patterns
because the musician's mind has been structured to
be sensitive to acoustic stimuli. Long-term accumulation of organized information and skills favors
the sudden appearance of new ideas and insight.
Perspiration and inspiration complement each other,
and it is a mistake to expect inspiration without
perspiration. Inspiration rarely comes unless an
individual has immersed him or herself in a subject,
and has a rich background of knowledge and experience in it.[40]

The fourth stage in the creative process in-

volves the actual implementation of ideas. The new
insight needs to be judged on its practical value.
This evaluation may be deferred in order to stimulate
creative ideas, but is inescapable in the implementation of new ideas. The creative person does not
fear criticism--for every innovation there is a host
of it--but works hard to communicate the new idea
to others, to get it accepted and recognized. Creativity is contagious, and the creative person wants
others to be creative also. The breakthrough must
be verified, implemented, and communicated to others.

As pointed out by historian Arnold Toynbee,
every emergence of a culture implies challenges from
the environment and responses by the "creative minority," who first withdraw from society to work,
then reenter society to implement their creative
ideas and gain acceptance and recognition.[41] Without reentry into society, the creative minority is
never really creative.

Completion of each new product or solution and
acceptance by society may be considered the end of
the creative process. But in fact, each ending begins a new creative process, just as each graduation
commences another stage of life. Each integration
requires further differentiation; each differentiation requires further integration; and each shift of
focus begins a new level of transcendence in the
spiral of life. Life is a continuous creative process, and the end of it is death.

5. Creativity and Religious Experience

As previously mentioned, creativity is tied
to the production of alpha brain waves, associated
with the relaxed state. A person experiencing alpha
waves feels like he or she is floating on air, "in
harmony with the universe" or a force flowing through
the body.[42] This feeling has mystical elements, and
is religiously significant. One of the characteristics of mysticism is passivity and "when the characteristic sort of consciousness once has set in,

the mystic feels as if his own will were in abeyance,
and indeed sometimes as if he were grasped and held
by a superior power," said William James.[43] Mystical states of consciousness "modify the inner life
of the subject between the times of their recur-
rence."[44] Phenomenally speaking, the creative state
of being is mystical, and the mystical state of being is creative. The mystical state expresses the
ideal of the human soul in search of unity and harmony with the universe, the penultimate and the Ultimate. In the Christian faith, salvation means reconciliation with God, with fellow human beings, and
with the whole of creation. In this sense, creativity is manifested in salvation. In traditional
Chinese culture, the ideal state of human consciousness is to be in harmony with Heaven and Earth by
identifying with the Tao. It is in a state of creativity.

     In the Judeo-Christian tradition, God is the
Creator of heaven and earth. Human creativity is
derived from God, and reflects divine Creativity.
Religion inspires art, literature, and music. Furthermore, significant scientific discoveries have
been made by religiously minded laymen or clergy.
Without returning to the bossom of "mother nature"
human creativity is futile: Without returning to the
Creator, human creativity misses its target and lacks
deeper dimensions. Outstanding artistic masterpieces
often contain something of exceptional qualities:
eternal, profound, and deeply religious, although
this something may not be expressed in recognizable
religious symbols. These outstanding masterpieces
symbolically reveals the religious sentiments and
aspirations of the artists, who seek to capture the
soul or spiritual climate of their times. Charles
Darwin did not reject his faith in God; he rejected
Karl Marx's offer to dedicate the first English edition of Das Kaptäl in his honor, for his scientific
contribution to evolutional theory because of Marx's
atheistic orientation.[45] Religion can be a creative
force in the life of the individual and in the civilization of modern life; such religion is a vital
religion, and not dead orthodoxy. Darwin prepared
himself to become a clergyman, but his vital crea-

tivity led him to natural science quite unexpectedly.

Creativity precedes material products; creativity is mental and spiritual. The material world needs to be understood in relation to the Creator Spirit. Creation happens in time and God is active in all its processes, but God is Spirit and Creativity, which transcends all beings in time and processes. God is sovereign Lord of the world which He has made and the work of creation expresses the love and power of God. The Creation story says, "The Spirit of God was moving over the face of the waters."[46] This symbolizes incubation in the creation of God, and all creative works are hatched by the Creator Spirit. This is significant to our understanding of human creativity and reminds us of the "subconscious incubation" in the creative process.

Furthermore, the Spirit is compared to the wind in Jesus' teaching about being born again: "the wind blows where it wills."[47] This reminds us of the unpredictability of creative insight; it often comes when we are relaxed and passive. The moment of discovery is beyond human control and prediction-- it comes like the wind and goes away like the wind. There is an element of transcendence in human creativity. If human creativity comes from the Creator Spirit, which transcends all beings and processes of creation, this element of transcendence is to be expected.

Dr. Paul Tournier is unique in his interpretation of human creativity. In contrast to popular ideas of creativity in the arts and sciences or problem-solving, he sees creativity in the human personality.[48] Psychotherapists tend to do the same. "The creation of the person" is the objective of psychotherapy. Creativity, an element of the "good life," is manifested in psychotherapy. It is "the expression of normal people in the act of actualizing themselves." In Christianity, God's salvation is believed to be a new creation of humanity. Anyone who sincerely believes in Jesus Christ and becomes transformed by Him, is a new creature, a new person, "born again" or "twice born." The God's power is manifested

253

in the transformation of personality available to all who truly repent. His creative activity is continuously operative in the lives of all believers. His creative power is love, which heals the wounds of human personality and resolves all inner conflicts through His acceptance and forgiveness. His love is eternal, and His creative power will continue to work until His purpose is fulfilled. Love is essential in the creation of human personality. There is no personality in isolation, only in interpersonal communion. "God is love" is manifested in interpersonal communion within the dynamism of the Holy Trinity --the Father, the Son, and the Holy Spirit, "One-in-Three," "Three-in-One." "God is love" not only to us, but in Himself. Love is the creative force in the universe.[49]

The opposite of creativity is stagnation. The reason for stagnation is often found in early childhood such as, "in excessive self-love based on a too strenously self-made personality" and "in the lack of some faith, some 'belief' in the species."[50] What blocks our own creativity is not somebody else: It is our egocentricity and excessive self-love. This is significant from the Christian perspective; human egocentricity is sinful. Salvation means liberation from egocentricity, and in this regard salvation liberates creativity. Thus, Christian-life is meant to be creative, and faith taps creativity and lets it flow like a river.

The expression of creativity in the church is spiritual renewal. If conservatism is tied to identity formation, liberalism is associated with creativity. Conservatism seeks to draw lines and close gates according to tradition, whereas liberalism lets one's mind open, acknowledging that there is new truth to be learned and that God continues to work His purpose in the world. Both conservatism and liberalism exist in Roman Catholicism and Protestantism. At the time of the Reformation, Protestantism was an expression of religious creativity renewing the life of the church, which triggered the Counter Reformation in the Roman Catholic Church later. Heresy is a distorted form of creativity; it is new, but not profound. Heresy is analogous to regression

without being at the service of the ego in the creative process. For creativity to be effective in
religious experience, it must be at the service of
eternal truth, which orthodoxy tries to capture and
defend.

Recently, new forms of ministry and worship
have appeared in the church, such as folk singing,
dance, or "becoming fools for Christ" by clowning,
etc.[51] Are they authentic expressions of religious
creativity? Or are they just faddish gimmicks to
attract people like the eye-catching ads?

NOTES

1. William Morris, ed., The American Heritage Dic-
    tionary of the English Language (Boston: Houghton
    Mifflin Co., 1973), p. 631.

2. George J. Seidel, The Crisis of Creativity (Notre
    Dame: Notre Dame University Press, 1966), p. 44.

3. "Year Out," Boston Globe, January 1, 1971, p. 1.

4. Harvey Lehman, Age and Achievement (Princeton,
    N.J.: Princeton University Press, 1953).

5. See, p. 140. Wayne Dennis, "Creative Productiv-
    ity between Ages of 20 and 80 Years," Journal of
    Gerontology, 21 (1) (1966), pp. 1-8.

6. Aron Copland, Music and Imagination (London:
    Oxford University Press, 1952), p. 41.

7. Erik H. Erikson, Childhood and Society (New York:
    W. W. Norton & Co., 1963), p. 267.

8. Richard Kostelanetz, Master Minds: Portraits of
    Contemporary American Artists and Intellectuals
    (New York: Macmillan Co., 1967), p. 5.

9. See, C. Taylor, "Creativity through Instructional
    Media: Universe of Challenges," Instructional
    Media and Creativity (New York: John Wiley and

Sons, 1969), pp. 43-70.

10. J. Douglas Brown, "The Development of Creative Teacher-Scholars," in Creativity and Learning ed. by Jerome Kagan (Boston" Houghton Mifflin Co., 1967), pp. 164-180.

11. Donald W. MacKinnon, "The Study of Creative Person," Creative Learning, pp. 20-35. Also, MacKinnon, "Personality and the Realization of Creative Potential," American Psychologists, 20 (1965), pp. 273-281.

12. Anthony Storr, The Dynamics of Creation (New York: Athenuem, 1972), p. 31.

13. Frank Barron, Creative Person and Creative Process (New York: D. Van Nostrand, 1969).

14. R. C. Richols and J. L. Holland, "Prediction of First Year College Performance of High Aptitude Students," Psychological Monographs,77 (1963), No. 570. Creative science students were found to be more responsible and self-controlled. See, M. B. Parloff and L. Datta, "Personality Characteristics Which Differentiates Creative Male Adolescents and Adults," Personality, 36 (1968), pp. 528-551.

15. M. Gilchrist, The Psychology of Creativity (Melbourne, Australia: Melbourne University Press, 1972), pp. 82-83.

16. R. B. Cattell and J. B. Drevdahl, "A Comparison of the Personality Profile of Eminent Researchers and Administrators and the General Population," British Journal of Psychology, 46 (1955), pp. 456-459.

17. Ronald W. Clark, Einstein: The Life and Time (New York: The World Publishing Co., 1971), p. 29.

18. Anne Roe, "The Psychology of the Scientist," Science, 134 (1961), pp. 456-459.

19. Howard Gardner, *The Arts and Human Development* (New York: John Wiley and Sons, 1973), pp. 317-323.

20. Rollo May, *Paulus* (New York: Harper & Row, 1973), p. 70. See also, Anthony Storr, *The Dynamics of Creation* (New York: Atheneum, 1972), p. 191.

21. Frank Barron, *Creativity and Psychological Health* (New York: D. Van Nostrand, 1963), p. 123.

22. Anthony Storr, *The Dynamics of Creation*, p. 181.

23. Mary Henle, "The Birth and Death of Ideas," *Contemporary Approaches to Creative Thinking* ed. H. E. Gruber et al. (New York: Atherton Press, 1962).

24. Silvano Arieti, *Creativity: The Magic Synthesis* (New York: Basic Books, 1976).

25. Philip H. Abelson, "Relation of Group Activity to Creativity and Learning," *Creativity and Learning*, pp. 191-202.

26. Anthony Storr, *The Dynamics of Creation*, p. 182.

27. Pitirim A. Sorokin, *Altruistic Love* (Boston: Beacon Press, 1950), p. 81.

28. S. J. Parnes, "Education and Creativity," *Creativity* ed. by P.E. Vernon (Baltimore, Md.: Penguin Books, 1970), p. 341.

29. Robert W. White, *Lives in Progress* (New York: Holt, Rinehart and Winston, 1966), p. 66.

30. H. Poincare, "Mathematical Creation," *The Foundation of Science* (New York: Science Press, 1913), pp. 383-394. Also cp., the General Electric Company conducted for its staff of engineers, physicists and chemists a school of creativity and found two major principles--1) physical passivity, which relieved the body from tensions completely, 2) a state of mental alertness, which

was characterized by concentration on the subject without tension. Those who participated
in it were three times as productive as those
who did not. See, Standwood Cobb, The Importance of Creativity (Methuchen, N.J.: The Scare-
crow Press, 1967), p. 95.

31. Wolfang Köhler, The Task of Gestalt Psychology
     (Princeton, N.J.: Princeton University Press,
     1969), pp. 160-163.

32. I. Stein Morris, Stimulating Creativity (2 Vols;
     New York: Academic Press, 1975), II, pp. 7-18.

33. R. B. Cattell and H. J. Butcher, "Creativity
     and Personality," Creativity ed. by P.E. Veron,
     p. 315.

34. Gordon W. Allport, Personality: A Psychological
     Interpretation (New York: Henry Holt & Co., Inc.,
     1937), p. 213. See also, Marie Jahoda, Current
     Concepts of Positive Mental Health (New York:
     Basic Books, 1958), p. 23. In describing mental
     health, Jahoda points out six categories--1) the
     attitudes of an individual toward his or her own
     self, 2) the individual's manner and degree of
     growth, development or self-actualization, 3)
     integration, 4) autonomy, 5) adequacy of an in-
     dividual's perception of reality, and 6) environ-
     mental mastery.

35. Whitt N. Schultz, "How to Use That Wonderful
     Gold Mine between Your Ears--Every Day," Have
     an Affair with Your Mind ed. by Angelo M. Brondi
     (The Creative Education Foundation, Inc., 1974),
     p. 46.

36. Ibid.

37. Gardner Murphy, Human Potentialities (New York:
     Basic Books, 1958), p. 166. Cp. in a conference
     on creative thinking, a participant said, "I
     need time alone if I am going to be creative,"
     "a time to let things gestate." See, Calvin W.
     Taylor and Frank W. Williams, ed., Instructional
     Media and Creativity (New York: John Wiley and

Sons, 1966), pp. 31-46.

38. E. Kris, "On Preconscious Mental Processes," in
Organization and Pathology of Thought ed. by D.
Rappaport (New York: Comumbia University Press,
1951); L. S. Kubie, Neurotic Distortion of the
Creative Process (Lawrence, Kansas: University
of Kansas Press, 1958).

39. Bertrand Russell, Portraits from Memory and Other
Essays (London: Allen and Unwin, 1965), p. 195.

40. Edmund W. Sinnott, "The Creativeness of Life,"
Creativity and Its Cultivation ed. by Harold
H. Anderson (New York: Harper and Brothers, 195'
pp. 12-29. Cp. G.G. Birch, "The Relation of Previous Experiences to Insightful Problem-Solving
Journal of Comparative Psychology, 38 (1945),
pp. 367-383. "The man close to the job is ofter
in the best position to find a better way,"
commented G. A. Price, President of Westinhouse
See, R. P. Crawford, The Technique of Creative
Thinking (New York: Horthorn Books, 1954), p.
219.

41. Arnold Toynbee, The Study of History (London:
Oxford University Press, 1934), II, pp. 18ff.;
III, pp. 248-263, 366-377. Sorokin recognized
the existence of pluralism of values in any
social institution in the creation of new culture. If such pluralism is not preserved in
forming a basis for ideological succession, the
culture will not make the transition from one
basic form to another. Thus, there will be
petrification and the culture will stagnate. See
Pitirim A. Sorokin, The Crisis of Our Age: The
Social and Cultural Outlook (New York: E. P.
Dutton, 1941, 1957), p. 25.

42. E. L. Hoover, "Alpha: The First Step to a New
Level of Reality," Human Behavior, May-June
1972, pp. 8-15.

43. William James, The Varieties of Religious Experience (New York: Longmans, Green & Co., 1928
pp. 381-382.

44. Ibid.

45. Gavin de Beer, Charles Darwin (New York: Double-
    day & Co., Inc., 1964), p. 266.

46. Gen. 1:2.

47. John 3:8.

48. Paul Tournier, A Place for You (New York: Harper
    & Row, 1968), p. 137. Cp. Carl Rogers, On Be-
    coming a Person (Boston: Houghton Mifflin Co.,
    1961), p. 193. Also, Rollo May, The Courage to
    Create (New York: W. W. Norton & Co., 1975),
    p. 40.

49. Jen (human-heartedness) is an important concept
    in Confucianism. It has been translated as hu-
    manity, goodness, love, altruism, etc. To Neo-
    Confucianists, it meant "the character of pro-
    duction and reproduction, consciousness, seeds
    that generate, the will to grow," implying crea-
    tivity. See, Wing-tsit Chan, A Source Book in
    Chinese Philosophy (Princeton, N.J.: Princeton
    University Press, 1963), pp. 523-525.

50. Erikson, Childhood and Society, p. 267.

51. "Becoming Fools for Christ," Time, September 1,
    1980, pp. 52-53.

CHAPTER

VIII

REALITY PERCEPTION

Another important issue in our discussion on maturity and maturation is reality perception. A sign of maturity is accurate perceptions of reality, internal or external. As a clinical psychologist points out, mentally sick patients have distorted perceptions of the world and people around them. They consider all people malevolent. Failure to perceive reality can be detrimental when the issue one confronts is really a matter of life and death. Therefore, it is important for us to differentiate between truth and falsity; we must learn not only how to read, but to read between the lines. In interpersonal relationships, we often misperceive reality, misunderstand other people, and do not understand ourselves. Mistakes in human perception are unavoilable, but the mature person is less likely to make serious mistakes in perceiving reality.

Perception is a subject as wide and old as philosophy; almost all human learning can be related to it, and every aspect of our life is affected by it. Almost all branches of academic research have contributed to our grasp of reality. It is beyond the scope of this chapter to give a summary of perception theories, to say nothing of the detailed treatment of it in philosophy and psychology. We can only briefly analyze the dynamics of human perception and their religious implications in relation to maturity and maturation.

Some behavioral scientists emphasize physiological operations in human perception and interpret perception as sensory mechanisms detected in lab experiments. But in daily life, perception implies cognition, insight, intuition, and knowledge. Perception refers to "any process by which we gain im-

mediate awareness of what is happening outside ourselves."[1] The Middle English "perceiven" comes from
the Latin "percipere" (to seize wholly, see all the
way through). Perception is not just sensory. As
pointed out by Dr. Floyd H. Allport, who has made a
comprehensive study of theories of perception, perception of meaning is indeed a "vital but neglected
aspect."[2] We cannot rule out this vital aspect of
perception from our consideration.

1. Perception and Emotion

Perception is not purely physiological, it is
always accompanied by emotion. Emotion provides
energy and substance for the construction of mental
images of the external world. In every experience,
we do not only record the images of things, persons,
or events, but also the emotional impact they have
on our feelings and mood at the time. Perception is
always accompanied and conditioned by emotion, and
it is inevitably distorted by it.

Moreover, our sensory perception is often limited and distorted itself. We depend on our five
senses to give us signals of danger, safety, friendliness, care, concern, etc. and to take action under
certain circumstances. But our senses are not perfect. As pointed out by philosopher and mathematician Arnold N. Whitehead, "our sense perceptions are
extraordinarily vague and confused modes of experience."[3] The moon on the horizon looks much larger
than it is at its zenith. When we compare two objects of the same gray color, one surrounded by a
white surface and the other by black, we are likely
to find that the gray-on-white object looks darker
than the gray-on-black one.[4] On a cloudy day, the
sky is more flattened in appearance than it is on a
sunny day. In psychological literature on perception, we find the Muller-Lyer illusion, Ponzo illusion, Wundt illusion, etc. which illustrate how our
perception can be easily fooled by illusions.[5]

Human perception is also affected by personal

factors such as emotion. Our court system is based
on the assumption that witnesses are capable of giving accurate evidence. It is generally recognized
that better educated witnesses give more accurate
testimony, but they are also more inclined to fill
in the blanks with subjective inferences. When a
lawyer interviews witnesses before a trial, even a
casual remark from other witnesses may cause one to
adapt his or her perception to that of others.[6] Based
on personal observation, William James said that even
abstract thoughts were more indebted to the thinker's
emotions than usually realized.[7] Emotions have great
impact on perception, and our minds impose "reality"
on the data of the senses. Our perception is largely
shaped by our emotion. Consequently, fantasy often
takes the place of reality. Human emotion, cognition,
and perception are all interrelated, and depend on
each other.[8]

We attach specific emotions to certain objects,
persons, or events. These emotions are related to
our experiences of pain or pleasure, reward or punishment, distress or delight. Through repeated experiences, we learn to associate subjective feelings
with objective events, persons, or things. This
learning is important to our survival. In The Expression of the Emotions in Man and Animals, Charles
Darwin indicated that many of our emotional expressions could be a leftover from ancient times when
such behavior was crucial to human survival. Fear
makes us flee from danger, and anger makes us fight
against enemies.

Perception of meaning and emotion are interrelated. The stronger the emotion, the more meaningful to the perceiver, either positive or negative;
when we perceive something very meaningful, we are
strongly attracted by it emotionally. It draws us
into it and makes us committed to it. When a person
finds a lover, he or she is attracted to the lover;
Seeing is perceiving, and the act of perceiving focuses our emotions. Whatever is focused in human
perception is meaningful. Focusing is the process
of integration; visual or emotional. What is meaningful is valuable, and what is valuable is some-

thing we love.

The intimate relation between perception and
emotion cannot be over-estimated. Invariably, we
experience emotional impact on perception. A frightened bank robber may perceive an ambulance as the
police, and a blind lonely man may perceive the ordinary sympathetic gesture of a female social worker
as a sign of romantic love. A friend may be perceived as an enemy, and an enemy as a friend, when
the friend scorns and the enemy flatters. Our emotional needs make us vulnerable to perceptual distortion. We perceive what we are motivated to see,
and remember what we want to hear.

Words have special meanings, as well as emotional impact for those who hear, read, or speak,
because linguistic symbols carry us back to concrete
experiences and memories of anger, joy, happiness,
or sadness. We hear expressions of highly emotional
nature such as "killing a proposal," "economic war,"
and the like. Normally, these words remind us of
the blood, pain, and cruelty of the worst kind. They
stir strong emotions, and by using the word "killing"
or "war" we are likely to enhance emotional states
to abnormal heights, and manipulate the response of
the hearer or reader. Political propaganda is full
of linguistic manipulation that creates perceptual
distortion, and the key to such distortion is stimulation to emotions. Political propaganda is highly
dangerous, although it is very effective with the
emotionally unstable people.

Meanings are attached to each stimulus we perceive, but the same stimulus does not have the same
meaning at all times. We may find a cup of water
delightful when we are thirsty, but the same cup of
water is likely to be a nuisance if we have to carry
it when our hands are full. Since the same things
does not always have the same meaning to the same
person, it does not have the same emotional impact.
Our perception is dynamic, and our emotion is likewise dynamic. Two people may see the same thing,
but they perceive and respond to it differently.
The perceptual evaluation of the same situation dif-

264

fers from person to person and from time to time.

In brief, our perceptions and emotions are interwoven, and an emotional state is more or less accompanied by bodily changes and sensations.

2. Perceptual Development

We are emotional animals. At birth, infants' expressions are unfocused. The child makes a general response to the change in one's body and the environment. As the child grows and experiences more of the world, he or she begins to differentiate among the emotional states of anger, joy, happiness, etc. The first expression of emotion is general excitement. Then distress and delight develop. Later anger, disgust, fear, and jealousy develop from distress. Likewise, affection for adults, then affection for children develops from delight.[9]

Our emotions and cognition are involved in perceptual development, which is characterized by increasing differentiation. The more emotions we experience, the more we learn to modify and verify our responses to perception. The more we learn, the more we are capable of making the right responses and interpretations of meanings for us. At first, the child may be interested in everything and afraid of nothing, but gradually he or she begins to know what to fear and what not. The child develops the emotion of fear and becomes apprehensive. Emotional development is generally accompanied by cognitive development. Gradually, the child begins to use his or her intellectual power, reflecting on past experiences and responses to perception.

Perceptual development is based on physical growth. The world appears different as we grow from infancy to adulthood, because of differences in our physical structure and sensory system--the skin surface of a baby is much smaller than that of an adult, the locus of touch on the baby is uncertain due to its rapid growth, and the localization of precise

265

sound sources is also uncertain due to the rapid
growth changes of distance between the ears. The
lens of adults' eyes change shape to allow precise
focusing at different distances so as to create
clear pictures, but the lens of infants' eyes do
not; the infant's eyes are somewhat shorter or shal-
lower than adult's eyes; the size perception mechanism is subject to growth change, and creates differences between the child's size perception and
the adult's size perception. The child has difficulty perceiving size accurately and absolute size
information, but the adult does not. But as the
child gets older, the accuracy of the child's perception gets better, and information from the senses
is gradually differentiated from the immediate sensory experiences.[10]

Perceptual development primarily refers to the
increase of differentiative ability. The infant's
world is undifferentiated. By the fifth month or so,
the child learns to make distinctions between real
heads and artificial dummies. The order of distin-
guishing the nature of things becomes clearer and
more differentiated as the child grows older. As
pointed out by perception theorists James and Eleanor Gibson, "perceptual learning leads to increased
specificity or differentiation of the perceptual
act, i.e., the individual becomes more sensitive to
the variables of the stimulus array."[11] The more
we develop perceptually, the more we can discern distinctive features. Perceptual learning consists of
sharpening and differentiating the perceptual acts.
It is comparable to the process of refining and putting a new cutting edge on already existing responses. The perceptually undeveloped style is undifferentiated and totalistic, inarticulate and global.

How does the process of differentiation, distinction, or discernment develop? Developmental
psychologists have been greatly concerned with this.
Recent trends discredit the view that the infant's
visual field is a formless blur or confusion and
stress the fact that the infant sees the world with
the limited means at his or her command. The infant's visual system has the capacity to distinguish

266

figures from background, but not to distinguish the identity of different features or patterns. These innate capacities and tendencies become sources for perceptual maturation and development. The following studies illustrate some changes in perceptual development among children.

A study by child psychologists R. G. Suchman and R. Trasbasso showed that children up to four years of age preferred to match slides on the basis of color, whereas older children chose to match on the basis of form.[12] The change from color to form preference is accompanied by changes in other spheres of cognitive development. Children who preferred form tended to have higher mental test scores, and performed better on a variety of classification and concept-formation tasks than children who preferred color. This was particularly true for American and European children. The conversion from color to form preference generally happens between 4 and 5 years of age. In other cultures, form preference may not always occur.

A study conducted with children and adolescents ranging from 6 to 22 years of age--roughly from the first grade through college--presented subjects with simple dot patterns which could be organized in one way or more ways. The study attempted to find whether principles of visual organization changed with age. Continuity of patterns increased in efficiency up to about 14 years of age, then dropped off. Similarity and proximity steadily increased in efficiency with age, and there was a gradual shift from a horizontal emphasis in visual organization to a vertical emphasis, i.e., a shift from seeing equally spaced dot patterns as rows to seeing them as columns. How these changes take place needs further investigation.[13]

The characteristics of young children's perception are summarized by Eleanor J. Gibson and her associate as: 1) "stuck"--nontransformable, 2) "autistic"--subject to the influence of affect, 3) "diffuse" in organization, 4) "dynamic"--being closely related to action, 5) concrete rather than abstract,

6) "egocentric"--having a central reference to the distractability, 8) organized around a minimal number of cues.[14]

Because the young child is stuck with what he or she sees, it is easy for him or her to become a victim of camouflage. The child below the age of 10 finds it difficult to break down complex geometrical figures into components. The child of three, for example, cannot reconstruct a picture from its parts or complete it from partial cues.[15] As the age increases, the ability to recognize incomplete pictures also increases. Although children under 6 have great difficulty recognizing familiar dotted outlines and figures as wholes, their ability to maintain the integrity of an outline increases steadily. There is less formulation of perceptual representations in early childhood because of the child's inability to reconstruct a whole from parts of a picture.

Children between 5 and 8 years of age perceive more autistically than older children.[16] They organize the figure-ground compound stimulus so that the rewarded stimulus becomes figure in reward-neutral and reward-punishment situations, and the neutral stimulus becomes figure in punishment-neutral situations. In general, they tend visually organize with the rewarded stimulus as figure and the punished stimulus as ground. They organize according to the pleasure principle, whereas adults organize on reality principle.

Children are unable to view the world from perspectives other than their own. When an identical toy landscape is rotated 90 degrees away from its original axis, a six-year-old child has great difficulty in matching the original landscape to the rotated landscape, because the child considers himself or herself to be the center of all coordinating systems that constitute the perceptual field. The child cannot have other perspectives.[17] In contrast, adults are more capable of seeing things from other people's perspectives. Emotionally, they are capable of experiencing empathy.

268

As noted previously, all aspects of human development are interwoven and none can be treated as an entity itself. Perception is tied to the senses, and its development is related to physical growth and cognitive development. Young children's perception is diffuse in organization and closely related to action. It is concrete, unsteady and organized around a minimal number of cues. Infants (10 to 11 months old) begin to link their perceptions of objects with their actions in an effort to find the significance by constantly dropping, throwing, kicking, or floating them on water. The child's perceptual development and memories of particular objects are closely related. Striking features of similar objects schematize into categories with names as verbalization increases. Children learn to differentiate aspects of objects and classify them into categories. Children aged 4 to 5 tend to classify idiosyncratically based on nonessential and incidental similarities. Children 5 to 6 years of age pay relatively more attention to single identifying cues when viewing miniature objects. But older children (up to 8 or 9 years of age) classify them according to function and usage, and only after that, by abstract generalization. Older children are more concerned with principal characteristics.[18]

Perceptual development is related not only to our autonomy but also to our independence, because our perceptual discrimination is affectively compounded at the very beginning of infancy.[19] With increasing age, our autism gradually lessens, and our realistic perceptions improve. From middle and late childhood to adolescence, our patterns of relating to our environment change significantly through perceptual development. As pointed out by H. A. Witkin and others, "Children between eight and ten years of age perceive an item very largely in terms of surrounding context; between ten and thirteen there is a marked decrease in the influence of the surroundings; between thirteen and seventeen there are still further decrease; and after seventeen there is a slight return to some context influence."[20] This shift has been described as "field-dependence" and "field-independence." But the return to context influence is another stage, "field-interdependence,"

reflecting the move first from dependence to independence, then from independence to interdependence,
in maturation. As previously discussed, maturity
implies interdependence.

Perceptual development is important to creativity as well as to autonomy. Every creative insight
is an important perceptual development, and every perceptual development brings us closer to reality and
the moment of discovery in the creative process.
Primary refinforcement in perceptual development is
not external; it comes from the joy of "eureka" and
the satisfaction of curiosity. Perception is not
just adaptive; it is also assimilative.

3. Perceptual Set and Distortion

Externally, perception centers on the reception
of sensory input; but internally, perception centers
on the incorporation and interpretation of that input.
Externally, perceptual development means an increasing differentiation of sensory input; internally,
perceptual development means strengthening the integration of perceptual set. If perception depends
only on the flux of sensory impressions, it disintegrates. The perceived meanings of new experiences
need to be integrated into the total mental structure
and accepted as its part. Perceptual set is the "radar" of our mental structure, or the detective system
of our "inner mansion," as well as the "code" system
of our brain computer.

The formation of perceptual set is a process
that consolidates the mental "storage" of external
experiences. Since each person has unique experiences, each has different perceptual set and sees
and interprets differently. Each person builds his
or her own mental "fortress" to "fight" the "invasion" of sensory input, to protect inner harmony and
to ensure security and peace. The ancients believed
that objects transmitted copies of themselves into
the human mind. The mind is no longer considered a
passive "clean slate." Each person has his or her

270

innate potential, and each sensory input needs to be
scrutinized before being integrated into the mental
structure as a meaningful part. Each person has a
unique way of doing this. Thus, perception is always
selective, and the perceiver takes an active role in
an effort to master the environment.

Perceptual sets can be interpreted as "habitual patterns" capable of being programmed by such
symbolic activities as language. Each perceptual
set is the "orienting reflex" built on action and
followed by imagery and symbols. Action, imagery,
and symbol are the three representation systems which
are unique in themselves, but are capable of "partial
translation one into the other," as pointed out by
Dr. Jerome S. Bruner.[21] When two systems of representation do not correspond, perceptual set is modified by disequilibrium and cognitive growth takes
place.

"Disequilibrium" in perceptual experience is
by nature non-veridical; it is "stimulus-deformation"
rather than "stimulus information." Perceptual set
is a "state that is preparatory for, or facilitative
of, some definite act of behavior," says Dr. Floyd
H. Allport. "It is an incipient stage of the act
itself."[22] Perceptual set itself is internal, yet
responsive to external stimulus. When the internal
is confirmed by the external, the percept is formed
as if the right piece were fitted into a jigsaw
puzzle, and then becomes integrated into one's mental
structure. Percept is back-formation from perception:
it is the product of perception, an impression of
something perceived by the senses: it is the basic
ingredient in the formation of perceptual set. No
percept is isolated. Each is tied to a chain of per-
cepts from the moment of birth, and each connects
differently. So, each person's perceptual set represents the total of accumulated and organized structure of his or her chain of perceptions. Some per-
cepts are associated with pleasure, others with pain.

Perception is characterized by organization.
The perceptual field is organized into figure and
ground. The distinctive features of something per-

271

ceived stand out from the rest and formulate the
figure. In each perceptual experience, certain un-
spoken steps can be conceptually analyzed, but these
are practically inseparable: 1) expectation, 2) exposure to the sensory stimuli, 3) selection of input,
4) "trial-and-check" of input, 5) formation of the
percept. "Disequilibrium" occurs when the process
is disrupted. In the process of perceiving, perceptual set plays the key role in determining expectations, selection, reception, and interpretation.
Functionally, each person's perceptual set is retrospectively and prospectively unique. But perceptual
organization is commonly based on contiguity and
similarity, frequency and relevance.

Each person has a unique perceptual set; each
reflects a combination of objective reality and subjective distortion of it. The world is always a
"world-as-experienced-and-constituted-by-a-perceiving-
subject," as philosopher Edmund Husserl points out.[23]
What is perceived depends greatly on one's emotional
needs, motivation, as well as perceptual set. So,
perceptual diversity and distortion are inevitable.
The following studies are good examples.

An empirical study by E.M. Siipola showed how
our perceptions are influenced by our expectations.[24]
The participants were divided into two groups and
shown nonsense words, i.e., "sael," "dack" and "wharl."
The researcher told the first group that they would
be shown words related to animals. As a result, most
of them perceived these words as "seal," "duck," and
"whale." The researcher told the second group they
would be shown words related to boats. Most of them
saw these words as "sail," "deck," and "wharf."

Similarly, a study by Sheldon Bach and George
S. Klein showed how the ideas that come to our attention at the time of perceiving have considerable impact on perception. In this study, participants were
all shown the same drawing of a human face and asked
whether the face looked angry or happy. The first
group was shown the picture without any particular
simultaneous stimulus. Their answers were evenly di-
divded. The second group was shown the same face, but

was simultaneously flashed the word, "angry." A significantly greater number of them reported that the face showed anger. The third group was shown the same face, and was simultaneously flashed the word, "happy." A significantly greater number of them said that the face was "happy."[25]

Another form of perceptual distortion has been tested by Jerome S. Bruner and C. G. Goodman. In their study, participants were divided into two groups; the first group were children of the poor, and the second group of the rich. All were asked to estimate the size of coins. The children of the poor consistently overestimated the size.[26] Why? Money has much greater value and importance to those who need it than those who have it in abundance. Our emotional needs may severely distort our perception.

Sometimes our perception is distorted by group influence. People in a group influence each other by creating a group norm regarding certain things, and this norm influences individual perceptions. A small minority can influence the majority enough to create new norms.[27] This small minority can be called the "creative minority" creating new culture. A vocal and creative minority can have an effect on our perception.

What we see depends greatly on our social orientation, which plays an important role in the formation of perceptual set. This can be illustrated by a picture drawn in such a way that it may be interpreted either as a "rat" or a "professor"--the rat's body can be seen as the professor's nose, and the rat's ears can be seen as the professor's eyes--depending on one's social orientation. The picture indicates the "role of frequency in developing perceptual sets."[28] Those who live on farms or who are professionally involved with rats in the lab may see the picture as an animal, whereas an academician may see a symbolic expression of an old man on the same faculty. The key factor is our perceptual set.

Formation of a perceptual set is an on-going process, constantly modified or restructured on the

conscious or unconscious levels. Perception seeks
wholeness and closure; but wholeness and closure cannot be achieved all the time, when there are new perceptual inputs. A mature person is open for new perceptual experiences so that he or she may add new
"blood" to his or her perceptual set. Naturally, we
are in control of perceptual additions. The nature
of the relationship between perceptual set and new
perceptual input is comparable to that of in-groups
and out-groups in social organizations and that of
personnel executive and new job applicants. As long
as the organization is alive and healthy, one can
expect continuing restructuring of manpower and personnel guided by in-groups or executives. Likewise,
human perception always restructures its expectations,
selection, and reception of new inputs guided by perceptual set, which continues to change, develop, and
integrate as well as expand and differentiate. In
the process of integrating new perceptual inputs, we
may mature and get closer to reality. Accurate perception of people around us and their accurate perception of us are necessary for mature living and
fulfillment.

4.   Perception and Culture

        Culture is the totality of socially transmitted
behavior patterns, arts, beliefs, institutions, and
other products of human creativity. It is often a
collective effort of a particular people struggling
for survival individually and as a species under
certain geographical conditions over a period of
time. As pointed out by historian Arnold Toynbee,
a culture may be the product of a creative minority
of people responding to challenges from the environment.

        Perception has two interrelated parts: sensory
and mental. The sensory part is primarily physical,
and is the instrument by which we contact the external environment. The mental part is an affective
attachment and cognitive interpretation of our senses.
Likewise, cultural formation has two interrelated

parts: physical and mental. No culture forms in a vacuum. It is always created in a physical environment, including climate, availability of food and shelter, potentiality for economic and industrial development, esthetic attraction, and other factors significant to the physical well-being and mental values of the people. Through encounters with the same environment over a long period of time, people gradually form common styles and patterns of perception. These common styles and patterns are not only tested individually but also collectively scrutinized by many generations until they crystalize and become powerful enough to be perceptual set for the people. Each culture has a unique "collective perceptual set" for monitoring new input, which French philosopher and social anthropologist Lucien Levy-Bruhl called "collective representations" in his discussion on how primitive people think,[29] The "collective perceptual set" regulates thoughts and shapes the patterns of emotional responses of the people.

Formation of a perceptual set is not entirely dependent on visual perception. In a study by R. Held and A. Hein, two kittens were kept in the dark until they were ten weeks old, preventing visual learning experiences. Both were exposed to the same environment, but one kitten was confined to a harnessing instrument, while the other was left free to move around. After ten days, the unharnessed kitten was able to put out his paws when he was carried toward a table, and blinked at approaching objects, whereas the harnessed could not.[30] Visually, both had same environment, but their total experiences differed, and they behaved differently. We respond to the environment with all our senses, not just with our eyes.

In reporting some observations regarding the experiences and behavior of the Ba Mbuti pygmies, C. M. Turnbull said that when a pygmy was taken from the forests of Congo to a vast plain and shown a herd of buffalo several hundreds yards away, the pygmy asked, "What kind of insects are they?" He had never been exposed to such a wide space before, nor had he any experience with distance of this meas-

sure. This totally new experience baffled his perception.[31] He was accustomed to the forest, not a
vast plain. When we travel to a country with a different culture, we may be shocked because our perceptual set is not sufficient for us to cope with the
new experience.

In their study on culture and thought, Michael
Cole and Silvia Scribner reported that, among the
Kpelle people of Liberia--literate and illiterate,
cash workers and farmer, road villagers and bush
dwellers--each group had its own way of recalling.
The literate group relied heavily on taxonomic categories as a basis for grouping, beginning with the
broadest and most inclusive and ending with the nar-
rowest, but the illiterate made little use of them.[32]
More educated people are likely to recall by way of
finding or imposing a structure on which to base
their recall.

Similarly, in an interview a minister of education, who had served two churches in the same city--
one middle class, and the other, lower class, said
that he had found a distinctive difference among the
children of these two churches: Children from the
middle class were more cognitively oriented, whereas
children from the lower class more affectively oriented.

Our perception is shaped by our physical environment as well as by our cultural environment.
The process of human perception is universal, but
its contents are not. People perceive the world differently in accordance with the cultural forces
around them, and formulate habits of inference and
interpretation. During World War II, the United
States sent soldiers to Algeria. When the soldiers
arrived, they were shocked by the physical dirtiness
of impoverished Algerian laborers--who had neither
water nor soap. On the other hand, the Algerians
were horrified by the cultural dirtiness of Americans
who violated one of their most deeply ingrained ta-
boos by eating with their right hands. Algerians
are severely punished (even as babies) when they eat
with the right hand. The same right hand should not

be used for eating as well as urinating, they believed. What the Americans saw as natural was a
serious violation of an Algerian taboo.[33]

Once a retired missionary reported that the
father of a fellow missionary visited his university
in mainland China prior to the communist revolution,
and was introduced to the university community at
morning worship. The father was greatly excited and
said how proud he was of his son. The audience was
amazed, and his son felt deeply embarrassed. Later
the father learned that what he saw as perfectly
natural was culturally embarrassing to his audience.
Traditionally, the Chinese are not accustomed to
praise their sons in public. When the father introduced his son to friends, he was supposed to humble
himself and say, "This is my little dog."

What we perceive is invariably conditioned by
our cultural upbringing. In an experiment with a
device that simultaneously showed a different picture
to each eye, psychologist Jerome D. Frank made a
group of American teachers and a group of Mexican
teachers to see a picture of baseball player and a
picture of bullfighter. An overwhelming proportion
of the Americans saw the baseball player, whereas
an overwhelming proportion of Mexican teachers saw
the bullfighter. These teachers saw what they were
accustomed and wanted to see culturally.[34]

We all conform to cultural expectations without
really being aware of it, and cultural conformity
makes our behavior predictable and social order de-
pendable. Sometimes the effect of cultural conformity goes deeper than we imagine, even in sensing and
responding to pain. Perception involves all the
senses, not just the sight and sound. Our skin is
another channel by which we perceive what is happening to us, and there are cultural differences in the
way we respond to and perceive pain. Each ethnic
group has a cultural heritage which influences perception and response. In a study of Jewish, Anglo-
Saxon, Irish, and Italian patients, Dr. Mark Abrowski
found significant differences in the way these four
ethnic groups responded to pain. In general, Irish

patients tended to endure pain in silence; Anglo-Saxon patients gritted their teeth to show as little pain as possible; Jewish and Italian patients expressed complaints loudly, bitterly, and with great emotion. Culturally, the Jews and Italians had no reason to keep suffering to themselves, but Anglo-Saxons believed that silence was proper. The Jewish and Anglo-Saxon patients refused to accept analgesic drugs until they had had an explanation and a diagnosis of their pain; they were more concerned with the meaning and significance of their symptoms. In contrast, the Italians welcomed analgesic drugs because they cared only for relief from the pain, whereas the Irish patients did not even try to see what the pain was, but just accepted it or tried to show that it did not really hurt too much.[35]

Culture influences the perception of occupations. In a study of Japanese and American perceptions of occupations, two sociologists, Charles E. Ramsey and Robert J. Smith, found that ratings of 23 occupations by high school seniors in Japan and in the United States were different. The rating of each occupation on a 5 point scale from "very high" to "very low" prestige showed:[36]

Japan	United States
1. College professor	1. Doctor
2. Doctor	2. Lawyer
3. Lawyer	3. Priest (minister)
4. Corporate executive	4. College professor
5. Author	5. Corporate executive
6. Union leader	6. Author
7. Primary school teacher	7. Movie performer
8. Policeman	8. Union leader
9. Small factory owner	9. Nurse
10. Private secretary	10. Primary school teacher
11. Government clerk	11. Private secretary
12. Nurse	12. Policeman
13. Priest (minister)	13. Soldier
14. Office worker	14. Government clerk
15. Beautician	15. Small factory owner
16. Movie performer	16. Farm owner

17. Department store clerk	17. Carpenter
18. Small shopkeepr	18. Office worker
19. Soldier	19. Beautician
20. Farm owner	20. Small shopkeeper

21. Small shop sales
    clerk
	21. Department store
	    clerk

22. Carpenter	22. Small shop sales clerk
23. Farm laborer	23. Farm laborer

The greatest difference was the high estimation of priest (minister) in the United States, which is predominantly Christian. Religion is an important ingredient of culture.

One study hypothesized that children who received religious upbringing would be more inclined than other children to manifest animistic and anthropomorphic tendencies in connection with non-religious ideas, in view of the fact that Protestantism, Roman Catholicism, and Judaism contain both animistic and anthropomorphic elements. The study used story completion, multi-choice items, and a questionnaire for parents. Children from the religious homes were significantly more anthropomorphic and animistic in their responses.[37]

Language is another important ingredient of culture. Without language, we can hardly find any form of intelligent communication and modern civilization. The ability to express thought in linguistic symbols is the watershed in human development, just as the discovery of fire was the watershed in the development of civilization. Language is a sign of human transcendence from self and the physical environment; it changes the quality of life, and raises the level of human experience; it liberates human beings from the bondage of physical limitations for abstract thinking and generalization. The process of linguistic development is interwoven with perceptual development.

Language plays an important role in cognitively shaping perceptual set. As pointed out by cognitive psychologist Jerome S. Bruner, "language predisposes

279

a mind to entertain modes of thought and certain way of arranging the shared subjective reality of a linguistic community."[38] The same word may mean different things to different people in different cultures. We see things through the eyes of our minds, not just our physical eyes; and the eyes of our minds are shaped by the language we use. The word "pluralism" is libertarian in democratic culture, but it is "a mechanism not for fostering equality but for preserving inequality" in authoritarian culture.[39] Culture shapes the meaning of the word. Language can never be just an instrument of expression; it becomes part of us, our modes of thinking and perceptual set.

What our language communicates is culturally conditioned. By the time we reach adulthood, we are well-inducted into the mainstream of our culutre. Prejudices are cultural products which reflect subjective distortions of objective reality. A study of ethnic prejudice showed that Jews were considered to be intelligent and ambitious; Italians unintelligent and deficient of character; and Anglo-Saxons beautiful. Thirty photographs of pretty but otherwise hardly identifiable young women were shown to a group of Columbia-Barnard students. They were asked to rate each photograph in terms of "general liking," "beauty," "intelligence," "ambition," and "character." Two months later, the same photographs were shown to them under different surnames, five Jewish names, five Italian names, five Irish names, and fifteen Anglo-Saxon names. When the ratings were compared, the pictures with Irish names had lost their beauty.[40]

Our perception is distorted individually and culturally. To be mature is to be aware of this fact and to take proper measures to guard against unrealistic inaccurate perceptions of reality. Too much cultural conditioning sterilizes imagination and creativity, and distorts perception and future vision; too much cultural indoctrination may make us "dead" conservatives and blind followers of traditions and noninnovative persons. The highly cultured may become blinded by their culture. In his recent book

Outgrowing Self-Deception, Dr. Gardner Murphy raises
the seemingly facetious question whether Americans
could be taught by groups of preliterates who could
serve as "informants" on American life.[41] Perhaps,
we are so conditioned by modern scientific and technological culture that we have lost the capability
of seeing ourselves realistically and objectively.
Those uncivilized preliterates may be in a better
position to see our flaws and teach us what is to be
human, because they have not been corrupted by modern
civilization. "Those who know no culture other than
their own cannot know their own," as Dr. Ralph Linton
pointed out.[42] It is important that we open ourselves
to others so that we may know ourselves better and
have less distorted perceptions of ourselves and the
world. By nature our perception is culturally distorted, but this does not mean that we should destroy
all cultures and go back to a primtive state. On
the contrary, we need to cherish what is good, re-
form what is evil, and re-create our culture, because
we cannot live in a cultural vacuum. At the same
time, we need to encounter people from other cultures.

     Each culture has social manners that guide
interpersonal relationships. In spite of cultural
differences in interpersonal relationships, there
is one common phenomenon--we tend to perceive other
people like us. Sometimes we make mistakes because
we assume other people are more like ourselves than
they actually are. In a study, children at a camp
were asked to describe each other individually, and
their descriptions were analyzed. Each child tended
to use the same characteristics no matter whom he or
she described.[43] In another study, students were
divided into two groups; "secure" and "insecure."
Each group was asked to look at 200 photographs and
to judge each as "very warm," "warm," "cold," "very
cold." The "secure" group made a significantly
greater number of "warm" judgments than the "insecure"
group.[44] This indicates the egocentricity of social
perception. Our personality characteristics have a
significant effect on our perceptions of others.

     To be mature in social perception is to be a
good judge of other people. People who are good

judges of others tend to be intelligent, emotionally
well adjusted, and to have esthetic and dramatic interests.[45] As pointed out by Gordon W. Allport, good
judges of other people tend to have particular characteristics, such as breadth of personal experience,
intelligence, cognitive complexity, self-insight, social skill and adjustment, detachment, esthetic attitudes, and so on.[46] In response to the question
"How do you judge people?" the chief executive of a
professional school said, "Well, some people have
special skills of judging others, but some don't. I
tend to trust others until they prove otherwise.
Sometimes it is too late." There is no particular
thing which makes us perceptually mature and accurate.
Experience may help, but we may still misperceive
others and are misperceived by others, because the
culture in which we live is constantly changing.

5.   Perception and Religious
Experience

        The religious dimension of perception is divine
revelation and human response to it. God's revelation is historical, factual, and concrete; it makes
its appeal to human senses. God reveals through nature.
Christians believe that Jesus Christ is God's revelation, and faith is needed to perceive and understand its meaning. As pointed out by Reinhold Niebuhr, the life and death of Jesus Christ is the supremely luminous point in human history, "a source
and center of an interpretation of life," which em-
braces "all of life's antinomies and contradictions
into a system of meaning and is conducive to a renewal of life."[47] For those who believe, Jesus of
Nazareth reveals God's love, power, and purpose in human history, which makes life meaningful in spite of
countless unspeakable human miseries in this world.
History is like an incomprehensible book , but for
those who believe in the crucified and risen Lord
Jesus, his life becomes the "luminous sentence" from
which one can go forward and backward in comprehending the true meaning of it.[48] In religious experience, to believe is to perceive.

282

This does not imply that there is no meaning in historical events other than Jesus Christ's life, death, and resurrection. Each historical event has a different meaning for different individuals and communities. Each event, whether big or small, is a potential means for divine revelation by which we know God's purpose in history and in our personal lives. In looking at each new historical event, we may formulate meaningful perceptions. When this takes place, the event stands out like a pole in the flux of time. We regain spiritual strength and the courage to go forward in life's adventure. At the same time we reconstruct our inner self. Dr. Roger L. Shinn of Union Theological Seminary describes this spiritual "check-and-trial" as the "circular processes in theology."[49] In an effort to find the meaning of an event, or even to formulate beliefs out of it, we go back and forth, inward and outward, wrestling with the event. In religious experiences, our beliefs are derived from perceptions of life's events; on the other hand, our perceptions of life's events depend on religious beliefs. Moreover, our ethical living is involved in the happening of the event and the interpretation of the event.

For us--living in the twentieth century--the "Christ-event" is remote and unrelated to our life except through Scripture, dogma, creeds, worship, church architecture, and so on, by which we create an atmosphere to recapture the divine revelation to the ancient Apostles. In this recapturing experience, the past becomes a present reality. When divine revelation takes place in the lives of men and women, they change their perception of themselves, of the world, and of reality; they become new creatures, and their point of view is no longer of this world. "The old has passed away, behold, the new has come. All this is from God, . . ."[50] Personal experience of divine revelation is sometimes ecstatic, overwhelming, and immediate. But not always. Dr. John Baillie, an outstanding preacher, theologian, and Co-President of the World Council of Churches, described his own experience of revelation: "Certainly it did not come 'out of the blue.' I heard no voice from the skies." The divine revelation came from

283

what he called "the spiritual climate of the home."
"It came from my parents' walk and conversation."[51]
This is the mode of experiencing God's revelation
for the majority of people. But some may have unusual experiences. Among those whom I have interviewed, there are three men who had somewhat mystical experiences in their young adulthood.

What makes the "Christ-event" of the past relevant to the present is the work of the Spirit, who
transcends time and space, and is immanent and active
here and now. The Spirit makes the past meaningful.
Since we think, act, and do all things through present consciousness, the past and future are unreal
unless they are contained in present consciousness.
The presence of the Spirit in the lives of Christians
makes celebrating Christmas, Easter, Pentecost meaningful and significant: These religious festivals
are no mere rituals from the past, but are alive with
new meaning at each celebration.

Dr. Thomas Barclay was a physicist, missionary,
and founder of Tainan Theological College, Taiwan.
The most decisive moment in his life was his sixteenth
birthday, when he pulled himself together and made a
covenant with God. He renewed it every year on his
birthday. God's revelation became personal and vivid
and alive after his sixteenth birthday.

The historical "Christ event" is objective,
while the personal experience of its meaning is subjective. The dichotomy between objectivity and subjectivity of revelation has been the focal point in
various theological controversies. From the perceptual point of view, this dichotomy should not exist.
Dichotomy implies that the perceptual process can be
divided into two isolated entities: subjective and
objective. In experience, this cannot be done. No
matter what is perceived or who is the perceiver, the
perceptual process has to be treated as a whole.

No objective arguments about the existence of
God can reveal God. The objective understanding of
God's revelation must be subjectively internalized
through the presence of the Spirit. The Spirit is

believed to be a subjective presence of the transcendent God, and in the presence of the Spirit there
is a synthesis and integration of the subjective and
the objective. Human perception is an integrating
and synthesizing process, an ongoing process. The
existence of God is subjectively perceived, not just
objectively argued. Religion is caught, not taught.
Faith is also an ongoing process, and the presence
of the Spirit is not caught once and for all, but
again and again.

As previously mentioned, besides the special
revelation in the life of Jesus, Christians also
affirm general revelation through nature; the Creator
is known through His creation. "We can be led from
them to know that God exists," said Saint Thomas
Aquinas.[52] Jesus' disciples are asked to "look at
the birds of the air" and to "consider the lilies of
the field."[53] The Psalmist exclaims, "O Lord, our
Lord, how majestic is thy name in all the earth,"
because "the heavens are telling the glory of God;
and the firmament proclaims His handiwork."[54] In an
interview in Massachusetts, a school principal recall
the awesome experience of God's presence during her
visit to one of the New Hampshire mountain areas.
She found the experience there complementary to her
worship experience in the church every Sunday. An
argument about the existence of God is hardly adequate. The presence of the Spirit has a direct and
personal impact. The road to the knowledge of God's
revelation cuts through sensory and intellectual
barriers.

Faith like perception is subjective, personal,
and direct. Martin Luther heard a fellow monk re-
peating the words of the Creed: "I believe in the
forgiveness of sins, and straightaway I felt as if
I were born anew. It was as if I had found the door
of paradise thrown wide open."[55] Faith is supra-
rational, not irrational; it is existential. Reduc-
ing religious experience to mere philosophical argument misses the point and overlooks the cutting edge
of religious faith.

Drug abuse is of great social concern. Some

people experiment with drugs to escape the monotony
of life and to experience ecstasy. In 1953 English
novelist Aldous Huxley reached and wrote about an unusual state of consciousness by taking mescaline.
He named his book The Doors of Perception. Suspicious
of this type of mystical experience, R. G. Zaehner
of Oxford tested it for himself and declared he was
not impressed; at best, the drug induced ecstasy can
only be called natural mysticism.

        In a historical survey of revelation theology,
Catholic theologian Avery Dulles points out three
basic mentalities accounting for various interpretations of revelation among leading modern theologians
in England, Europe, and the United States. The first
type is called the "positive or factual mind," and it
emphasizes revelation as a concrete event, particularly the historical event of Jesus Christ. The second type is called the "conceptual or abstract mind"
stressing the eternal truths in revelation. And the
third type is called the "intuitive or mystical mind,"
inclined to depict revelation as an ineffable encounter with God.[56] This indicates that revelation
is three dimensional--mystical, factual, and rational.
Over-emphasizing one of them at the expense of the
others is misleading just as it is misleading to say
that perception involves only the expectation and
attention to what to be seen, or only the reception
of the sensory input, or only the "check-and-tiral"
and formation of percept. Perception involves all
of them.

        At the end of an interview with a successful
construction manager, I asked "What has been the most
important thing in your life so far?" After thinking
for a while, he answered quietly and affirmatively,
"Faith! Faith has been the most important thing in
my life." Faith is religious perception. It involves
three dimensions: the factual, the conceptual, and
the intuitive.

                            NOTES

1. T. G. R. Bower, The Perceptual World of the Child

(Cambridge, MA: Harvard University Press, 1977), p. 1.

2. Floyd H. Allport, Theories of Perception and the Concept of Structure (New York: John Wiley and Sons, 1955), pp. 531-575.

3. Merton White, ed., Age of Analysis (New York: Mentor Books, 1955), p. 94.

4. Wolfang Köhler, The Task of Gestalt Psychology (Princeton, N.J.: Princeton University Press, 1969), pp. 39-41, 46.

5. Lloyd Kaufman, Perception (New York: Oxford University Press, 1979), pp. 355ff.

6. James Marshall, "The Evidence: Do We See and Hear What Is? Or Do Our Senses Lie?" Psychology Today, 6 (2) (1969), pp. 48-52.

7. Way Wilson Allen, William James: A Biography (New York: Simon and Schuster, 1969), p. 197.

8. Paul Tibbetts, ed., Perception (Chicago: Quadrangle Books, 1969), p. 77. Human emotion, cognition, and perception are interrelated because they are all controlled by the brain. In a discussion about engrams, it is hypothesized that "all of the cells of the brain must be in almost constant activity, either firing or actively inhibited," that "every instance of recall requires the activity of literally millions of neurons," and that "the same neurons which retain the memory traces of one experience must also participate in countless other activities." This may explain the dynamism in human perception.

9. Katharine M. Banham Bridges, "Emotional Development in Early Infancy," Child Development, 3 (1932), pp. 324-341.

10. Bower, Ibid., passim.

11. James J. Gibson and Eleanor J. Gibson, "Perceptual Learning: Differentiation or Enrichment," Psychological Review, 62 (1955), pp. 32-41. Also, Eleanor J. Gibson, Principles of Perceptual Learning and Development (New York: Appleton-Century-Crofts, 1969), pp. 450-471.

12. R. G. Suchman and T. Trasbasso, "Color and Form Preference in Young Children," Journal of Experimental Child Psychology, 4 (3) (1966), pp. 177-187. Also, Michael Cole and Sylvia Scribner, Culture and Thought (New York: John Wiley and Sons, 1974), p. 90.

13. R. Rush, "Visual Grouping in Relation to Age," Arch. Psychol., 31 (217) (1937-1938), p. 95. Quoted by Charles M. Solley and Gardner Murphy, Development of the Perceptual World (New York: Basic Books, 1960), pp. 142-143.

14. Eleanor J. Gibson and Vivian Clum, "Experimental Methods of Studying Perception in Children," in Handbook of Research Methods in Child Development ed. by P. H. Mussen (New York: John Wiley and Sons, 1960).

15. C. M. Mooney, "Age in the Development of Closure Ability in Children," Canadian Journal of Psychology, 11 (1957), pp. 219-226.

16. Solley and Murphy, Ibid., pp. 139-141. Also, Charles M. Solley and R. Sommer, "Perceptual Autism in Children," Journal of General Psychology, 56 (1957), pp. 3-11.

17. J. Piaget and B. Inhelder, The Child's Conception of Space (London: Routledge and Kegan Paul, 1956).

18. M. D. Vernon, "Perception in Relation to Cognition," in Perceptual Development in Children ed. by Aline H. Kidd and Robert M. Rivorce (New York: International Universities Press, 1966), pp. 394-397.

288

19. E. R. Hilgard, "The Role of Learning in Perception," in Perception: An Approach to Personality ed. R. R. Blake and G. V. Ramsey (New York: Ronald Press, 1951), pp. 95-120.

20. H. A. Witkin, et al. Psychological Differentiation: Studies of Development (New York: John Wiley and Sons, 1962), p. 374. Also, Solley and Gardner, Ibid., pp. 137-138.

21. Jerome S. Bruner, et al. Studies in Cogntive Growth (New York: John Wiley and Sons, 1967), pp. 1-67.

22. Floyd H. Allport, Ibid., pp. 407-413.

23. Paul Tibbetts, Ibid., p. 205.

24. E. M. Siipola, "A Group Study of Some Effects of Preparatory Set," Psychological Monographs, 46 (210) (1935), pp. 27-38.

25. Sheldon Bach and George S. Klein, "Conscious Effects of Prolonged Subliminal Exposures of Words," American Psychologist, 12 (1957), p. 397.

26. Jerome S. Bruner and C. G. Goodman, "Value and Need as Organizing Factors in Perception," Journal of Abnormal and Social Psychology, 42 (1947), pp. 33-44.

27. S. Moscovici, E. Lage, and M. Vaffrechoux, "Influence of a Consistent Minority in a Color Perception Task," Sociometry, 32 (1969), pp. 365-380.

28. B. R. Bugelski and D. A. Alampay, "The Role of Frequency in Developing Perceptual Sets," Canadian Journal of Psychology, 15 (1961), pp. 205-211. Cp. Picasso's "Head of a Bull."

29. Lucien Levy-Bruhl, How Natives Think (New York: Washington Square Press, 1966), ch. 3.

30. R. Held and A. Hein, "Movement-Produced Stimula-

tion in the Development of Visually Controlled Movement by Selective Exposure during Rearing," Jounral of Comparative and Physiological Psychology, 56 (1963), pp. 872-876.

31. C. M. Turnbull, "Some Observations regarding the Experiences and Behavior of the Ba Mbuti Pygmies," American Journal of Psychology, 74 (1961), pp. 304-308. Cp. Zulu people, conditioned by rounded huts, excluded angular things in their perception. See, Gordon W. Allport and T. F. Pettigrew, "Cultural Influence on the Perception of Movement: The Trapezoidal Illusion among Zulus," Journal of Abnormal and Social Psychology, 55 (1957), pp. 104-113.

32. Michael Cole and Silvia Scribner, Culture and Thought (New York: John Wiley and Sons, 1974), pp. 136-138.

33. Ibid.

34. Jerome D. Frank, "The Face of the Enemy," Psychology Today, 5 (11) (1968), pp. 24-29.

35. Quoted by Richard Stiller, Pain: Why It Hurts, Where It Hurts, When It Hurts (New York: Thomas Nelson Inc., 1975), pp. 27-28.

36. Charles E. Ramsey and Robert J. Smith, "Japanese and American Perceptions of Occupations," American Journal of Sociology, 65 (1960), pp. 475-482.

37. M. Ezer, "The Effect of Religion on Children's Responses to Questions Involving Physical Causalty," in The Cause of Behavior ed. J. Rosenblith and W. Allensmith (Boston: Allyn and Bacon, 1961), pp. 481-487.

38. Jerome S. Bruner, On Knowing (Cambridge, MA: Harvard University Press, 1962), p. 137.

39. Kalman H. Silvert, Man's Power (New York: The Viking Press, 1970), pp. 132-136.

290

40. Gerhart Aenger, The Social Psychology of Prejudice (New York: Harper and Brothers, 1953), p.
150.

41. Gardner Murphy, Outgrowing Self-Deception (New
York: Basic Books, 1975), p. 44. Cp. a professor's awareness of self-deception, Benjamin
Demott, "Onward and Downward from the Ivory Tower," Psychology Today, 14 (9) (1977), pp. 60-
62.

42. Quoted by Stuart Chase, The Proper Study of Man
(New York: Harper & Row, 1956), p. 82.

43. S. M. Dornbush, et al. "The Perceiver and the
Perceived: Their Relative Influence on the Categories of Interpersonal Cognition," Journal of
Personality and Social Psychology, 1 (1965),
pp. 434-440.

44. J. Bossom and A. Maslow, "Security of Judges as
a Factor in Impressions of Warmth in Others,"
Journal of Abnormal and Social Psychology, 55,
(1957), pp. 147-148.

45. R. Taft, "The Ability to Judge People," Psychological Bulletin, 52 (1959), pp. 1-23.

46. Gordon W. Allport, Patterns of Growth in Personality (New York: Holt, 1961), pp. 497-522.

47. Reinhold Niebuhr, Faith and History (New York:
Charles Scribner's Sons, 1949).

48. H. Richard Niebuhr, The Meaning of Revelation
(New York: The Macmillan Co., 1960), pp. 68-69.

49. Roger L. Shinn, "Perception and Belief," Union
Seminary Review, 34 (1978), pp. 13-21.

50. II Cor. 5:16-18.

51. John Baillie, Our Knowledge of God(New York: Char-
less Scribner's Sons, 1959), p. 182.

291

52. Thomas Aquinas, _Summa Theologica_ (London: Bums Oates and Washburne Ltd., 1920), i. 12, xii.

53. Mt. 6:26-30.

54. Ps. 8:9, 19:1.

55. Quoted by William James, _The Varieties of Religious Experience_ (New York: Longman's Green and Co., 1928), p. 382.

56. Avery Albert Dulles, _Revelation Theology_ (New York: Herder and Herder, 1969), p. 177-180.

CHAPTER

IX

SUFFERING AND COPING

Life's journey is full of stress and suffering.
Shakespeare wrote:

> "To be, or not to be: that is the question:
> Whether 'tis nobler in mind to suffer. . .
> Or to take arms against a sea of troubles,
> . . . and, by a sleep we say we end
> The heart-ache and the thousand natural shocks
> That flesh is heir to, . . ."[1]

"Life is a tough proposition," said Prof. H. A. Wolfson of Harvard University, as he was remembered by
students in counseling them. The crying of a new
born baby signifies life's stress; silent mourning
of the bereaved affirms life's suffering; the deep
sighs of the oppressed echo human agony and miseries. Every day we are bombarded with news of suffering through what we read, hear, and see. As we look
back, around or beyond, we cannot escape from the
reality of human suffering. Although we may be elated
by occasional experience of joy, goodness or hope,
we are often dragged down by the cries of the wounded,
the hungry, the desolate, the sick, the unemployed,
the uprooted, and the helpless. How many times have
we tried to alleviate human suffering and found that
we may win some battles but never the war. After all
our efforts, we suffer more than ever, and feel dis-
tressed more than ever. This is what has been, and,
perhaps, will always be. The rich suffer; the poor
suffer; in different ways we all suffer. Suffering
has been a fact of life for people of all ages; it
was a stark human phenomenon in preindustrial society;
our postindustrial life is full of it. It has been a
problem for philosophers and theologians ever since
Homo sapiens began to think and ask questions. As
pointed out by Fyodor Dostoyevsky, "Suffering is the
sole origin of consciousness."

1. Suffering, Pain, and Stress

Pain is an inevitable part of the creative process and human growth. The pangs of childbirth are
an example. In every stage of human growth there is
a central problem, a painful crisis, a developmental
task. Each person is bound to experience "growing
pains," at one time or another.

Pain is an unpleasant sensation, but it occurs
in varying degrees of severity as a consequence of
injury, disease, or emotional distress. The sensation of pain is an annoying, but useful "warning signal against potential or actual damage to tissue
cells," as pointed out by J. S. White and W. H. Sweet
in their discussion on pain, its mechanisms and neuro-
surgical control.[2] Pain is an effective indicator of
extreme stimulation, intrusion, and attack from the
outside, or disharmony of bodily functions inside.
Pain means "telic decentralization is taking place,"
Dr. David Bakan interprets.[3] Pains tell us that
our body is in trouble; its homeostasis is disrupted
and needs to be restored. The centralized human
organism functions properly; whenever there is a sign
of decentralization, pain is felt. Pain signals differentiation. If this differentiation is not accompanied by integration, our body will decay. Our body
assumes sovereignty and wants to stop the local decentralization and total disintegration. Pain teaches
what should be avoided, increasing our chance of survival. Occasionally we are insensitive to pain. At
other times, pain is too great to bear, and we require
the assistance of a painkiller.

Psychologically pain has its locus in the conscious ego: pain is the price we pay for consciousness. Every pain has two not very clearly differentiated components--1) pain per se, 2) a sense of annihilation. In the early stage of ego development,
pain and the sense of annihilation are not differentiated. As we grow cognitively, the two become more
differentiated and our consciousness transcends from
pains. This development may have correlations with
the findings of Kenneth A. Holroyd and Frank Andrasik

in their study of 39 community residents with chronic
tension headaches. They reported that both self-
control treatment and the headache discussion pro-
cedure produced substantial reductions in headache
pain.[4] It seems Stoicism is based on the effective-
ness of cognitively-oriented therapeutic procedures,
that is, the transcendence of ego-consciousness over
pain and the sense of annihilation.

Pain makes positive contributions to our well-
being, although the experience of pain is annoying.
If our body did not experience pain, we would not
be aware of disasters. Pain also benefits animals.
A study by R. Melzack and T. H. Scott on the response
of dogs to pain is significant. One group of dogs
was raised in a normal environment of which pain was
a part of growing experience, while the other group
of dogs was raised in an artificial, painless environment. Then, all of the dogs were put into a situation in which they might be struck by an electrified
car. Those raised in a normal environment received
an average of 6 shocks, whereas those raised in the
painless environment received an average of 24.7
shocks.[5]

Pain prompts our consciousness, teaching us
what hurts; it increases our sense of autonomy of
the ego, producing a sense of transcendence from
the mechanism of sensory response itself; it facilitates the birth of selfhood through negative routes
and the process of differentiation in cognitive development. Pain eventually creates its own center
and facilitates the process of individuation. But
the newly created telic center must harmonize with
the larger telic center, be it that of the body,
the family, the community, the nation, the species,
or of the universe. Otherwise, the individualized
telic center can be cancerous, and there would be no
communication between the individualized telic center and the larger telic center. Pain teaches us
the importance of communication between the two. Socially, the telic center of criminals is always in
conclict with that of the family, the community, and
the universe. Learning from pain is good as long as
the pain does not create an isolated telic center independent from the larger telic center. Autism is

is an extreme form of learning from too much pain.

This psychological phenomenon of building an independent telic center through too much pain is comparable to the development of cancer cells in human body. Biologically, normal cells stop growing when they touch each other, but cancer cells continue to grow. Normal cells communicate with each other, and the telic center of the normal tissue harmonizes with the larger telic center of the organism. But cancer cells are "imperialistic," and their growth cannot be stopped. In their study of intercellular communication and the control of tissue growth, W. R. Loewenstein and Y. Kanno of Columbia University passed a current of ions into a cell and assessed the current leakage which spread to adjacent cells, in an attempt to probe this phenomenon. The normal cells stopped growing upon mutual contact because "some kind of signal must be transmitted from cell to cell." But there was no such communication between the cancer cells. They found that the electric measurements among the cancer cells were negligible--"the effective membrane resistence in cancer cells is 20-200 times greater than in normal cells."[6]

Politically, this is manifested in revolution and rebellion. If oppressed people experience too much pain, they attempt to formulate a totally independent telic center of their own, in opposition to the larger telic center, namely, the government.

In human personality, the ego is the larger telic center. In the course of normal maturation, the ego emerges from the undifferentiated state of experiencing pain per se and its sense of annihilation as one, to the differentiated state of localizing where and what the pain is, separating pain from its sense of annihilation without being overwhelmed by it. When the ego develops, pain is experienced more precisely, is separated from the ego, and is under the scrutiny of the ego according to reality principle. Some years ago, I visited a teenage boy who had an operation. In a conversation, the surgeon said, "Some patients cannot tell what and where the pain is, but Ken is exceptional. He can pinpoint every bit of pain in great details." His ego was not overwhelmed by it.

In the underdeveloped stage, the ego is overwhelmed by pain so much so that pain is unrealisti-
cally exaggerated by emotionally intensified anxiety.
In responding to the same shot at the clinic, children are panic and cry loudly, but adutls are self-
controlled and keep silence. Therefore, how we handle pain is an indication of our maturity. The mature ego is separated from the pain per se and transcended from its sense of annihilation. Thus, inner
composure is maintained. The ego is above the pain.

Similarly, the mature ego is above all "complexes" and subjugates them; they may be a connected
group of repressed ideas, habitual patterns of thought,
feeling or action, exaggerated obsessive concern or
fear, which assert independence from the ego. These
"complexes" want to build independent telic centers
of their own in conflict with the larger telic center of human personality, namely, the ego. The mature ego does not allow them to do so.

Our pain may not be stressful, but if the pain
persists, it becomes mentally or emotionally dis-
ruptive and disquieting. Stress tests our strength
and integrity. In exploring the psychology of stress
and anxiety, C. P. Crowley says "The scientist learns
about matter when he puts it under stress, and the
poet learns about words when he puts them under stress.
So we learn about man when we put him under stress."[7]
When we are put under stress, our integrity is tested.
Integrity is a sign of maturity. This mature state
of mind is "the fruit" which gradually ripens in the
later years of life. Erikson calls it "ego integrity" and describes it as "a post-narcissistic love
of the human ego--not of the self--as an experience
which conveys some world order and spiritual sense,
no matter how dearly paid for."[8] We want to defend
our integrity against all kinds of threats. Based
on his empirical medical research of stress, Dr.
Hans Selye gives advice not very different from
Socrates' "Know thyself." He quotes English poet
and educator Matthew Arnold: "Resolve to be thyself;
and know that he who finds himself, loses his misery."[9]

297

Some people suffer because of their love of
others: The pain they bear is sacrificial. Altruistic love is a sign of maturity. But other people
suffer because of their immaturity. The pain they
have to bear from car accidents may be caused by
careless driving, mischievous conduct, misjudgment,
or too much alcohol. Suffering does not tell us
what maturity is, but why we suffer and how we cope
with it may well show our maturity.

2. Successful Coping

Modern society is proud of its scientific and
technological advancement, but life in modern society
is full of stress and tension. People turn to yoga,
transcendental meditation, and seek help from drugs.
There are numerous techniques for relaxation. But
coping with stress, we need more than techniques,
because coping invovles our total personality. Successful coping requires maturity. At the same time
coping with stress is a maturing experience.

Aware of the destructive forces inherent in
modern living, a highly "successful" psychiatrist
I interviewed decided to step down at the age of
forty. A close friend and colleague of his had died
of heart attack not long before, and he could not
bear to think of himself as the next victim. Society
seems "insane," people are exhausted too young, their
coronary arteries harden too early, and their blood
pressure is chronically too high. He resigned from
a high post and accepted a new position as the director of a small counseling center.

Dr. Orlo Strunk of Boston University had two
basic convictions--1) "life is more a mystery to be
lived than a problem to be solved," and 2) "life is
more important than profession."[10] At every turn
of life's journey, we become critical of the present
situation and see things more clearly than ever. A
new perception leads us to a new life style and new
ways of coping.

There are three stages in coping with stress

298

as pointed out by Dr. Hans Selye in his discussion on the stress of life.[11] The first stage is "alarm reaction." The activity of the autonomous nervous system increases alarmingly, but only for short periods of exertion. The second stage is "resistence." In this stage, we attempt to resist stress by increasing the glandular secretion. But if the original stressful factors do not disappear, or if new stressful factors are added to the situation, we reach the third stage, "exhaustion." The glandular system cannot continue to function at a high rate, and we have to withdraw. So, if there is proportionately too much stress in any dimension of life, we need diversion or rest, because human nature is both psychosomatic and somatopsychic. Healthy mature living is well-balanced and not centered around trivialities. Too much differentiation is stressful, and leads to exhaustion. Differentiation needs to be supplemented by integration and transcendence, before stress reaches the final stage.

Stress is a two-edged sword. Stress can energize, but it can also inhibit. Stress can facilitate, but it can also disrupt. Stress can be "the key to veridical perception or, equally, the key to misperception," according to Dr. Charles M. Solley's study of the effects of stress on perceptual attention.[12] He concludes that mild stress is ideal for improving perception. Twelve volunteers participated in his experiments and were shown 20 typewritten words; each word appeared for 2 seconds. During the first 10 presentations, participants were given an electric shock. During the last 10 presentations, there was no electric shock. Eight of the twelve participants did not see any words during the shock period. Stress can lead to misperception or obstruct perception. Nevertheless, mild stress can improve our perception.

On the other hand, whether we can cope with a stressful situation or not depends on how we perceive ourselves in relation to it. If we are overwhelmed by stress and feel threatened, our anxiety mounts and affects our ability to cope with it. In a discussion on "empirical findings and theoretical problems in the use of anxiety scales," I. G. Sarason said that high anxiety subjects were "affected more detrimentally by motivating conditions or failure reports than" the subjects lower in anxiety score distribution. High anxiety subjects had been "more self-preoccupied and generally less content with themselves."[13] Our self-image is an important factor in coping with stressful situations. If we are self-confident, we will generally succeed. So, personality plays an important role in the determination of success or failure. What seems to be a stressful situation for one person may be a welcoming challenge for another.[14] A person may be provoked to fight, while another is awakened to flight. Some people cripple, or even destroy themselves by constantly anticipating threats. They react regressively rather than realistically, and are haunted by painful memories.[15]

Most of our coping patterns have been learned in childhood. The Coping Project headed by child psychologist Louis Barclay Murphy at the Menninger Foundation demonstrated this.[16] Thirty two children (aged 2.5 to 5.5) were studied with regard to how they handled stressful situations at home and at school. The study showed that a child's ability to cope with stress came from the parent who could be depended on when the child needed support, and who could let the child cope with problems when the child was ready to do so. Parent who tried to force children before they were ready deprived them of some of their coping ability. We often find that small children cling to their parents when meeting new people, until they are sure of themselves and of the situation. They learn coping skills almost instincitvely. When they sense that the situation is too difficult to handle, they will stand back until they have the inner strength and self-confidence to cope with it. Our coping experiences in early childhood are powerful forces shaping the patterns of our responses to stressful situations. Some people think of their failures more than their successes, while others remember their successes more than their failures. Those who remember failures more than successes are likely to blame themselves or others, and are less likely to cope successfully when they are frustrated.

In a study of "mastery of stress," Funkenstein, King and Drolette of Harvard Health Service found four kinds of people--1) those who master stressful situations quickly and without much difficulty, 2) those who master stressful situations after a prolonged struggle, 3) those who cannot master stressful situations with increasing difficulty and changing patterns, 4) those who cannot master stressful situations with increasing difficulty but no changing patterns. There are also four patterns of emotional reactions in coping: 1) "no emotion," 2) "anger-out," 3) "anger-in," and 4) "severe anxiety."[17] Those who handle stressful situations successfully belong to the first two emotional patterns: "no emotion" and "anger-out." They are either self-controlled and self-confident, or express their anger outwardly. They are not internally threatened. The people of "no emotion" type are mature and capable of maintaining inner composure under difficult circumstances; they perceive the situation realistically and take measures to overcoming it; they are patient. Protesters and strikers are "anger-out" types; they are not internally threatened, but they cannot maintain inner composure. But the "anger-in" and the "severe anxiety" types are internally threatened by stressful situations.

A professor's wife indicated that her husband's emotional reaction to frustration was typically "anger-in"--"When he was angry, he wouldn't say anything." Sometimes it is difficult to differentiate "no emotion" and "anger-in." When our anger turns inward, or when we blame ourselves indiscriminately, we suffer great psychological pain and pay a high price for social harmony and civilization. Physically, "anger-in" may be tied to the secretion of "epinephrine-like substance."[18] Philosophically, it may be related to fatalism.

How we perceive ourselves and our relationship with our parents is important to our mastery of stress. Based on the study of Funkenstein, King and Drolette, we may hypothesize that "anger-out" types perceive

301

their fathers as the chief authority figures and role-model, and their mothers as the chief sources of affection. "Severe anxiety" types perceive their mothers as the chief authority figures, role-model, as well as the chief source of affection. By seeing the father as the authority figure and the mother as the source of affection, the "anger-out" type tends to dichotomize masculine and feminine roles. There is no such differentiation of roles in the "severe anxiety" type who may still be dominated by the mother-child symbiosis of infancy. Furthermore, we may also hypothesize that for the "anger-in" type, the father lets the mother share the role of being the source of authority, while the mother lets the father share the role of being the source of affection. Consequently, there is little distinction between masculine and feminine roles. The more the mother appears to be the authority figures, the greater is the likelihood of responding to stress with anxiety, whereas the more the father emerges as the authority figure, the greater is the likelihood of responding to stress with "anger-out." However, in view of the current change in sexual roles we may have to wait to see the psychological impact on the patterns of coping.

H. G. Wells had two secret weapons to fight adversities: one was his self-confidence, optimism, and spirit of adventure; and the other was "the principle that had helped him as a child--laughter is the best protection against absurd world."[19] A sense of humor can help us transcend pain and suffering and analyze the situation properly. In other words, humor may make the "distalization" of pain and stress possible.

Successful coping depends on our ability to transcend ourselves and see things objectively and realistically; it depends on our ability to be self-objectified. As pointed out by an old minister, coping with stress is like swimming. The swimmer has to lift up his or her head above the water and see what is coming up. There are times when we seem to be overwhelmed by unsurmountable waves, but after the waves subside, our head is above the water again.

Humor is an expression of self-objectification and helps us handle stress. When stress seems unsurmountable, we need to keep our heads above the water by having a sense of humor.

Hans Selye, who has devoted his life to the study of stress, tells this story of his childhood: His grandmother found him crying, about what he could no longer recall. She regarded at him with a particularly benevolent and protective look, and said, "anytime you feel that low, just try to smile with your face, and you'll see. . . . Soon your whole being will be smiling." Later he wrote in The Stress of Life: "I tried. It works."[20]

The same way of coping with stress can be found in other autobiographical works. During his seven years in a Chinese communist labor camp, Bao Ruo-Wang experienced manifold hardships and went through various stressful situations. In his Prisoner of Mao, he said "The best way to confront hardship is with humor."[21] This was also true for Dr. Morris Fishbein. As a boy he lost control of his anal sphincter and soiled himself on his way home from a playground. He felt ashamed and frightened, but his mother, whose best way of coping with stress was laughter and humor, just laughed. On another occasion he complained bitterly to his mother about how he was mistreated at school. To his great surprise, his mother just laughed. In his autobiography, he said, "I, too, learned to laugh off annoyances."[22]

More than half a century ago, psychologist Boris Sidis reminded us that "when some source of energy is tapped by an appropriate stimulus the result is joy and consequently laughter."[23] Laughter is a release of psychic energy. "Laughter is good medicine" is an ancient saying. This is also the experience of Norman Cousins who wrote Anatomy of an Illness as Perceived by the Patient: Reflection on Healing and Regeneration. He depended on laughter and humor in coping with illness, believing that laughter and other positive emotions enhance body chemistry.[24]

303

Our creativity is often inhibited by fear, anxiety, and other negative emotions. When our creativity is released, true power and wit comes into our minds. Successful coping depends on our creative imagination.

Modern life is dynamic, complex, and unpredictable. At no time in human history has Homo sapiens been so conscious of physical and emotional tension and stress. This is particularly true for executives and professionals. In coping with stress, we need to know the principle that satisfaction from work is much more important than prestige. Another principle is that it is better to do a few things at a satisfying pace than to do many things under pressure with no real satisfaction. Those who practice these principles are less vulnerable to stress. Based on their study of coping with job stress, psychologists Salvatore Maddi and Suzanne Kobasa advised individuals in high stress positions to be tough with themselves, to examine their job experiences, and to get involved in what they were doing. They need to know the impact of their jobs on them as persons. "Hearty individuals" use their stress constructively. It is important for us to believe in our autonomy, if we want to cope with stress successfully. Becoming convinced that we can take care of our own life and exterting some control over it helps us cope with stress. If we do so, we will stay healthier than passive individuals who think life is totally under the control of external forces. An adventurous spirit is another positive force which helps us cope with stress, and successful coping depends also on our interest in new experiences.[25] This implies what Dr. Robert W. White called "competence."[26]

Another coping strategy is being concerned with the interrelationship between the past and future as they impinge on the present. We should look ahead and see clearly. We should be able to distinguish short-term and long-range goals, and formulate viable intermediate goals that provide satisfaction and indicate progress. We should be able to distinguish major demands and minor requirements, and to subordinate minor interests to basic

commitments and major goals. This strategy also
nurtures our powers of concentration. If a disturbance becomes intolerable, we may change our schedule
or plans, but we must never give up the task as a
whole. Whenever we should start to solve a problem,
we quickly sort out extraneous details, and grasp
the heart of the matter. The problem should be man-
ageable, so we can be optimistic about it. Those
who fail to master stress often think their peers
unhelpful and malevolent. A healthy person is generally more cooperative; threatened individuals tend
to withdraw. The more we get involved in the world,
the more accurate are our perceptions of the interrelationship between the past and future. The less
mature person assesses the future vaguely and con-
fusedly. Thus, he or she is less likely to cope
with stress successfully. A healthy person has communicated well with parents in childhood, and has
learned positive patterns of coping. Sensitivity
to others is enhanced by positive parent-child relationships.

        If we are convinced that the worst in life may
turn out to be the best, we can cope better. A state
of impasse is stressful. When an electrical engineer
was deeply in debt, he wanted to take his own life
by jumping out of the window of his eight-dollar-a-
week room in Brooklyn. He brooded, "but death is so
permanent." Pacing the floor, he tried to think of
something useful and constructive. He thought about
a problem related to radio and came up with a proposal, which he presented to an RCA representative.
He got five hundred dollars in advance to buy materials, and in two weeks he was back with the first
radio receiver. "This was the beginning of the
'magic brain' for which RCA radio sets became fa-
mous."[27] His suicidal impulse gave way to positive
thinking, and his pessimistic brooding was replaced
by constructive action. The worst turned out to be
the best.

        Looking for the best in the worst is another
way of coping with stress. This was the approach of
a Chinese woman. In her autobiographical narrative,
she described her unhappy marriage and life as a

beggar. How could a person with human dignity and pride cope with her life situations? She was a positive thinker. "The life of the beggar is not the hardest," said she, "There is freedom. Today perhaps there is not enough to eat, but tomorrow there will be more." "When there is drama on the open-air stage, no lady can get as close to the stage as a beggar." "No woman but a beggar woman could see the magistrate in his embroidered ceremonial robes ride to the temples to offer sacrifices."[28] Perhaps she unconsciously drew resources from the common ancient Chinese belief in Heaven and the goodness of the Universe, as many people of her villiage would do in times of trouble.

One of the basic themes in Lao-Tzu is that "Reversal is the movement of Tao." The pendulum will swing back when it reaches an extreme. The Book of Changes says, "When the cold goes, the warmth comes; when the warmth comes, the cold goes." "When the sun has reached its meridian, it declines, and when the moon has become full, it wanes."[29] This natural principle seems to make Chinese people cautious in times of prosperity, and hopeful in times of hardship. This teaching provided them with a psychological weapon to fight despair, particularly during the darkest hours of World War II--"The dawn will soon come."

A positive attitude is indispensible for coping with stress successfully. Despite her three marital failures, one woman still considered herself "blessed, happy, and grateful."[30] "I have no regrets. That's the way I've grown and learned." This is also true of coping with illness, retardation, and other physical problems. In a study of "parents, physicians, and spina bifida," Rosalyn B. Darling investigated the problems and adjustments of families of children with spina bifida, cerebral palsy, congenital blindness, Down's syndrome, and other forms of moderate to severe psychosomatic retardation.[31] How can the parents cope with their stress and suffering? All the parents who defined their situations positively had suceeded in coping with the widespread stigma placed on the physically and mentally handi-

306

capped. They seemed to draw support from other members of the family, friends, and others in a positive way. The mother of a severely handicapped son
emphatically felt that her son should live as long
as possible in spite of his physician's advice that
he should be allowed to die. Physicians appeared
significant to parents only when they were able to
offer a positive definition of the child as a person.

Melvin Schoonover of the New York Seminary was
a victim of a bone disease called osteogenesis im-
perfecta. Writing to his daughter Polly, who was
only three days old when she suffered her first broken leg, he said, "In many ways I consider myself to
be among the most privileged" in spite of the pain
and loneliness and agony known only by the handicapped. He shared some of his own experiences with
her so that she would preserve the hope that "the
end of the struggle is not despair, but hope and
joy."[32] As a handicapped person, he experienced
"the gift of affliction." He learned that "we find
our lives only by throwing them away by taking all
kinds of stupid risks not only with physical well-
being but also with any self-centered notion that
we can somehow be independent of other men." He was
convinced that independence is a product of interdependence, and that self-centeredness is a mistake.
His positive attitude was the source of his strength
to cope with the pain, loneliness, and agony known
only to himself.

A positive attitude was the psychological weapon by which the first woman in Congress, Jeannette
Rankin, protected herself from depression when she
was defeated in her bid for a second term in 1919.
Looking back fifty years later, she found two things
saved her from feeling depressed: a firm belief that
her legislative career was not over, and a sense that
there was important work for her to do as a woman
and a pacifist.[33]

In coping with stress, we may need to re-exam-
ine our goals, interests, potential, opportunities,
and the ways we achieve them. Coping involves redefinition of our identity, and above all we need a

positive identity. If we feel bad about ourselves,
we are vulnerable to stress. When we fail, we are
likely to look back. But if we have had positive
achievements in the past, we can tell ourselves,
"You have made it, and you are going to make it in
the future too." Then, we may recapture our confidence and competence.

A young college professor became unemployed in
his mid-thirties. He had gone through many agonizing
job-hunting experiences and was discouraged by constant rejection. He was over-qualified and lacked
practical experience. He felt humiliated. He sent
resumes out by the hundreds, but they were thrown
in waste paper baskets. He went to employment agencies, but he was just a guinea pig for career coun-
selors. He responded to newspaper ads in vain. He
made contacts through friends but they could not help
him out. He began to ask, "Who am I? Why am I here?
What do I want to do with my life? What do I enjoy
doing most? What can I do best? Where can I do it?
etc." He sat down and worked out a job-hunting strategy and proceeded step by step, feeling that he was
in command of his own life. He identified his goals
and his commitments whole-heartedly, but modified
them until he carved out a career in business as a
writer.

Successful coping requires proper balance of
differentiation, integration, and transcendence.
Failure often comes from fixation to only one of
these. Transcendence is needed most when we lose
perspective and are overwhelmed by our situation. Integration is needed most when we become isolated,
egocentric and self-pitying. Differentiation is
needed most when we lose positive self-image, freedom, and autonomy. Stress and suffering can become
a stepping stone for further maturation.

3. Loneliness, Love, and
Suffering

The title of Harvard sociologist David Riesman's

book, <u>The Lonely Crowd</u>, indicates the predicament of
modern men and women. Life is full of frustration.
We feel frustrated and lonely, when we encounter
painful rejection, defeat, and failure. Modern society is characterized by differentiation, individuality, and competition. Self-assertion proclaimed in
the name of "equality" increases social conflict and
hostility. At home, happiness is replaced by "Who's
Afraid of Virginia Woolf?" syndrome; the strongest
"castle" for coping is deserted, and the word "love"
becomes irrelevant. The divorce rate increases and
homes are broken. True friends are hard to find;
interpersonal relationships are superficial and poi-
soned by utilitarianism. There is no simple answer
to the stress caused by loneliness and isolation.

Loneliness is an extreme form of differentiation, and its remedy is love, the manifestation of
integration. If we are loved and can love, we cannot be victimized by loneliness. Love is the source
of our strength to buffet stressful situations. A
loveless life is bitterly lonely. Love provides us
with the courage to take on new ventures; it drives
fear away. When we dare to venture, "the battle is
half over."[34] Love is both kind and firm. "Happiness is love, not just laughter." If we have no love,
we can have a million close "friends" and still be
lonely. "Love has more power to unite the world than
the hydrogen bomb does to destroy it." "You can be
the best looking, most popular, most successful person on earth and still be lonely. No matter what
you do, where you go, or what you try to be, loneliness still eats your heart," said Duane Pederson who
mingled among the people moving around the most glam-
orous place called Hollywood.[35] Love and loneliness
are inseparable; "love has no meaning without loneliness; loneliness becomes real only as a response to
love," said Clark E. Moustakas in his discussion on
loneliness and love.[36] Love, in all its forms, is
produced by the interaction of human beings and the
most intense form of love is spontaneously produced
in the family, among close friends, or in small face-
to-face groups. Human love can never be pure; it is
produced for the most part haphazardly side by side
with hate of various kinds. Human love is always

ambivalent. Even so, we cannot live without love.

        To cope with suffering, stress, pain, and sor-
row, we need to cultivate a new receptivity to others.
We must open our hearts as much as possible and welcome the touch, trust, and understanding of others
who are genuinely loving and concerned. The acceptance of love is beneficial not only to the receiver
but also the giver. The power of love is manifested
most strongly in times of trouble. The loving care
that friends and members of the family give has a
healing power to the sufferer. A minister in his
fifties witnessed this healing power of love. His
first wife died of cancer at the age of thirty-one.
He grieved deeply. His mother-in-law said to him,
"Don, we love you so much!" He was touched by the
fact that her first words to him were not about her
daughter or herself, but him. He was recently hospitalized. His teenaged children came and expressed
genuine love for him, friends came and showed such
deep concern that he said, "If you live without being loved, it is no use no matter how long you live.
If you are loved, you don't worry when you will die.
You have got it." Love and care helped him overcome
loneliness and despair.

        A happy family can help us withstand the stress
and strains of modern life. Dr. Richard C. Cabot was
described in Work, Play, Love, Worship, a biographical statement on his life and work, as "a supremely
happy man. His spontaneous, hearty laugh was never
cynical. The exhaustless source of his happiness
was his married life."[37] In order to overcome loneliness, we need the collective "we" spontaneously
united into one "family" by mutual sympathy and responsibility in which our suffering or joy, creative
achievement or failure is fully and willingly shared
by the others, and in which everyone feels an indispensible partner of the whole. What we need today
is unifying and inspiring family relationships.

        In response to the question of how one copes
with stress, a middle-aged junior college president
said that there were three things which had helped
him withstand the assaults of modern life: 1) a sup-

portive family, 2) a summer cottage to retreat, and
3) good sleeping habits. We all need supportive
families, whether we are married or single.

Loneliness is not just a psychological problem
but also a social phenomenon. We are responsible
for the loneliness that we feel, but we are also
responsible for our fear of love. We need to accept
responsibility and take risks. Drugs may give us
ecstatic feelings and excitement, and alcohol may
intoxicate us, but neither can disperse deep rooted
loneliness. By reaching out, we can establish a
happy family, and find supportive friends. Those
who use power to control others may be the most insecure and lonely people of all, although they would
hardly admit it. If they were loved and secure,
they would not need to struggle for power over others
as a means of seeking recognition.

Love can heal painful loneliness, but loving
is also painful. Love can save a person from being
destroyed by stress and suffering, but loving ex-
poses us to rejection, and rejection is painful.
We can only find fulfillment of our human nature by
loving others, but this is risky and threatening.
Love is paradoxical; it is a mystery. Love is beyond reason and intellect. The human mind does not
fully comprehend the mystery that "He who loves his
life loses it, and he who hates his life in this
world will keep it for eternal life."[38]

To love is to know another person. Knowing
is not purely cognitive; it involves the knower
emotionally as well as intellectually. Because love
is self-giving and self-forgetful, love does not
insist on subjectivity only but respects the validity of other persons' existence; it is a remedy for
perceptual distortion. Love enhances our understanding of other persons. Egocentricity creates
loneliness, and distorts perception. To truly know
is to listen to the truth, which is independent from
the knower. In loving, we overcome loneliness and
transcend our egocentricity and subjective biases.
In some ways, those who love truth and pursue it
wholeheartedly are so self-forgetful that there is
no room in their minds for empty and lonely feelings.

311

In this psychodynamic, loneliness is oriented to differentiation, love is oriented to integration, and
knowledge is oriented to transcendence.

There are differences in the ways individuals
react to suffering. Furthermore, there are differences in the ways particular individuals react to
suffering at one time and the ways they react at other times, although the differences may be small.
Nevertheless, we are often locked in our egocentricity
because of pain, stress, and suffering. And it takes
time for us to become unlocked from a state of emotional isolation and egocentricity. In this unlock-
ing process, cognitive understanding is important.
Liberation from loneliness comes when we understand
the situation anew.

A mother, whose son committed suicide because
of a long term illness after an accident, blamed herself for pushing him to do the things which he was
not capable of doing. One day she realized that, by
committing suicide, her son mistreated her as much
as she mistreated him. This made her feel better and
less guilty about his death. She was liberated from
emotional entanglement and her confused state of mind,
and began to see things more objectively.

Before long, she was able to find constructive
channels for reestablishing her relationships with the
world through work as a writer and volunteer. Her
loneliness disappeared shortly. Naturally, she received emotional support from others close to her.
But the moment she objectively assessed the situation
was the turning point. It was a moment of detachment
and transcendence.

Love overcomes fear, and in this sense, love
implies autonomy and independence. The most important concern of those who love is not avoiding of
suffering; they embrace suffering voluntarily. As
German theologian Dorothee Soelle points out, "love
does not 'require' the cross, but de facto it ends
up on the cross."[39] A loving mother voluntarily en-
dures pain and suffers for the birth of her child,
and continues to bear burdens for the child's growth.

Readiness to sacrifice for others indicates the intensity and purity of love. When a person is filled with love and ready to sacrifice their life for others, nothing is powerful enough to stop him or her. Our "true autonomy is the possibility of disposing fully of oneself to give oneself to others," and the fear of giving ourself makes us less autonomous, able to do what is right and loving.[40] This indicates that human autonomy is partly rooted in the capacity to suffer for the sake of others as well as for truth, goodness, and love. Moral suffering is a source of human progress. Without moral suffering, we have no power for renewal.

At one time or another, we all aspire to a Utopia free from suffering. It is not enough to advise our youth to have fun and to enjoy themselves. This gives them a distorted view of reality. They need to suffer for noble causes. Noble people always risk their lives for their causes, rather than live untroubled lives. Sometimes, we need challenge more than anything else. Peace cannot be found by escaping the suffering of the world, but by embracing it with courage and love.

Suffering may make us feel isolated. But if suffering becomes a means by which our compassion and love for others is conveyed, we can accept it wholeheartedly. Innumerable heroes and heroines have endured pain and suffering for those they wanted to help. Suffering communicates our love and helps us relate to others. A testimony of this suffering can be found in some of the last letters of those condemned to death by the Nazis in the years 1939-1945. Those who suffered in the closed prison were not so closed to themselves to make them feel self-pity as we might think. "You imagine that a person condemned to die constantly dwells on it and regrets it. That's not true. From the beginning I thought about the possibility of death. . . . Death is always bad only for the living, for those who are left behind. Therefore I must wish you power and courage. I kiss and embrace you all till we meet again." Another wrote to his wife: "Farewell, I ask you to tell everyone that nothing is ended. I shall die, but you will live."[41] Suffering is universal, but does not always make the sufferer egocentric and self-pitying. On the contrary, suffering may make us turn toward others, our loved ones and friends, and even the whole of humanity.

In learning the universality of suffering, the sufferer may find what is to be truly human and be united with others by the bond of suffering. Ultimate suffering is altruism. In his study of stress, medical scientist Hans Selye learned not only biological truths but also "the evolution of intercellular altruism" and "the evolution of interpersonal altruism."[42] Normal maturation of human personality is altruistic in its direction, and suffering is an important element in this growth. In his study of altruism, sociologist Pitirim A. Sorokin has found: "for 46.9% of the students who experienced a notable change in their life, the catastrophic precipitants were as follows: illness, 8.6%; bereavement, 6.2%; dear person's misfortune or illness, 3.9%; accident, 2.3%; family breakdown, 1.6%; military service, 1.6%; war, 2.3%; disappointment in love, 2.3%."[43] Suffering made them altruistic and mature.

Even though we may succeed in coping with pain, stress, and suffering, we are not immortal. Life prepares us for the eventual moment of departure from this world, death. The homeostatic mechanism of our body is evidently self-preservative, and yet, it leads to disintegration and death eventually, as the new cycle begins. When the fruit is ripe, it returns to where it began--the earth--as a seed to a new life and cycle. In the wisdom of the body, the organism follows its own path to death. If living becomes pointless, it is because we make it so. The larger telic center of the whole universe permits us to wear out gradually, do our work with a sense of fulfillment; it replaces us when the time comes.

4. Suffering and Religious
Experience

How we cope with suffering depends on our maturity, and both suffering and maturity are important subjects for religious experience. Some people suffer without asking questions about God and our place in history or the meaning of life. But others cannot help seeking to understand human suffering in religious terms. If there is a good Lord, who is the Creator and Sustainer of the universe, why do the wicked and unprincipled seize the goods of the earth for themselves while the morally conscientious go away empty-handed; why do earthquakes, floods, and fires destroy good and bad indiscriminately? Moreover, some religious beliefs about God seem inconsistent with the realities of human suffering. Virtue is not rewarded, and evil is not punished. "The hinge that squeaks gets the grease," and the child who cries gets candy, but the docile child gets nothing for obedience, politeness, and goodness. What kind of heavenly Father is this God? Why do we suffer if He is the Living God? Why do the righteous suffer as much as the wicked, if not more? Why do the innocent suffer for evil they have not done? Why does not God always intervene to help his faithful people?

The most common answer to these questions from the earliest days in Judaism is that suffering is a test of faith. In this way, suffering is made purposeful and meaningful. Another approach is acknowledging that suffering is a problem quite beyond human understanding. The classical view is questioned by the book of Job; suffering is not necessarily the result of sin. Job struggled with the problem of suffering and the religious convictions his friends represented, but finally found that the individual is a tiny part of the whole creation and cannot possibly comprehend the design of the Creator. We are too small a fragment of the universe to know the mystery of God's design. There are those who look toward life after death for hope and consolation, and put emphasis on future reward, thus making the present world less significant. Such an eschatological solution to the problem of suffering can be found among political revolutionaries in their endurance of pain and hardship. They are oriented to the future. But for Christians, the future transcends this world.

A religious breakthrough in suffering can be
found in the life of Jesus of Nazareth: He met the
realities of suffering in his own person and was defeated by them; he knew where his life was leading--
to the cross on the Calvary--and he died there; yet
he rose from the dead, in a victory over suffering
and death. Throughout his life, Jesus met the facts
of suffering in a direct and practical way and showed
compassion through healing, feeding, and understanding others. He accepted actively and positively the
facts of suffering and made suffering a means of redemptive love. He was not interested in discussions
about why suffering should exist. The truly creative approach to suffering is not primarily theoretical, but experiential.

The facts of suffering are real. Nobody can
respond creatively by pretending that suffering does
not exist. The truly creative approach to suffering
is a quality of life characterized by faith, hope,
and love. Such a quality of life can be illustrated
by the experience of Leonard Wilson, a missionary in
Asia. During World War II, he was imprisoned by the
Japanese military police for many months, was beaten
and tortured. In a speech on radio in 1946, he summarized these experiences in a Biblical phrase, "more
than conquerors." He overcame suffering by his faith,
hope, and love. The ordeal he went through was a
spiritual experience. It was a challenge to his
courage and love. He said, "Without God's help I
doubt whether I would have come through. Long hours
of ignoble pain were a severe test."[44] Suffering is
particularly important to Christianity, because Jesus'
suffering reveals the true nature of God and human
existence. In Christianity, God is revealed to be
the Suffering Servant. Divine power is not the dic-
tatorial power of domination, control, and violence.
In Jesus, God reveals the power of love and suffering.
As pointed out by Harvard theologian Arthur C. McGill
in his discussion on suffering, "the distinctive mark
of God's power is service and self-giving. And in
this world such power belongs only to him who serves."[45] God is revealed as a sufferer, a servant;

316

but in serving and loving, God remains as divine in his glory, majesty, and power. In this God reveals the perfect paradoxical triune dynamism of differentiation, integration, and transcendence; "self-giving" maintains the paradox between differentiation (self) and integration (giving), and at the same time, "divine" implies transcendence. God is the prototype of Christian maturity.

Should this view of God make us masochistic? It would be a mistake to prohibit the use of drugs in alleviating pains and suffering of those who are dying of cancer or undergoing surgery, just because Jesus suffered on the cross. Jesus was not a masochist who loved to be punished by others or suffered for the sake of suffering; he did not suffer because of low self-esteem or psychological problems. His suffering is believed to be redemptive because it is self-giving for the redemption of the sins of the world in accordance with God's scheme. The cross of Jesus does not make physical suffering itself sacred and redemptive. The act of endurance of pain, poverty, or discomfort has no moral value in and of itself, unless it is borne out of a moral conscience for some altruistic purposes. It has moral value only when it is an expression of self-giving love for others. We have no need to learn deprivation when we have enough food and shelter. The ascetic act cannot be <u>de facto</u> redemptive, unless it is manifested in concrete behavior of altruistic motives. To argue that technology has created a crisis for spiritual leaders today because it alleviates human suffering by producing labor saving devices, and thereby the church is confronted with a harder task of developing Christian spirituality, is questionable.

Physical suffering is not the highest or the hardest kind of suffering in the world; mental and spiritual suffering may well be more painful. Spiritually, Alan Paton of South Africa faced great disappointment in the way his country had been unjust to people of other races. He was beset by attacks of melancholy. After years of struggling against injustice, he learned that active loving saved him from a "morbid preoccupation with the shortcomings of society and the waywardness of men."[46] Active love is truly powerful. We should not love poverty and suffering for their own sake. Suffering must be for the sake of love. The more we love, the more we experience the possibility of suffering. It would be a mistake to think of God whose existence is to serve us, and not vice versa. We cannot really comprehend and endure manifold suffering in this world unless we have come to know the nature of God through Jesus, the Suffering Servant.

In view of the amount of human suffering we hear daily, the 18th century Scottish philosopher and historian David Hume was not off the mark when he raised the question, "Might not the Deity exterminate all ill, wherever it were to be found; and produce all good, without any preparation or long progress of cause and effect?"[47] On the other hand, suffering may be the channel by which we know God. When we reach the "rock beneath," we may find God there. Our extremity is God's opportunity. In this experience, there is a change of attitude, a form of "repentence." Then, we may find an unshakable conviction of enduring value emerging from the depth of suffering. This is the secret of triumphant coping; this is the way the saints coped with life situations, not only in choosing how to respond to unavoidable suffering, but in voluntarily go into situations in which suffering was inevitable; this is how martyrs have responded to suffering--they confront, accept, and carry human suffering with a vision of enduring value which has no parallel in the world, the reality of God. We may not be responsible for the suffering into which life has thrust us, but we are entirely accountable for the attitude we choose.

There is koinonia (communion) in suffering. In suffering we may experience the presence of the Spirit in a way not commonly found in ordinary life. Suffering has the spiritual power to break down barriers between people in order to make them reach out to each other in mutual support and communion. In suffering, we experience new kinds of fellowship, often beyond our expectations. People became friendlier during the blizzard in Massachusetts in February 1978. Snow piled up quickly, cars were stalled, roads were closed, a state emergency was declared, casualties were reported, coastal towns were damaged, and everything seemed paralyzed. Soon people began to help each other. Older people were cared for by young volunteers. Walking on the snowbound streets, people smiled at each other. "It is too bad it took a blizzard to bring out these good qualities in people," commented a news reporter. There was indeed fellowship in suffering, a wonderful reward for the catastrophes people had encountered. Unfortunately, when everything became "normal," people no longer smiled at each other. Suffering suspends social differentiation for the time being, and lets integration have full play in creating harmony, communion, and mutual-smiling. Before long, differentiation resumes in social life. But in the process some people experience fundamental changes in their attitudes and purpose of life through the presence of the Spirit in the event, and the combination and interplay of integration and differentiation turn into transcendence. Then suffering experience becomes the base for further growth.

Character is an important element of human personality. As pointed out by Dr. Leslie D. Weatherhead, "happiness is not a true end. It is always byproduct. Character is the end, for our character development contributes to the glory of God which is the end of all human existence."[48] Character is like gold purified by fire, and suffering is the purifying fire. Many of our troubles are caused by our carelessness, misuse of freedom, selfish desire, or pure ignorance. "Fire" is needed to purify them. "If our days were all sunshine--our lives would become a desert, our streams of sympathy would dry up, our eyes would become spiritually blind and our nature swinishly selfish," said churchman Ralph Sockman.[49] In suffering we find "the deeper meanings and richer resources of life." Indomitable spirits do not come ordinarily from affluent untested lives. "Storms make strong oaks," and unconquerable spirits are forged by countless suffering experiences. Personal suffering played an important role in the rise of great leaders such as Abraham Lincoln, Franklin D. Roosevelt. Poverty is a seedbed for crime, but a

319

number of great men and women have come from poor families.

To the grieved, everything seems negative, but those who have gone through bereavement are inclined to be more understanding and eager to make themselves available to anyone who may suffer likewise. They are more sensitive to the futility of advising the bereaved to be brave, knowing that in due time the bereaved will accept death. Although death is a painful event, it is also a great creator of sympathy and understanding. We want to know "Why me? Why mine?" and yet we do not get answers no matter how hard we try, because there will always be questions unanswered in this world.

Growing pains must be accepted as part of the growing process; their presence is an important stimulus in the process of maturation. Adversity makes us mature. When we experience pain and suffering, we may need it rather than we deserve it. However, it is not a good policy to suffer without complaining. Unquestioning submission to pain and suffering is masochism. We can learn nothing from suffering unless we question it and work through it somehow. Working through it, we may increase our capacity for love. This is the strength of weakness, action of non-action, usefulness of the useless. Growth is a form of change, and suffering accelerates that change. In the process of maturation we must die to egocentricity so that we may become more receptive to what is communicated by the external world and by our true selfhood, and above all become more sensitive to what God is doing. Mencius learned this and said, "When Heaven is about to bestow great responsibility on any man, it trains his mind with suffering, his sinews and bones with hard work, his body with hunger; it puts him to poverty, places obstacles in the paths of his doing, so as to make his mind alert, harden his character, and improve whatever is incompetent."[50]

"Man is born to trouble as the sparks fly upwards," said Eliphaz to Job.[51] Suffering became part of human destiny after the loss of Paradise. Saint Augustine believed that God created a pefect

320

world before the Fall, but another ancient church
father, Irenaeus, saw our world as the divinely ap-
pointed environment in which human beings were to
grow to a mature state signifying the fulfillment
of God's purpose on earth.[52] Although suffering
should not be endured passively, but fought, it may
make us grow toward maturity and become less egocentric. A college football player suffering from tuberculosis had to be hospitalized for about a year.
Although his time seemed wasted, he said later, "I
can see now that it was an important part of my
training. It gave me a new sense of the value of
life, not only my own but of all." Recovering from
illness in 1929, Albert Einstein said, "Illness has
its advantages: one learns to think. I have just
begun to think."[53] Suffering may become a turning
point in life. Suffering may crack our egocentric
shell and release the power of love, bringing us
true joy and happiness.

Maturity is not measured by age but by the
quality of life. Jesus epitomizes this quality. His
life embodied not only suffering for love's sake but
also love itself, the fulfillment of human life.

To love is to tear selfishness apart. That
tearing is painful, but not self-destructive: rather
it is self-fulfilling. When a person becomes unselfish and is ready to die, he or she is capable
of releasing great power. This power is the power
of love, which is redemptive and has the capacity
to heal.

NOTES

1. The Oxford Dictionary of Quotations (London:
    Oxford University Press, 1966), p. 434.

2. J. C. White and W. H. Sweet, Pain: Its Mechanism
    and Neurosurgical Control (Springfield, Ill.:
    Charles C. Thomas, 1955), p. 68.

3. David Bakan, Disease, Pain, and Sacrifice (Chi-

cago: University of Chicago Press, 1968), pp. 68-69.

4. Kenneth A. Holroyd and Frank Andrasik, "Coping and the Self-Control of Chronic Tension Headache," Journal of Consulting and Clinical Psychology, 46 (5) (1978), pp. 1036-1045.

5. R. Melzack and T. H. Scott, "The Effects of Early Experience on the Response to Pain," Journal of Comparative and Physiological Psychology, 50 (1957), pp. 155-161.

6. W. R. Loewenstein and Y. Kanno, "Intercellular Communication and the Control of Tissue Growth: Lack of Communication between Cancer Cells," Nature, 209 (1966), pp. 1248-1249.

7. C. P. Crowley, "Stress and Structure," in Explorations in the Psychology of Stress and Anxiety ed. Byron P. Rouke (Toronto: Longman's Canada Ltd., 1969), pp. 171-178.

8. Erik H. Erikson, Childhood and Society (New York: W. W. Norton & Co., 1963), pp. 268-269.

9. Hans Selye, The Stress of Life (New York: McGraw-Hill, 1956), pp. 260, 282.

10. Orlo Strunk, Jr., "All Things Hold Together," in Psychology and Faith ed. H. Newton Maloney (Washington, D.C.: University Press of America, 1978), pp. 234-242.

11. Selye, The Stress of Life, pp. 31-32, 271.

12. Charles M. Solley, "Effects of Stress on Perceptual Attention," in Explorations in the Psychology of Stress and Anxiety ed. Bryon P. Rouke (Toronto: Longmans Canada Ltd., 1969), pp. 1-14.

13. I. G. Sarason, "Empirical Findings and Theoretical Problems in the Use of Anxiety Scales," Psychological Bulletin, 57 (1960), pp. 403-412.

14. M. Arnold, "Stress and Emotion," in Psychologi-

cal Stress: Issues in Research ed. M. H. Appley
and R. Trumbull (New York: Appleton-Century-
Crofts, 1967), p. 126.

15. T. S. Langer and S. T. Michael, Life Stress and
Mental Health (Glencoe, Ill.: Free Press, 1963).

16. L. B. Murphy, "The Problem of Defense and the
Concept of Coping," The Child in His Family ed.
E. J. Anthony and C. Kouperr (New York: John
Wiley and Sons, 1970).

17. D. H. Funkenstein, S. H. King, and M. E. Drolette, Mastery of Stress (Cambridge, MA: Harvard
University Press, 1957).

18. Ibid.

19. Antonnia Vallentine, H. G. Wells, Prophet of Our
Day (New York: Doubleday & Co., 1959), pp. 105-
114.

20. Selye, The Stress of Life, p. 263.

21. Ruo-Wang Bao and Kudolph Chelminski, Prisoner
of Mao (New York: Coward, McCann and Geoghegan,
1973), p. 7.

22. Morris Fishbein, An Autobiography (New York:
Doubleday & Co., 1969), p. 30.

23. Boris Sidis, The Psychology of Laughter (New
York: Appleton, 1923), pp. 68-69. See also,
Morris M. Brody, "The Meaning of Laughter," Psy-
choanalytic Quarterly, 19 (1949), pp. 224-225.

24. Norman Cousins, Anatomy of an Illness as Perceived by the Patient: Reflections on Healing
and Regeneration (New York: W. W. Norton & Co.,
1979).

25. S. Maddi and S. Kobasa, "Coping with Job Stress,"
Boston Sunday Globe, September 4, 1977, p. 31.

26. Robert W. White, "Motivation Reconsidered: The
Concept of Competence," Pyschological Review, 66
(1959), pp. 297-333.
323

27. V. Boesen, <u>They Said It Couldn't Be Done</u> (New York: Doubleday & Co., 1971), pp. 29-30.

28. Ida Pruit, <u>A Daughter of Han: The Autobiography of a Chinese Working Woman</u> (New Haven: Yale University Press, 1945), pp. 72-73.

29. <u>Lao Tzu</u>, ch. 40. See also, <u>The Book of Changes</u> Appendix iii, i. Fung Yu-lan, <u>A Short History of Chinese Philosophy</u> (New York: Macmillan Co., 1948), p. 19. Cp. Kwang-kuo Hwang, "The Patterns of Coping Strategies in a Chinese Society," <u>Acta Psychologica Taiwanica</u>, 19 (1977), pp. 61-73.

30. Lloyd Shearer, "Doris Day: The Woman behind the Image," <u>Parade</u>, February 8, 1976, pp. 8-9.

31. Rosalyn B. Darling, "Parents, Physicians, and Spina Bifida," <u>The Hastings Center Report,</u> 7 (4) (1977), pp. 10-13.

32. Melvin Schoonover, <u>Letters to Polly</u> (Grand Rapid, Mich.: William B. Erdmans Publishing Co., 1971).

33. Hannah Josephson, <u>Jeannette Rankin: First Lady in Congress</u> (Indianapolis, Ind.: Bobbs-Merrill Co., 1974), p. 105.

34. Cyril H. Powell, <u>The Lonely Heart</u> (Nashville: Abingdon Press, 1960), p. 33.

35. Duane Pederson, <u>On Lonely Street with God</u> (New York: Hawthorn Books, Inc., 1973), p. 31.

36. Clark E. Moustakas, <u>Loneliness and Love</u>(Englewood Cliffs, NJ: Prentice-Hall, 1946), p. 143.

37. <u>Work, Play, Love, Worship</u> (Ella Lyman Cabot Trust, Cambridge, Massachussetts, 1961), p. 9.

38. John 12:25.

39. Dorothee Soelle, <u>Suffering</u> (Philadelphia: Fortress Press, 1973), p. 163.

40. Louis Evely, <u>Suffering</u> (New York: Doubleday &

Co., 1974), p. 92.

41. Soelle, _Suffering_, pp. 135-136.

42. Selye, _The Stress of Life_, pp. 260-282.

43. Pitirim A. Sorokin, _The Ways and Power of Love_ (Boston: Beacon Press, 1954), p. 222.

44. John Bowker, _Problems of Suffering in Religions of the World_ (New York: Cambridge University Press, 1970), p. 76.

45. Arthur C. McGill, _Suffering: A Test of Theolgical Method_ (Philadelphia: Geneva Press, 1968), pp. 56-57.

46. Alan Paton, "The Challenge of Fear," in _What I Have Learned_ (New York: Simon and Schuster, 1968), pp. 257-259.

47. David Hume, _Dialogue Concerning Natural Religion_ (Oxford: Claredon Press, 1935), pt. xi, p. 253.

48. Leslie D. Weatherhead, _Salute to a Sufferer_ (Nashville: Abingdon Press, 1962), p. 28.

49. Ralph Sockman, _The Meaning of Suffering_ (Nashville: Abingdon Press, 1961), p. 78.

50. _The Book of Mencious_, 6B:15.

51. Job 5:7.

52. John Hick, _Evil and the God of Love_ (New York: Macmillan Co., 1966), pp. 207 ff.

53. Ronald W. Clark, _Eintein: The Life and Time_ (New York: World Publishing Co., 1971), p. 400.

CHAPTER

X

CONCLUSION

Human growth is a triune process, based on
three basic principles: differentiation, integration,
and transcendence. Growth is a dynamic multiple interaction of these, often with one dominating while
the other two remain inherently present and potently
active. This triune nature of the growing process is
uniquely human. In differentiation, we find integration and transcendence; in integration, we find differentiation and transcendence; and in transcendence, we
find integration and differentiation. We are not just
another organism, nor are we just physical beings.
We are capable of transcendence, and have a higher
level of complexity in our differentiation and integration. Such transcendence constitutes our spirituality.

Each stage of life has three dimensions: body,
mind, and spirit. These three dimensions are woven
around three polarities: subjectivity, objectivity,
and divinity. Every experience has unpredictable
dynamism operating in the interaction between the
internal and the external, the subjective and the
objective, whether this interaction is in the form
of an "I" and "thou," or "I" and "it" relationship.
In this unpredictable dynamism, we may find not only
human forces but also the power, wisdom, creativity,
and love of the Spirit. This unpredictable dynamism
makes human faith and spirituality possible and indispensible, and constitutes true religion.

The Spirit is both transcendent and immanent.
As we find integration and transcendence in differentiation, transcendence and differentiation in integration, and differentiation and integration in transcendence, the three polarities of subjectivity, objectivity, and divinity are also interwoven with each
other in constituting a dialectical and "three-in-one"

327

"one-in-three" triune dynamism. In human experience, this triune dynamism is manifested in the dialectical relationship of "I" and "thou," both divine and human, because, the Spirit, who is transcendent, is also immanent in us. In this triune dynamism, transcendence embodies both differentiation and integration; divinity embodies both subjectivity and objectivity. In Freudian understanding of human personality, the triune dynamism is composed of the id, the ego, and the superego: the id is oriented to differentiation; the ego, integration; and the superego, transcendence.

Human growth is divided into childhood, adolescence, young adulthood, middle adulthood, late adulthood. In childhood, maturation is oriented to differentiation so that the child becomes differentiated from parents as an individual. In adolescence, maturation is oriented to integration so that the adolescent integrates various self-images, forming an identity that will further integrate into the larger society in young adulthood, while differentiated from the parents and transcended from childhood. In adulthood, maturation is oriented to transcendence so that the mature adult transcends from self and society, achieving accurate and realistic perceptions, better planning, acting, evaluating, and eventually dying, while being differentiated as an individual and integrated into society. In each stage, differentiation, integration, and transcendence are present and manifest themselves differently. The triune dynamism of human growth is operative at each stage of life.

Conceptually, we may discuss the three principles of differentiation, integration, and transcendence as if they were separate entities. But experientially, they are interwoven. The more mature we become, the more differentiated, integrated, and transcended we are. If we are differentiated, we are at the same time integrated and transcended in the growing process. The more externally individualized we are, the more internally integrated we become, and the less egocentric we turn out to be. Growth implies transcendence, and maturation is a triune process.

Human growth is not just ego-centered assimilation, nor is it just adaptive socialization; it is a process of dynamic interaction between the subjective and the objective, and of self-objectified transcending process. To become independent, we must be nurtured by our parents and others, and depend on them. To be creative, we must depend on the environment and have thorough knowledge and experience of the field as well as a transcending vision, which expresses originality, excellence, and profoundness. True independence comes from interdependence, and true autonomy is nurtured by heteronomy. Identity is born of identifications, and identification leads to individuation. The growing experience is both joyful and painful. It is physical, emotional, and spiritual.

Life becomes meaningless when one of the three dimensions of human existence--the physical, the emotional, and the spiritual--is totally ignored, or one of the three basic principles--differentiation, integration, and transcendence--is totally disfunctional. We must constantly be aware of the importance of the physical, emotional, and spiritual dimensions of daily living. In principle, we must have differentiation, integration, and transcendence in our growing process.

The major themes which compose maturity and the process of maturation are "autonomy and independence," "identity and ego-ideal," "creativity and care," "reality perception," and "suffering and coping." All are mutually related. If a person is autonomous and independent, he or she is likely to have formed his or her identity and ego-ideal successfully, to be fairly creative, and to care for him or herself, for others as well for his or her products, just as he or she is capable of perceiving reality accurately and of coping with stress and suffering successfully. Naturally, maturity is more strongly manifested in some areas than others. If a person has kept the triune dynamism of differentiation, integration, and transcendence from disruption, he or she is wholesome and mature. He or she has inner strength, self-confidence, basic trust, integrity, and humor.

329

Maturity needs to be seen in two ways: 1) as a state of being, and 2) as a process of becoming. Maturity as a state of being symbolizes the state of perfection we can aspire to but never reach. In religion, God symbolizes perfection; in Christianity, God is the prototype of maturity. Although we may aspire to be as perfect as God is perfect, we can never be. By nature, God transcends all. No matter how mature we are, we are human.

Maturity as a process of becoming signifies the triune dynamism of differentiation, integration, and transcendence in human grwoth. Theologically, this "three-in-one" "one-in-three" triune dynamism is manifested in the Holy Trinity, one God in three persons--the Father, the Son, and the Holy Spirit, classically expressed in terms of "one substance in three persons" (una substantia, tres personae). The Holy Trinity symbolizes the triune perfection of differentiation, integration, and transcendence. Ecclesiastically, this triune dynamism is manifested in three types of church polity with their respective emphases and orientations to the three basic principles of human growth--1) Congregationalism (differentiation), 2) Presbyterianism (integration), and 3) Episcopacy (transcendence).

Finally, we see the triune dynamism of differentiation, integration, and transcendence in politics, education, and business. In politics, we see it in the triune system of the U.S. government--one government in three branches: Congress, the Chief Executive, and the Supreme Court. Although each branch of the government follows the triune dynamism of human grwoth, Congress is oriented to differentiation, representing each of the fifty states; the Chief Executive is oriented to integration, representing the nation; the Supreme Court is oriented to transcendence, representing legal justice. Likewise, we see differentiation in laissez faire education, integration in democratic education, and transcendence in authoritarian education. In business, we see differentiation in competition, integration in cooperation, and transcendence in innovation; in each company, the triune dyanism is manifested in labor, management, and R & D (research and development).

Thus, the triune dynamism of differentiation, integration, and transcendence is essential to human maturation and maturity; it determines every aspect of our life individually and collectively; it sheds light to our understanding of where we are socially and culturally; and it helps us decide our future direction. Above all, the triune dynamism points to the living God, the Ultimate of the universe.

BIBLIOGRAPHY

Allport, Floyd H. Theories of Perception and the Concept of Structure. New York: John Wiley & Sons, 1955.

Allport, Gordon W. The Individual and His Religion. New York: The Macmillan Co., 1950.

Allport, Gordon W. Personality: A Psychological Interpretation. New York: Holt, 1961.

Allport, Gordon W. Pattern and Growth in Personality. New York: Holt, 1961.

Allport, Gordon W. The Person in Psychology. Boston: Beacon Press, 1968.

Allport, Gordon W. The Use of Personal Documents in Psychological Science. New York: Social Science Research Council, 1942.

Allport, Gordon W. ed. Letters from Jenny. New York: Harcourt, Brace and World, 1965.

Allport, Gordon W. Becoming: Basic Considerations for a Psychology of Personality. New Haven, Conn.: Yale University Press, 1955.

Allport, G. W. and Ross, J. M. "Personal Religious Orientation and Prejudice." Journal of Personality and Social Psychology 5 (1967):432-443.

Baillie, John. Our Knowledge of God. New York: Charles Scribner's Sons, 1959.

Babin, Pierre. Faith and the Adolescent. New York: Herder and Herder, 1965.

Bales, Robert Freed. Personality and Interpersonal Behavior. New York: Holt, Rinehart and Winston, 1970.

Baltes, P. B. and Shaie, K. W., eds. Life Span Devel-

opmental Psychology: Personality and Socialization.
New York: Academic Press, 1973.

Barron, Frank. Creative Person and Creative Process.
New York: Holt, Rinehart and Winston, 1969.

Barron, Frank. Creativity and Psychological Health.
New York: D. Van Nostrand, 1963.

Bea, Cardinal Augustin, et al. What I Have Learned.
New York: Simon and Schuster, 1968.

Beard, Ruth M. Piaget's Developmental Psychology.
New York: Basic Books, 1969.

Beisser, Arnold R. "Identity Formation within Groups."
Journal of Humanistic Psychology, 9 (1971):133-146.

Belgum, David. Religion and Personality in the Spiral
of Life. Washington, D. C.: University Press of
America, 1979.

Berkowitz, L. The Development of Motives and Values
in the Child. New York: Basic Books, 1964.

Bertocci, P. A. and Millard, R. M. Personality and
the Good. New York: David McKay Co., 1965,

Birren, J. E. The Psychology of Aging. Englewood
Cliffs, N.J.: Prentice Hall, 1964.

Bischof, L. J. Adult Psychology. New York: Harper &
Row, 1969.

Blair, J. "Who Is Emotionally Mature?" Psychology
12 (1975):33-38.

Blake, R. R. and Ramsey, G. V. ed. Perception: An
Approach to Personality. New York: Ronald Press,
1951.

Boelen, Bernard. Personal Maturity. New York: Seabury
Press, 1978.

Botwinick, J. Cognitive Process in Maturity and Old

Age. New York: Springer, 1967.

Bower, T. G. R. The Perceptual World of the Child. Cambridge, Mass.: Harvard University Press, 1977.

Branden, N. "On the Concept of Mental Health." The Personalist 54 (1973):216-221.

Bronowski, J. The Identity of Man. New York: Double-day/National History Press, 1965.

Browning, Don S. Generative Man: Psychoanalytic Per-spectives. Philadelphia: Westminster Press, 1973.

Bruner, Jerome S. On Knowing. Cambridge, Mass.: Harvard University Press, 1962.

Bruner, Jerome S. et al. Studies in Cognitive Growth. New York: John Wiley & Sons, 1966.

Bull, Norman. Moral Judgment from Childhood to Ado-lescence. Beverly Hills, CA: Sage Publications, 1969.

Button, J. H. and Britton, J. O. Personality Changes in Aging. New York: Springer, 1972.

Cameron, Norman. Personality Development and Psycho-pathology. Boston: Houghton Mifflin Co., 1963.

Chaplin, D. P. Children and Religion. New York: Charles Scribner's Sons, 1961.

Chase, Stuart. The Proper Study of Mankind. New York: Harper & Row, 1956.

Cobb, E. "Childhood Religion." Daelalus 86 (1956): 582-600.

Cole, M. and Scribner, S. Culture and Thought. New York: John Wiley & Sons, 1974.

Colm, H. "Religious Symbolism in Childhood Analysis." American Journal of Psychoanalysis 12 (1953):39-56.

Daly, Mary. Beyond God the Father. Boston: Beacon

Press, 1973.

Deutscher, Irwin. "The Quality of Postparental Life:
Definitions of the Situation." _Journal of Marriage
and the Family_ 26 (1964):52-59.

Dignan, M. H. "Ego Identity and Maternal Identification." _Journal of Personality and Social Psychology_
1 (1965):476-483.

Dittes, J. "Justification by Faith and the Experimental Psychologist." _Religion in Life_ 28 (1959):
567-576.

Dollard, John. _Criteria for the Life History_. New
Haven, Conn.: Yale University Press, 1935.

Dupre, Louis. _Transcendental Selfhood_. New York:
Seabury Press, 1976.

Eisdorfer, C. and Lawton, M. P. eds. _The Psychology
of Adult Development and Aging_. Washington, D. C.:
The American Psychological Association, 1973.

Elkin, D. and Elkin, S. "Varieties of Religious Experience in Young Adolescents." _Journal for the
Scientific Study of Religion_ 2 (1962):102-112.

Erikson, Erik H. _Childhood and Society_. New York:
W. W. Norton & Co., 1950.

Erikson, Erik H. _Young Man Luther_. New York: W. W.
Norton & Co., 1958.

Erikson, Erik H. _Identity and the Life Cycle: Psychological Issues_. New York: International Universities Press, 1959.

Erikson, Erik H. _Identity, Youth and Crisis_. New
York: W. W. Norton & Co., 1968.

Erikson, Erik H. _Dimensions of a New Identity_. New
York: W. W. Norton & Co., 1974.

Erikson, Erik H. ed. _Adulthood_. New York: W. W. Norton & Co., 1978.

Fitcher, J. "Religion and Socialization among Children." Review of Religious Research 6 (1962):24-33.

Fowler, James W. and Keen, S. Life Maps: Conversations on the Journey of Faith. Waco, Texas: Word Books, 1978.

Fowler, James W. et al. Trajectories in Faith: Five Life Stories. Nashville, Tenn.: Abingdon Press, 1980.

Frankl, Victor E. Man's Search for Meaning. Boston: Beacon Press, 1958.

Freud, Sigmund. Civilization and Its Discontents. New York: W. W. Norton & Co., 1952.

Freud, Sigmund. The Future of an Illusion. New York: Doubleday & Co., 1953.

Freud, S. and Bullitt, W. C. Thomas Woodrow Wilson: A Psychological Study. Boston: Houghton Mifflin Co., 1967.

Fried, B. The Middle Age Crisis. New York: Harper & Row, 1967.

Gesell, Arnold. The First Five Years of Life. New York: Harper & Row, 1940.

Gibson, Eleanor. Principles of Perceptual Learning and Development. New York: Appleton-Century-Crofts, 1969.

Gilligan, Carol. "In a Different Voice." Harvard Educational Review 47 (1977):481-517.

Gilchrist, M. The Psychology of Creativity. Melbourne, Australia: Melbourne University Press, 1972.

Glasser, William. The Identity Society. New York: Harper & Row, 1972.

Goethals, G. W. and Klos, D. S. Experiencing Youth:

First Person Account. Boston: Little, Brown and
Co., 1971.

Goldman, Ronald. Religious Thinking from Childhood
to Adolescence. New York: Seabury Press, 1964.

Goldman, Ronald. Readiness for Religion. New York:
Seabury Press, 1965.

Gould, Roger. Transformations: Growth and Change in
Adult Life. New York: Simon and Schuster, 1978.

Green, Richard. Sexual Identity Conflict in Children
and Adults. New York: Basic Books, 1974.

Hall, C. S. and Lindzey, G. Theories of Personality.
New York: John Wiley & Sons, 1965.

Hann, N. Coping and Defending. New York: Academic
Press, 1977.

Hanson, R. P. C. God: Creator, Saviour, Spirit.
Richmond, Va.: John Knox Press, 1973.

Harris, Ralph N. "The Meaning of Personal Identity."
American Journal of Psychoanalysis 31 (1971):39-47.

Hauser, S. T. Black and White Identity Formation.
New York: John Wiley & Sons, 1971.

Havighurst, Robert J. Developmental Tasks and Education. Chicago: University of Chicago Press, 1972.

Heath, Douglas H. Explorations of Maturity: Studies
of Mature and Immature College Men. New York:
Appleton-Century-Crofts, 1965.

Heath, Douglas H. Maturity and Competence: A Trans-
cultural View. New York: Halsted Press, 1977.

Hennessey, Thomas. Studies in Moral Development.
New York: Paulist Press, 1976.

Hick, John. Evil and the God of Love. New York:
Macmillan Co., 1966.

Hodgson, Leonard. The Doctrine of the Trinity. New York: Charles Scribner's Sons, 1944.

Hsu, Francis L. K. Clan, Caste, and Club. Princeton, N.J.: D. Van Nostrand, 1963.

Hus, Francis L. K. The Challenge of the American Dream. Belmont, CA: Wadsworth Publishing Co., 1970.

Jahoda, Marie. Current Concepts of Positive Mental Health. New York: Basic Books, 1958.

James, William. The Varieties of Religious Experience. New York: Longmans, Green and Co., 1928.

Johnson, Paul E. Personality and Religion. Nashville, Tenn.: Abingdon Press, 1957.

Jung, Carl G. Modern Man in Search of a Soul. London: Routledge and Kegan Paul, 1933.

Kagan, Jerome. The Growth of Child. New York: W. W. Norton & Co., 1978.

Kagan, Jerome and Moss, H. Birth to Maturity: A Study in Psychological Development. New York: John Wiley & Sons, 1962.

Kagan, Jerome ed. Creativity and Learning. Boston: Houghton Mifflin Co., 1967.

Kao, Charles C. L. Search for Maturity. Philadelphia: Westminster Press, 1975.

Kao, Charles C. L. "Identity, Faith, and Maturity." Journal of Psychology and Theology 3 (1975):42-48.

Kaufman, Gordon D. Systematic Theology: A Historicist's Perspective. New York: Charles Scribner's Sons, 1968.

Kaufman, Gordon D. The Problem of God. Cambridge, Mass.: Harvard University Press, 1972.

Keniston, Kenneth. The Uncommitted: Alienated Youth in American Society. New York: Dell, 1960.

Kiev, A. A Strategy for Handling Executive Stress.
Chicago: Nelson Hall, 1974.

Kilpatrick, William. Identity and Intimacy. New
York: Doubleday & Co., 1975.

Kimmel, Douglas C. Adulthood and Aging. New York:
John Wiley & Sons, 1973.

King, Stanley H. Five Lives at Harvard. Cambridge,
Mass.: Harvard University Press, 1973.

King, S. H.; Funkenstein, D. D.; and Drolette, M. E.
Mastery of Stress. Cambridge, Mass.: Harvard University Press, 1957.

Klapp, Orrin E. Collective Search for Identity.
New York: Holt, Rinehart and Winston, 1969.

Klink, J. L. Your Child and Religion. Richmond, Va.:
John Knox Press, 1972.

Kohlberg, Lawrence. "Development of Moral Character
and Moral Ideology." In Review of Child Development Research, edited by W. L. Hoffman and L. W.
Hoffman. New York: Russell Sage Foundation, 1959.

Köhler, Wolfang. The Task of Gestalt Psychology.
Princeton, N.J.: Princeton University Press, 1969.

Kunkel, F. In Search of Maturity. New York: Charles
Scribner's Sons, 1943.

Lehman, Harvey. Age and Achievement. Princeton, N.J.:
Princeton University Press, 1953.

Lenski, Gehard. The Religious Factor. New York:
Doubleday & Co., 1961.

LeShan, Eda J. The Wonderful Crisis of Middle Age.
New York: David McKay Co., 1973.

Levinson, Daniel J. et al. The Seasons of a Man's
Life. New York: Alfred A. Knopf, 1978.

Lickona, Thomas ed. Moral Development and Behavior.

New York: Holt, Rinehart and Winston, 1976.

Lidz, Theodore. The Person: Stages of Life Cycle.
New York: Basic Books, 1976.

Loevinger, Jane and Wessler, Ruth. Measuring Ego-
Development. San Francisco: Jossey-Bass, 1970.

Lomas, P. "Family Role and Identity Formation."
International Journal of Psychoanalysis 42 (1961):
371-380.

Lowenthal, M. F. "Social Isolation and Mental Illness in Old Age." American Sociological Review
29 (1964):54-70.

Lowenthal, M. F. and C. Hawen. "Interaction and
Adaptation: Intimacy as a Critical Variable."
American Sociological Review 33 (1968):20-30.

MacKinnon, Donald W. "Personality and the Realization of Creative Potential." American Psychologist
20 (1965):273-281.

Maddi, Salvatore R. Personality Theories: A Comparative Analysis. Homewood, Ill.: Dorsey Press, 1968.

Malony, H. Newton. Psychology and Faith: The Christian Experience of Eighteen Psychologists. Washington, D. C.: University Press of America, 1979.

Martinich, A. P. "Identity and Trinity." The Journal
of Religion 58 (1978):169-181.

Maslow, Abraham H. Motivation and Personality. New
York: Harper and Brothers, 1954.

Maslow, Abraham H. Toward a Psychology of Being.
New York: D. Van Nostrand, 1962.

Maslow, Abraham H. Values and Peak Experiences.
New York: Viking Press, 1970.

May, Rollo. Love and Will. New York: W. W. Norton
& Co., 1969.

May, Rollo. The Courage to Create. New York: W. W. Norton & Co., 1975.

Maynard, Donald M. Your Home Can Be Christian. Nashville, Tenn.: Abingdon Press, 1952.

Mayer, N. The Male Mid-Life Crisis: Fresh Starts after 40. New York: Doubleday & Co., 1978.

McClelland, D. C. The Roots of Consciousness. New York: D. Van Nostrand, 1964.

McClelland, D. C.; Rindlisbacher, A.; and deCharms, R. "Religious and Other Sources of Parental Attitudes toward Independence Training." In Studies in Motivation, edited by D. C. McClelland. New York: Appleton-Century-Crofts, 1955.

McGhee, Paul E. "Moral Development and Children's Appreciation of Humor." Developmental Psychology 10 (1974):514-525.

McGill, Arthur C. Suffering: A Test of Theological Method. Philadelphia: Geneva Press, 1968.

McLeish, John A. B. The Ulyssean Adult. Toronto: McGraw-Hill Ryerson, 1976.

Meynall, Hugo. "The Holy Trinity and the Corrupted Consciousness." Theology 79 (1976):143-151.

Miller, Randolph C. Your Child's Religion. New York: Doubleday & Co., 1962.

Mischel, T. ed. Cognitive Development and Epstemology. New York: Academic Press, 1971.

Morris, Charles W. Varieties of Human Values. Chicago: University of Chicago Press, 1956.

Moustakas, Clark E. The Self. New York: Harper & Row, 1956.

Murphy, Gardner. Outgrowing Self-Deception. New York: Basic Books, 1975.

Murphy, Gardner. *Human Potentialities*. New York: Basic Books, 1958.

Nelson, James ed. *Wisdom*. New York: W. W. Norton & Co., 1958.

Neugarten, Bernice L. ed. *Middle Age and Aging*. Chicago: University of Chicago Press, 1968.

Niebuhr, H. Richard. *The Meaning of Revelation*. New York: Macmillan Co., 1967.

Niebuhr, H. Richard. *The Responsible Self*. New York: Harper & Row, 1963.

Niebuhr, Reinhold. *Faith and History*. New York: Charles Scribner's Sons, 1949.

Niebuhr, Richard R. *Experiential Religion*. New York: Harper & Row, 1972.

Nouwen, Henri J. M. *Reaching Out*. New York: Doubleday & Co., 1975.

O'Connell, Agnes H. "The Relationships between Life Style and Identity Synthesis and Resynthesis in Traditional, Neotraditional, and Nontraditional Women." *Journal of Personality* 44 (1976):482-486.

Ornstein, Robert. *The Psychology of Consciousness*. San Francisco: W. H. Freeman & Co., 1972.

Otto, R. *The Idea of Holy*. New York: Oxford University Press, 1958.

Overstreet, Harry A. *The Mature Mind*. New York: W. W. Norton & Co., 1949.

Palmore, Erdman ed. *Normal Aging*, Vol. 1 and 2. Durham, N.C.: Duke University Press, 1970, 1974.

Perry, Ralph Barton. *General Theory of Value*. Cambridge, Mass.: Harvard University Press, 1950.

Phenix, Philip Henry. *Education for the Common Good*.

New York: Harper and Brothers, 1961.

Piaget, Jean. The Construction of Reality in the Child. New York: Basic Books, 1954.

Piaget, Jean. The Origin of Intelligence in Children. New York: International Universities Press, 1956.

Piaget, Jean. Judgment and Reasoning in the Child. Totawa, J.N.: Littlefield, Adams & Co., 1966.

Piaget, Jean. Mental Image in the Child. London: Routledge and Kegan Paul, 1971.

Piaget, Jean. The Grasp of Consciousness. Cambridge, Mass.: Harvard University Press, 1973.

Prenter, Regin. Spiritus Creator. Philadelphia: Mulenberg Press, 1953.

Pruyser, Paul. A Dynamic Psychology of Religion. New York: Harper & Row, 1968.

Rahner, Karl. Foundations of Christian Faith. New York: Seabury Press, 1978.

Rawls, John. A Theory of Justice. Cambridge, Mass.: Harvard University Press, 1971.

Richardson, S. A. et al. Interviewing, Its Form and Functions. New York: Basic Books, 1965.

Rizzuto, Ana-Maria. The Birth of the Living God. Chicago: University of Chicago Press, 1979.

Rogers, Carl R. On Becoming a Person. Boston: Houghton Mifflin Co., 1961.

Rogers, William R. et al. Toward Moral and Religious Maturity. First International Conference on Moral and Religious Development, Abbey of Senanque, 1979. Morristown, N.J.: Silver Burdett & Co., 1980.

Ross, Murray. The Religious Beliefs of Youth. New York: Association Press, 1950.

Seidel, G. J. _The Crisis of Creativity_. London, Nortre Dame: University of Notre Dame Press, 1966.

Selye, Hans. _The Stress of Life_. New York: McGraw-Hill Book Co., 1956.

Sheehy, G. _Passages: Precitable Crises of Adult Life_. New York: E. P. Dutton, 1976.

Sherrill, Lewis J. _The Struggle of the Soul_. New York: Macmillan Co., 1961.

Sherrill, Lewis J. _The Gift of Power_. New York: Macmillan Co., 1955.

Sherrill, Lewis J. _Guilt and Redemption_. Richmond, Va.: John Knox Press, 1957.

Sizer, T. and Sizer, N. A. eds. _Moral Education_. Cambridge, Mass.: Harvard University Press, 1970.

Skinner, B. F. _Beyond Freedom and Dignity_. New York: Bantham Book, 1971.

Skura, M. "Creativity: Transgressing the Limits of Consciousness." _Daedalus_ 109 (1980):127-146.

Smith, Wilfred Cantwell. _Faith and Belief_. Princeton, N.J.: Princeton University Press, 1979.

Sockman, Ralph. _The Meaning of Suffering_. Nashville, Tenn.: Abingdon Press, 1961.

Soddy, Kenneth ed. _Identity: Mental Health and Value System_. London: Tavistock Publication, 1961.

Soddy, K. and Kidson, M. C. _Men in Middle Life_. Philadelphia: J. B. Lippincott, 1967.

Soelle, Dorothee. _Suffering_. Philadelphia: Fortress Press, 1973.

Sorokin, Pitirim A. _Altruistic Love_. Boston: Beacon Press, 1950.

Sorokin, Pitirim A. _The Ways and Power of Love_.

Boston: Beacon Press, 1954.

Sorokin, Pitirim A. The Crisis of Our Age: The Social and Cultural Outlook. New York: E. P. Dutton, 1957.

Spitz, Rene. The First Year of Life. New York: International Universities Press, 1965.

Spicer, Malcolm. "The Trinity: A Psychological God." Studies of Religion 5 (1975):117-133.

Starbuck, E. D. The Psychology of Religion. New York: Charles Scribner's Sons, 1900.

Stein, M.; Vidich, A. J.; and White, D. M. Identity and Anxiety. New York: Free Press, 1960.

Stein, M. I. Stimulating Creativity. New York: Academic Press, 1975.

Sternglanz, S. H. and Serbin, L. A. "Sex Role Stereotyping in Children's Television Programs." Developmental Psychology 10 (1974):710-715.

Stewart, Charles W. Adolescent Religion: A Developmental Study of the Religion of Youth. Nashville, Tenn.: Abingdon Press, 1967.

Stone, L. and Church, J. Childhood and Adolescence. New York: Random House, 1957.

Storr, A. The Dynamics of Creation. New York: Atheneum, 1972.

Strommen, Merton P. ed. Research on Religious Development: A Comprehensive Handbook. New York: Hawthorn Books, 1971.

Strunk, Orlo. Mature Religion: A Psychological Study. Nashville, Tenn.: Abingdon Press, 1965.

Sullivan, H. S. The Interpersonal Theory of Psychiatry. New York: W. W. Norton & Co., 1953.

Tillich, Paul. A Complete History of Christian Thought. New York: Harper & Row, 1968.

Tillich, Paul. On the Boundary: An Autobiographical Sketch. New York: Charles Scribner's Sons, 1966.

Tillich, Paul. Systematic Theology, 3 vols. Chicago: University of Chicago Press, 1967.

Tillich, Paul. Dynamics of Faith. New York: Harper & Row, 1957.

Tillich, Paul. The Courage to Be. New Haven, Conn.: Yale University Press, 1952.

Tournier, Paul. Learning to Grow Old. New York: Harper & Row, 1971.

Tournier, Paul. The Person Reborn. New York: Harper & Row, 1966.

Tournier, Paul. A Place for You: Psychology and Religion. New York: Harper & Row, 1968.

Tournier, Paul. The Strong and the Weak. Philadelphia: Westminster Press, 1963.

Turner, Dean. The Autonomous Man. St. Louis, Mo.: Bethany Press, 1970.

Ulanov, A. and B. Religion and the Unconscious. Philadelphia: Westminster Press, 1975.

Vaillant, George E. Adaptation to Life. Boston: Little, Brown and Co., 1977.

Van Dusen, Henry P. Dag Hammarskjöld: The Statesman and His Faith. New York: Harper & Row, 1964.

Van Over, Raymond. Unfinished Man. New York: World Publishing Co., 1972.

Vernon, P. E. ed. Creativity. Baltimore, Md.: Penguin Books, 1970.

Vigotsky, L. S. "Thought and Speech." Psychiatry 2 (1939):29-52.

Vigotsky, L. S. Thought and Language. New York:

Wiley/MIT Press, 1962.

Wallia, C. S. ed. Toward 21. New York: Basic Books, 1970.

Weatherhead, Leslie D. Salute to a Sufferer. Nashville, Tenn.: Abingdon Press, 1962.

Wheelis, Allen. The Quest for Identity. New York: W. W. Norton & Co., 1958.

White, Ernest. The Christian Life and the Unconscious. New York: Harper and Brothers, 1955.

White, Robert W. The Enterprise of Living: Growth and Organization in Personality. New York: Holt, Rinehart and Winston, 1972.

White, Robert W. Lives in Progress. New York: Holt, Rinehart and Winston, 1966.

White, Robert W. The Study of Lives. New York: Atherton Press, 1964.

White, Robert W. "Motivation Reconsidered: The Concept of Competence." Psychological Review 66 (1959): 297-333.

Whiting, Charles S. Creative Thinking. New York: Reinhold Publishing Co., 1958.

Wieman, Henry Nelson. Man's Ultimate Commitment. Carbondale, Ill.: Southern Illinois University Press, 1958.

Wilson, John et al. Introduction to Moral Education. Baltimore, Md.: Penguin Books, 1969.

Witkin, Herman A. et al. Psychological Differentiation. New York: John Wiley & Sons, 1962.

Wolff, Robert Paul. The Autonomy of Reason. New York: Harper & Row, 1973.

Yinger, J. Milton. The Scientific Study of Religion. New York: Macmillan Co., 1970.

INDEX

Abelson, Philip H., 243
Abrowski, Mark, 277
"acceptant-democratic" relationship, 15
action mode, 178-179
Adelson, Joseph, 118
adolescence: a cultural phenomenon, 108; analogy for modern culture, xii; and oedipal conflicts, 111-112; autonomy in, 181-182; characteristics of, 108; concept of God, 121-123; formal operation, 118-119,120; heterosexual relationships, 113; homosexuality, 113; idealism vs. cynicism, 116-117; identity formation, 109-110,206-211; intimacy vs. identity, 117-118; major tasks, 108-109; parent-child relationships, 110-111; peer culture, 110, 113, 114; physical growth, 115; "popularity neurosis," 114; religious dimension, 118-123; sex differences, 115; sublimation, 116; triune dynamism, 112
aggression, 84
Algeria, 276
Allport, Floyd H, 262,271
Allport, Gordon W., 123, 282
alpha wave: creativity, 244; receptive mode,173; religious experience, 251-252
altruism: and society,99; and suffering, 314;

children's, 100; Sorokin's study, 36-37; support for creativity, 314 (see also Good Samaritan)
American: and Algerian, 276-277; and Mexican, 277; perception of occupation, 278-279; perceptual improvement, 281
Andrasik, Frank, 294
anger: "anger-in" type, 301-302; "anger-out" type, 301-302
Anglo-Saxon: response to pain, 277-278; stereotypes of, 280
anxiety: and pain, 297; and self-preoccupation, 300; in young adulthood, 125; of the creative person, 237-239, 247; severe-anxiety type, 301-302
Aquinas, St. Thomas, 285
Arkwright, Richard, 228
Arnold, Matthew, 297
asceticism, 117
Asian theology, 219
assimilation, 76, 86
"associative play," 83
Augustin, St., 78, 146, 320
authenticity, 135, 244
anthropomorphism, 89-93, 279
autism, 267-269, 295
automation: and autonmy, 189-190; midlife crisis, 143
autonomy: and action mode, 178-180; and appreciation of humor, 184-185;

and basic trust, 180;
and coping, 304; and
creativity, 180; and
heteronomy, 182, 185-
186, 193-194; and hu-
man development, 178-
185; and isolation,
182-183; and integrity
197; and mastery of
language, 183; and ma-
turity, 171-177; and
perception, 269-270;
and self-confidence,
184; and religious ex-
perience, 191-197; and
social harmony, 190;
defined, 171-173; in
moral development,181;
vs. shame and doubt;
74, 77, 178-179

Ba Mbuti pygmy, 275
Babin, Pierre, 121
Bach, Sheldon, 272
Bacon, Francis, 186
Baillie, John, 196, 283
Bakan, David, 294
Baldwin, A. L., 15
Bales, Robert Freed, 25
Bao, Ruo-Wang, 303
Barclay, Thomas, 284
Barth, Karl, 219
basic trust: and auto-
nomy, 180; and crea-
tivity, 244; and pa-
rental love, 65-66
Beisser, Arnold R., 208-
209
Belgum, David, 107
Bell, Alexander Graham,
228
beta wave, 179
Bible, 39, 44, 46, 120,
·221 (see also church,
faith, God, and revela-
tion)

black theology, 219
Blai, Boris, 176
Boehm, Lenore, 185
Boelen, Bernard, 135
Bones, Jessie Woodrw, 205
Brady, K., 162
Bruner, E. M., 215
Bruner, Jerome S., 223,271,
273, 279
Brunner, Emil, 219
Breuer, Josef, 47
Buddhism, 35, 134, 162
Bultman, Rudolph, 219
Butler, Samuel, 190
Bunyan, John, 3, 242

Cabot, Richard C., 310
Canestaro, Carmen, 124
care: and creativity, 230;
and maturity, 232; in
educational context, 26-
34; teacher's, 29
Cartwright, Edmund, 228
Casals, Pablo, 21
castration anxiety, 81
Catell, Raymond B., 236
Caufield, Genevieve, 32-33,
129
challenge: and autonomy,
183-184; and creativity,
242-243; teacher's, 27-
28
character, 319-320
Chinese: 149, 229; and
Caucasian children, 68;
culture and perception;
277; creativity and art,
239; coping, 303, 305-
306; experience of the
church, 33, 35, 37, 41;
family context; 20; iden-
tity in Chinese culture,
212-213; independence
and revolution, 173; one-
ness with the Tao, 70,
252; shame, 74; young

intimacy and mutuality, 126-127; mentor-protege relationships, 129-130; pluralism and relativism, 162, 280

Erikson, Erik H., 60, 65, 72, 77, 97, 126, 140, 154, 155, 179, 209, 212, 232, 297

Evans, Luther H., 190

eureka, 270

existentialism, 134-135

faith: and autonomy, 180; and human nature, xiv; and perception, 282; anthropomorphic, 90-93; doubting, 118-120; existential, 132-136; integrated, 144-148; new faith and identity crisis, 220-221; simplified, 98-101

fantasy: and problem solving, 86; in toddlerhood, 78-79; oedipal, 81 (see also reality testing)

Fishbein, Morris, 303

first born, 68-69

Fowler, James W., 60, 91, 99

Fox, Nathan, 68

Fraiberg, Selma, 78

Frank, Jerome D., 277

Franklin, Benjamin, 234

free association, 249-250

free will, 193, 227, 241-242

French, Marilyn, 174

Freud, xi, xiv, 47, 60, 62, 70, 80, 83, 130, 192, 236, 297

Fulton, Robert, 228

Funkenstein, D. H. 300

Galileo, 192, 242

Garden of Eden, 69, 77-79

Gardner, Howard, 238

generativity, 140, 232

Gibson, James and Eleanor, 266, 267

Gilbert, G. M., 162

God: and creativity, 252; and suffering, 318; in infancy, 69-72; in late adulthood, 157-158; in middle adulthood, 144-148; in middle and late childhood, 118-120; in toddlerhood, 77-79; in young adulthood, 132-136; prototype of Christian maturity, 317; theonomy, 195; vision of, 192 (see also revelation, the Holy Trinity, etc.)

Goethals, George W., 126

Goethe, 240

Goldman, Ronald, 91, 119, 121

Good Samaritan: a Chinese girl's, 48; an immigrant's, 48; James'(W.), 45; Johnny's, 45; Niebuhr's (R.), 46; Thoreau's (H.), 45

Goodman, C. G., 273

Graham, Billy, 157

guilt, 82-83, 100

Hale, Hartley, 33

Handlin, Oscar, 214

Hargreaves, James, 228

Hein, A. 275

Held, R., 275

heterogeneity, 245-246

heteronomy: and autonomy in human development,

353

179-186; and conservatism, 193; and Enlightment, 194; and John Calvin, 195; defined, 194; religious, 194
Hick, John, 2
Hitler, xii
Hodge, Dean R., 119
Holroyd, Kenneth A., 294
Holy Trinity, 99-100, 254, 330
Hottentots, 186
Hume, David, 318
humor: and coping with stress, 302-303; autonomy and appreciation of, 184; in parent-child relationships, 24, 141
Hurlock, E.R., 100
Husserl, Edumund, 272
Huxley, Aldous, 286
hypothesis, 6-7, 121, 301

id, 82-83, 97
idea bank, 248
idealism, 116, 120, 128, 138
identity: and autonomy, 204; and basic values, 210; and conservatism, 254-255; and coping, 307-308; and creativity, 230-231; and melting pot, 213-214; and cultural crisis, 212, 215, 217; and social change, 210; and work, 188; collective, 212; foreclosure, 210-211; formation, 206-211; orthodox, 220-221; social matrix, 214-215; vs. religion, 218-223; vs. secularization, 221-222
illusion, 116, 262
incubation, 249, 253

independence, 131, 171, 172 (see also autonomy)
individuation, 134, 146, 203, 295-296
industry vs. inferiority, 97
infancy: and religious dimension, 69-72; concept of time, 68; first born, 68; perception, 66-68; psychomotor coordination, 63-65; psychosocial development, 65-66; symbiosis, 66-69
integration: and basic trust, 65; and meaning, 161; basic principle, 58-59; midlife, 137-138; need of, xiv-xv (see also triune dynamism)
interdependence: and maturity, 173, 232; autonomy, 197; in perceptual field, 269-270
intimacy: and identity, 117, 126; and meaning, 160; and old age adjustment, 155-156; in midlife, 139; in the church, 135; in young adulthood, 126-127; vs. "isolation," 126
invention, 228
Irish, 277-278, 280
Irenaeus, 321
Italian, 277-278, 280

James, William, 45, 123, 148, 149, 209-210, 234, 252, 263
Japanese: and Genevieve Caufield, 32-33; graduate student, 134; military police, 316
Jasper, Karl, 234
Jesus, 69, 124, 157, 196-

354

Malcolm X, 34
Mao Tse-tung, 173
marriage: choosing a mate, 132; happy, 131; midlife, 141; old age, 156; young adulthood, 125, 131
Marx, Karl, xiv, 252
Maslow, Abraham H., 151, 191
masochism, 317, 320
maturation, 55-168: adolescence, 108-124; basic principles, 58-59; early childhood, 80-93; infancy, 60-72; late adulthood, 148-158; middle adulthood, 136-148; middle and late childhood, 93-101; toddlerhood, 72-79; young adulthood, 124-136
maturity, 169-325: and culture, x, xv; and existentialism, 135; and meaning, 158-162; and old age, xii, 154; autonomy and independence, 171-197; church people's, 35-43; creativity and care, 227-255; identity and ego-ideal, 203-223; mentor's, 46; parental, 13-25, 127; reality perception, 261-286; suffering and coping, 293-321; teacher's, 26-34
May, Rollo, 238
McGhee, Paul E., 184
Mead, George Herbert, 83
meaning: and maturity, 146; and perception, 162; infant experience

of, 67; of suffering, 315-320; quest of, xiv, 1-2
melting pot, 213-214, 216, 222
Melzack, R., 295
Mencius, 320
Mendel, Gregor Johann, 234
menopause, 142
mentor: an electrical engineer's, 46; and midlife, 175; and professional autonomy and identity, 175, 207-208; institutional vs. personal, 130
Merton, Thomas, 31
Mexican, 277
middle adulthood: authenticity and integration, 138-139; career change, 142-143; creative years, 136; "generativity vs. stagnation," 140; integrity, 142; marriage life, 141-142; meaninglessness of life, 145-146; midlife crisis, 136-138, 142, 144-146; parent-child relationships, 141; philosophy of life, 138-140; physical decline, 142; postparental life, 143-144; power need, 140-141; religious conversion and faith, 144-145; unmarried life, 144
middle and late childhood: concrete operational stage, 97; cognitive development and sublimation, 97; "industry vs. inferiority," 97; moral judgment, 97-98; peer groups, 94; reli-

242; and new culture, 259; in democratic culture, 280; inequality, 280

Poincare, Jules Henri, 244

popularity neurosis, 114

Rahner, Karl, 192
Ramsey, Charles E., 278
Rankin, Jeannette, 150, 307
rationalism, 134-135
reaction formation, 96
reading: and creativity, 233-234; and maturation, 48; Dewey's, 48; Edison's, 48; Well's, 48; Washington's, 48; Wilson's, 206
reality testing, 64-65 (see also cognitive development)
receptive mode, 178-179
Reformation, 194, 254
regression, 249, 254
relativism, 98, 107, 159, 169
relaxation: and creativity, 244-245; Einstein's, 248; religious significance, 253
repentence, 146, 254, 318
retirement, 148-149, 152
retrospective method, 6-7
revelation: and Jesus Christ, 282-285; and drug, 285-286; and faith, 285, 286; and nature, 49, 285; and

perception, 282; and suffering, 316-318; Baillie's (John) experience, 283; Barclay's (Thomas) experience, 284; Russell's (Bertrand), 42, 250; types of mentality and theology, 286
Ricks, David F., 4
Riesman, David, 27, 308
Rockefeller, Nelson, 183
Roe, Anne, 238
Roff, Merrill, 6
Rogers, Carl R., 6, 139, 174, 211
Roosevelt, Franklin D., 319
Russell, Bertrand, 23, 42, 250

sadistic-anal, 73
salad bowl, 213-214
Sarason, I. G., 300
Sartre, Jean Paul, xiv, 134
Shoonover, Melvin, 307
Schopenhauer, Arthur, 1
Schultz, Whitt N., 248
Scotland, 19, 245
Scott, T. H., 295
Scribner, Silvia, 276
Seidel, George J., 227
self-actualization, 151, 191, 247, 253, 258
Selye, Hans, 297, 299, 303, 314
sex differences, 80, 95-96, 119, 121, 302
Shakespeare, 80, 293
shame and doubt, 74-75, 77, 79
Sherrill, Lewis J., x, 70, 108, 138
Shinn, Roger L., 283
Siao, Yu, 49

Sidis, Boris, 303
Siipola, E. M., 272
Skinner, B. F., 90, 186
Smartha, Stanley J., 219
Smith, Robert J., 278
Snyder, John I., 188
socialization: and church
  context, 40-41; and
  collective identity,
  212; and heteronomy,
  186; and traditional
  culture, 217; in mid-
  life, 137, 139-140;
  in old age, 150-151,
  155-156; in young
  adulthood, 126, 128;
  of Bill Lear, 42-43;
  of creative geniuses,
  234, 235, 236; peer
  groups, 93, 112-118;
  primary, 83-84; so-
  cializing faith, 98-
  101
Sockman, Ralph, 319
Socrates, 193, 235, 297
Soddy, Kenneth, 212
Soelle, Dorothee, 312
Solley, Charles M., 299
Sorokin, Pitirim A., 36,
  215, 314
soul, xi-xii, 129, 191,
  209, 212, 231, 252
space concept, 88-89
Spengler, Oswald, 217
spina bifida, 306-307
spouse, 46-47 (see also
  marriage)
stagnation, 254, 259
Starbuck, Edwin D., 123
Stewart, Charles W., 121
  -122
stress: and children,
  300; and humor, 302;
  and self-confidence,
  302; and self-image,
  300; executive, 304;

in modern culture, xiv;
  mastery of, 301-302;
  perceptual distortion,
  299; stages of coping,
  298-299 (see also coping,
  pain, and suffering)
Strommen, Merton, 118
Strunk, Orlo, 298
Stunpf, Carl, 209
sublimation: adaptive ego
  mechanism, 177; and cognitive development, 96-
  97; in adolescence, 115-
  116; transcendence, 162-
  163
suffering: and altruism,
  314; and masochism, 317;
  and maturity, 314; and
  religious experience,
  314-320; Jesus Christ's,
  316; koinonia of, 318-
  319; Nazi camp, 318;
  origin of consciousness,
  293; universality of, 293
  (see also coping, loneliness, pain, stress, etc.)
Sullivan, Anne, 32
Sullivan, Harry Stack, 60,
  126
superego, 82-83, 123
Sweet, W. H., 294
symbiosis: and American
  dream, 70; and creativ-
  ity in psychotherapy,
  103; and differentiation,
  66; and infant perception,
  67; and integration, 62;
  and personality development, 61-62; dissolution
  of, 68; human beings and
  computer, 191; mystical
  experience, 135; reli-
  gious significance of,
  69-72
synergistic society, 139
synod, 214

359

Witkin, H. A., 269
Wolfson, H. A., 293
Wright, Franklin Lloyd,
  20

young adulthood: defined,
  125; emotional wellbeing,
  125, 131; existential
  faith, 132-136; identity
  formation and career,
  128-129, 136; "intimacy
  vs. isolation," 126, 127,
  135; life structure, 131;
  major tasks, 125, 128;
  marriage, 125-131; men-
  tor-protege relation-
  ships, 130-131; parent-
  hood, 127-128; peer
  groups, 130-131, 132

Zaehner, R. G., 286
Zulu, 290

ABOUT THE AUTHOR

Charles Kao has studied at Tainan Theological College, Taiwan (1951-1955); St. Andrew's College, Selly Oak, England (1959-1960); and Westminster College, Cambridge, England (1960-1961). He was a PARS fellow at Union Theological Seminary, New York (1961-1962) and received the S.T.M. in 1962.

He has taught at Tainan Theological College as an Instructor (1957-1959), Assistant Professor (1963-1966), and Associate Professor (1966-1967); and at Emerson College as a Lecturer in Philosophy and Religion (1970, 1976). He has served in several pastorates in Taiwan, England, and the United States; and is currently a minister of The United Presbyterian Church in the U.S.A.

He has translated Marcus Ward's Outlines of Christian Doctrine Vol. 1 and 2 into Chinese (ATSSEA Textbook Program, 1965-1966), published articles in professional journals including Ethics in Science and Medicine, Journal of Psychology and Theology, and Theology and the Church (in Chinese); book reviews in South East Asia Journal of Theology; and meditation in The Upper Room. His first book is entitled Search for Maturity (Westminster Press, 1975).

He did his doctoral study at Boston University (1962-1963, 1967-1969), received a Ph.D. in 1969, and was a Visiting Scholar at Harvard University (1969-1970).

He is married and has a son. He was naturalized in 1974, and lives in Brookline, Massachusetts.

363